ORGANIZATIONAL
APPROACHES
TO STRATEGY

ORGANIZATIONAL APPROACHES TO STRATEGY

Edited by
GLENN R. CARROLL
DAVID VOGEL

BALLINGER PUBLISHING COMPANY
Cambridge, Massachusetts
A Subsidiary of Harper & Row, Publishers, Inc.

Contents

From the Editors

We are pleased to present this collection of analytical essays on strategy and organizations. *Organizational Approaches to Strategy*, the fourth book from the Berkeley Business School to be published by Ballinger, contains essays that were published as a special issue of the *California Management Review* (vol. 30, no. 1) in the Fall of 1987. The other three books are *Strategy and Organization: A West Coast Perspective* (edited by the two of us and also originally published by the *California Management Review*), *The Competitive Challenge: Strategies for Industrial Innovation and Renewal* (edited by David Teece as the outgrowth of the Transamerica Lecture Series at Berkeley), and *Ecological Models of Organizations* (edited by Glenn Carroll). The relationship between Ballinger and the Berkeley Business School is a special one that we hope will develop into a long-term tradition. Many of Ballinger's staff have aided us in numerous ways, but we are especially indebted to Marjorie Richman for her encouragement, advice, and support.

The intended audience for this book, as with the *California Management Review*, is both the executive and the academic worlds. Catering to these groups simultaneously requires a delicate balance of common sense and analytical rigor. As in the past, we sought to achieve this balance by asking some of the best talent in business schools and consulting firms to write state-of-the-art papers in a non-technical style. The superb chapters found between the covers of this book speak to the wisdom of that editorial policy.

It would be a mistake, however, to attribute the final product only to the efforts of the authors and the editors. Gundars Strads, *California Management Review*'s production editor, skillfully expanded the accessibility of each chapter with his thorough copyediting. Walda Thompson, the journal's office manager, competently administered the project. And Stephanie Lee assisted greatly with early clerical and secretarial support. To each we express our gratitude.

Glenn R. Carroll
Palo Alto, CA

David Vogel
Berkeley, CA

ORGANIZATIONAL
APPROACHES
TO STRATEGY

Chapter 1

Organizational Approaches to Strategy: An Introduction and Overview

Glenn R. Carroll

lmost anyone associated with a business school will tell you that strategy is one of the hottest topics of discussion and research these days. Students flock to strategy courses. Executives find strategy seminars stimulating. And many professors of business see strategy research as the academic world's greatest potential contribution to renewing the international competitiveness of American business.

While it seems that just about everyone wants strategy research, there is less agreement about what it actually is. The strategy appellation can be used to describe research on many different topics, ranging from corporate takeovers to small-group decision making. In fact, for research to be legitimately labelled as being in the strategy area, it appears that only one of several sufficient criteria need be satisfied. These are:

- a concern with *performance* as the outcome variable of major interest;
- a *normative* orientation to research problems leading to discussion (if not investigation) of implications for managers; and
- an emphasis on the issues of interest to *top management,* including especially the decisions they face.

Such a wide field of inquiry leads, of course, to disparate approaches to research. One fundamental distinction that can be found in strategy research concerns the difference between what might be called *economic* approaches and *organizational* approaches. Economic approaches, best exemplified by Michael Porter's penetrating books *Competitive Strategy* and *Competitive Advantage,*[1] concern themselves with the efficient posturing of a firm in the face of a given structure of competition. Questions about the availability of information, the costs of transactions, the "culture" of a firm, and the ease of implementation are usually finessed away by a set of convenient but stylized assumptions about human nature and organizational life.

Organizational approaches, by contrast, usually derive much of their insight by opening up the issues which economic approaches assume away. By relying on institutional and behavioral observations, organizational analysts of strategy seek to build theory from the ground up rather than the other way around. Much of the research conducted from this perspective begins with the recognition that organizational structures are problematic and that they severely constrain strategic decisions and their implementation. It is this orientation that characterizes the chapters in this book and that warrants its overall title.

The difference between the economic and organizational approaches to strategy is not simply one of emphasis. Porter's primary metatheoretical premise, for instance, is that firms which are "stuck in the middle" of any of several generic strategies—that is, firms without sharp strategic orientation towards cost leadership, product differentiation, or market focus—are doomed to failure. Yet a key finding of much organizational work shows that many successful strategies are stumbled into without much foresight and often with early failure.[2] The implication is that if these firms had not been able to "muddle through the middle" for a while, they would probably never have succeeded.

Despite their grouping together here, organizational approaches are a diverse lot. As Henry Mintzberg shows in the first chapter, this diversity extends even to the definition of strategy. He identifies five commonly used conceptualizations:

- strategy as *plan,* meaning a consciously intended course of action;
- strategy as *ploy,* defined as a specific maneuver intended to outwit a competitor;
- strategy as *pattern*—that is, consistency in behavior whether intended or not;
- strategy as *position,* or a means of locating an organization in an environment; and
- strategy as *perspective,* meaning an ingrained way of perceiving the world.

Obviously, there is some overlap in the definitions; they are not mutually exclusive. It is also true that any particular analysis of strategy is likely to involve the use of several of these conceptualizations. Nonetheless, a dominant conceptualization can usually be identified in any specific strategic analysis.

At the risk of offending the authors of the following chapters, I would venture that all five concepts of strategy are employed here and that the analyses might be classified by dominant conceptual usage in this way:

John Child's chapter (plan), the chapter by Bahrami and Evans (perspective and pattern), Powell's chapter (pattern and plan), Hambrick (ploy), Harrison (ploy), Gerlach (position), Bourgeois and Eisenhardt (perspective and pattern), Romanelli (pattern), and Eccles and Crane (pattern and perspective).

Alternatively, the chapters can be grouped by focus. The first five chapters—those by Mintzberg, Child, Bahrami and Evans, and Powell—are each concerned with issues of general strategic theory. The next four chapters—by Hambrick, Harrison, Gerlach, and Bourgeois and Eisenhardt—come down a level of abstraction and concern themselves with some particular special dimension of strategy. Finally, the last two chapters—by Romanelli, and Eccles and Crane—concentrate on particular industries, mini-computers and investment banking, respectively. Taken together, the chapters show the variety of ways strategic analysts can focus and refocus their theoretical lens. Enjoy your explorations into their perspectives on strategy.

References

1. Michael E. Porter, *Competitive Strategy* (New York, NY: Free Press, 1980); Michael E. Porter, *Competitive Advantage* (New York, NY: Free Press, 1985).
2. Richard T. Pascale, "Perspectives on Strategy: The Real Story Behind Honda's Success," *California Management Review*, 26/3 (Spring 1984): 47–72; Henry Mintzberg and Alexandra McHugh, "Strategy Formation in an Adhocracy," *Administrative Science Quarterly*, 30/2 (June 1985): 160–197.

PART I

GENERAL STRATEGIC THEORY

Chapter 2

The Strategy Concept I:
Five Ps For Strategy

Henry Mintzberg

Human nature insists on a definition for every concept. The
field of strategic management cannot afford to rely on a
single definition of strategy, indeed the word has long been
*used implicitly in different ways even if it has traditionally been
defined formally in only one. Explicit recognition of multiple*
definitions can help practitioners and researchers alike to maneuver through
this difficult field. Accordingly, this article presents five definitions of strategy—as plan, ploy, pattern, position, and perspective—and considers
some of their interrelationships.

Strategy as Plan

To almost anyone you care to ask, *strategy is a plan*—some sort of *consciously intended* course of action, a guideline (or set of guidelines) to deal
with a situation. A kid has a "strategy" to get over a fence, a corporation
has one to capture a market. By this definition, strategies have two essential
characteristics: they are made in advance of the actions to which they apply,
and they are developed consciously and purposefully. (They may, in addition, be stated explicitly, sometimes in formal documents known as "plans,"
although it need not be taken here as a necessary condition for "strategy as
plan.") To Drucker, strategy is "purposeful action"[1]; to Moore "design for
action," in essence, "conception preceding action."[2] A host of definitions in
a variety of fields reinforce this view. For example:

- in the military: Strategy is concerned with "draft[ing] the plan of war
  . . . shap[ing] the individual campaigns and within these, decid[ing] on
  the individual engagements."[3]

7

- in Game Theory: Strategy is "a complete plan: a plan which specifies what choices [the player] will make in every possible situation."[4]
- in management: "Strategy is a unified, comprehensive, and integrated plan . . . designed to ensure that the basic objectives of the enterprise are achieved."[5]
- and in the dictionary: strategy is (among other things) "a plan, method, or series of maneuvers or stratagems for obtaining a specific goal or result."[6]

As plans, strategies may be general or they can be specific. There is one use of the word in the specific sense that should be identified here. As plan, *a strategy can be a ploy*, too, really just a specific "maneuver" intended to outwit an opponent or competitor. The kid may use the fence as a ploy to draw a bully into his yard, where his Doberman Pincher awaits intruders. Likewise, a corporation may threaten to expand plant capacity to discourage a competitor from building a new plant. Here the real strategy (as plan, that is, the real intention) is the threat, not the expansion itself, and as such is a ploy.

In fact, there is a growing literature in the field of strategic management, as well as on the general process of bargaining, that views strategy in this way and so focusses attention on its most dynamic and competitive aspects. For example, in his popular book, *Competitive Strategy*, Porter devotes one chapter to "Market Signals" (including discussion of the effects of announcing moves, the use of "the fighting brand," and the use of threats of private antitrust suits) and another to "Competitive Moves" (including actions to preempt competitive response).[7] Likewise in his subsequent book, *Competitive Advantage*, there is a chapter on "Defensive Strategy" that discusses a variety of ploys for reducing the probability of competitor retaliation (or increasing his perception of your own).[8] And Schelling devotes much of his famous book, *The Strategy of Conflict*, to the topic of ploys to outwit rivals in a competitive or bargaining situation.[9]

Strategy as Pattern

But if strategies can be intended (whether as general plans or specific ploys), surely they can also be realized. In other words, defining strategy as a plan is not sufficient; we also need a definition that encompasses the resulting behavior. Thus a third definition is proposed: *strategy is a pattern*—specifically, a pattern in a stream of actions.[10] By this definition, when Picasso painted blue for a time, that was a strategy, just as was the behavior of the Ford Motor Company when Henry Ford offered his Model T only in black. In other words, by this definition, strategy is *consistency* in behavior, *whether or not* intended.

This may sound like a strange definition for a word that has been so bound up with free will ("strategos" in Greek, the art of the army general[11]). But the fact of the matter is that while hardly anyone defines strategy in this way,[12] many people seem at one time or another to so use it. Consider this quotation form a business executive:

> Gradually the successful approaches merge into a pattern of action that becomes our strategy. We certainly don't have an overall strategy on this.[13]

This comment is inconsistent only if we restrict ourselves to one definition of strategy: what this man seems to be saying is that his firm has strategy as pattern, but not as plan. Or consider this comment in *Business Week* on a joint venture between General Motors and Toyota:

> The tentative Toyota deal may be most significant because it is another example of how GM's strategy boils down to doing a little bit of everything until the market decides where it is going.[14]

A journalist has inferred a pattern in the behavior of a corporation, and labelled it strategy.

The point is that every time a journalist imputes a strategy to a corporation or to a government, and every time a manager does the same thing to a competitor or even to the senior management of his own firm, they are implicitly defining strategy as pattern in action—that is, inferring consistency in behavior and labelling it strategy. They may, of course, go further and impute intention to that consistency—that is, assume there is a plan behind the pattern. But that is an assumption, which may prove false.

Thus, the definitions of strategy as plan and pattern can be quite independent of each other: plans may go unrealized, while patterns may appear without preconception. To paraphrase Hume, strategies may result from human actions but not human designs.[15] If we label the first definition *intended* strategy and the second *realized* strategy, as shown in Figure 1, then we can distinguish *deliberate* strategies, where intentions that existed previously were realized, from *emergent* strategies, where patterns developed in the absence of intentions, or despite them (which went *unrealized*).

Strategies About What?—Labelling strategies as plans or patterns still begs one basic question: *strategies about what?* Many writers respond by discussing the deployment of resources (e.g., Chandler, in one of the best known definitions[16]), but the question remains: which resources and for what purposes? An army may plan to reduce the number of nails in its shoes, or a corporation may realize a pattern of marketing only products painted black, but these hardly meet the lofty label "strategy." Or do they?

As the word has been handed down from the military, "strategy" refers to the important things, "tactics" to the details (more formally, "tactics teaches the use of armed forces in the engagement, strategy the use of engagements for the object of the war"[17]). Nails in shoes, colors of cars: these are certainly details. The problem is that in retrospect details can sometimes prove "strategic." Even in the military: "For want of a Nail, the Shoe was lost; for want of a Shoe the Horse was lost . . . " and so on through

Figure 1. Deliberate and Emergent Strategies

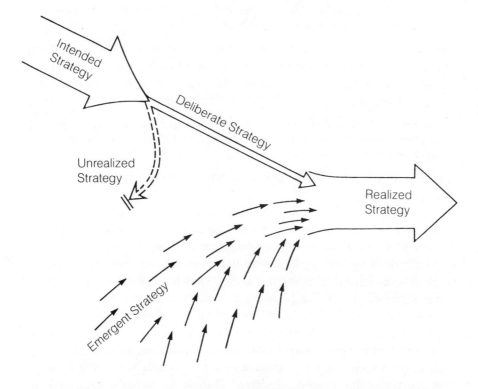

the rider and general to the battle, "all for want of Care about a Horseshoe Nail."[18] Indeed one of the reasons Henry Ford lost his war with General Motors was that he refused to paint his cars anything but black.

Rumelt notes that "one person's strategies are another's tactics—that what is strategic depends on where you sit."[19] It also depends on *when* you sit: what seems tactical today may prove strategic tomorrow. The point is that these sorts of distinctions can be arbitrary and misleading, that labels should not be used to imply that some issues are *inevitably* more important than others. There are times when it pays to manage the details and let the strategies emerge for themselves. Thus there is good reason to drop the word "tactics" altogether and simply refer to issues as more or less "strategic," in other words, more or less "important" in some context, whether as intended before acting or as realized after it.[20] Accordingly, the answer to the question, strategy about what, is: potentially about anything. About products and processes, customers and citizens, social responsibilities and self interests, control and color.

Two aspects of the content of strategies must, however, be singled out because they are of particular importance and, accordingly, play major roles in the literature.

Strategy as Position

The fourth definition is that *strategy is a position*—specifically, a means of locating an organization in what organization theorists like to call an "environment." By this definition, strategy becomes the mediating force—or "match," according to Hofer and Schendel[21]—between organization and environment, that is, between the internal and the external context. In ecological terms, strategy becomes a "niche"; in economic terms, a place that generates "rent" (that is "returns to [being] in a 'unique' place"[22]); in management terms, formally, a product-market "domain,"[23] the place in the environment where resources are concentrated (leading McNichols to call this "root strategy"[24]).

Note that this definition of strategy can be compatible with either (or all) of the preceding ones: a position can be preselected and aspired to through a plan (or ploy) and/or it can be reached, perhaps even found, through a pattern of behavior ("the concept of strategy need not be tied to rational planning or even conscious decision-making assumptions. Strategy is essentially a descriptive idea that includes an organization's choice of niche and its primary decision rules . . . for coping with that niche"[25]).

In military and game theory views of strategy, it is generally used in the context of what is called a "two-person game," better known in business as head-on competition (where ploys are especially common). The definition of strategy as position, however, implicitly allows us to open up the concept, to so-called n-person games (that is, many players), and beyond. In other words, while position can always be defined with respect to a single competitor (literally so in the military, where position becomes the site of battle), it can also be considered in the context of a number of competitors or simply with respect to markets or an environment at large.[26] Since head-on competition is not the usual case in business, management theorists have generally focussed on the n-person situation, although they have tended to retain the notion of economic competition.[27] But strategy as position can extend beyond competition too, economic and otherwise. Indeed, what is the meaning of the word "niche" but a position that is occupied to *avoid* competition.

Thus, we can move from the definition employed by General Ulysses Grant in the 1860s, "Strategy [is] the deployment of one's resources in a manner which is most likely to defeat the enemy," to that of Professor Rumelt in the 1980s, "Strategy is creating situations for economic rents and finding ways to sustain them,"[28] that is, any viable position, whether or not directly competitive.

Astley and Fombrun, in fact, take the next logical step by introducing the notion of "collective" strategy, that is, strategy pursued to promote cooperation between organizations, even would-be competitors (equivalent in biology to animals herding together for protection).[29] Such strategies can range "from informal arrangements and discussions to formal devices such as interlocking directorates, joint ventures, and mergers."[30] In fact, considered from a slightly different angle, these can sometimes be described as *political* strategies, that is strategies to subvert the legitimate forces of competition.

Strategy as Perspective

While the fourth definition of strategy looks out, seeking to locate the organization in the external environment, the fifth looks inside the organization, indeed inside the heads of the collective strategist. Here, *strategy is a perspective*, its content consisting not just of a chosen position, but of an ingrained way of perceiving the world. Some organizations, for example, are aggressive pacesetters, creating new technologies and exploiting new markets; others perceive the world as set and stable, and so sit back in long established markets and build protective shells around themselves, relying more on political influence than economic efficiency. There are organizations that favor marketing and build a whole ideology around that (an IBM); others treat engineering in this way (a Hewlett-Packard); and then there are those that concentrate on sheer productive efficiency (a McDonald's).

Strategy in this respect is to the organization what personality is to the individual. Indeed, one of the earliest and most influential writers on strategy (at least as his ideas have been reflected in more popular writings) was Philip Selznick, who wrote about the "character" of an organization—distinct and integrated "commitments to ways of acting and responding" that are built right into it.[31] A variety of concepts from other fields also capture this notion: psychologists refer to an individual's mental frame, cognitive structure, and a variety of other expressions for "relatively fixed patterns for experiencing [the] world"[32]; anthropologists refer to the "culture" of a society and sociologists to its "ideology"; military theorists write of the "grand strategy" of armies; while management theorists have used terms such as the "theory of the business"[33] and its "driving force"[34]; behavioral scientists who have read Kuhn[35] on the philosophy of science refer to the "paradigm" of a community of scholars; and Germans perhaps capture it best with their word "Weltanschauung," literally "worldview," meaning collective intuition about how the world works.

This fifth definition suggests above all that strategy is a *concept*. This has one important implication, namely, that all strategies are abstractions which exist only in the minds of interested parties—those who pursue them, are influenced by that pursuit, or care to observe others doing so. It is important to remember that no-one has ever seen a strategy or touched one; every strategy is an invention, a figment of someone's imagination, whether conceived of as intentions to regulate behavior before it takes place or inferred as patterns to describe behavior that has already occurred.

What is of key importance about this fifth definition, however, is that the perspective is *shared*. As implied in the words Weltanschauung, culture, and ideology (with respect to a society) or paradigm (with respect to a community of scholars), but not the word personality, strategy is a perspective shared by the members of an organization, through their intentions and/or by their actions. In effect, when we are talking of strategy in this context, we are entering the realm of the *collective mind*—individuals united by common thinking and/or behavior. A major issue in the study of strategy formation becomes, therefore, how to read that collective mind— to understand how intentions diffuse through the system called organization to become shared and how actions come to be exercised on a collective yet consistent basis.

Interrelating the Ps

As suggested above, strategy as both position and perspective can be compatible with strategy as plan and/or pattern. But, in fact, the relationships between these different definitions can be more involved than that. For example, while some consider perspective to *be* a plan (Lapierre writes of strategies as "dreams in search of reality"[36]; Summer, more prosaically, as "a comprehensive, holistic, gestalt, logical vision of some future alignment"[37]), others describe it as *giving rise* to plans (for example, as positions and/or patterns in some kind of implicit hierarchy). This is shown in Figure 2a. Thus, Majone writes of "basic principles, commitments, and norms" that form the "policy core," while "plans, programs, and decisions" serve as the "protective belt."[38] Likewise, Hedberg and Jonsson claim that strategies, by which they mean "more or less well integrated sets of ideas and constructs" (in our terms, perspectives) are "the causes that mold streams of decisions into patterns."[39] This is similar to Tregoe and Zimmerman who define strategy as "vision directed"—"the framework which guides those choices that determine the nature and direction of an organization."[40] Note in the second and third of these quotations that, strictly speaking, the hierarchy can skip a step, with perspective dictating pattern, not necessarily through formally intended plans.

Consider the example of the Honda Company, which has been described in one highly publicized consulting report[41] as parlaying a particular perspective (being a low cost producer, seeking to attack new markets in aggressive ways) into a plan, in the form of an intended position (to capture the traditional motorcycle market in the United States and create a new one for small family motorcycles), which was in turn realized through an integrated set of patterns (lining up distributorships, developing the appropriate advertising campaign of "You meet the nicest people on a Honda," etc.). All of this matches the conventional prescriptive view of how strategies are supposed to get made.[42]

Figure 2. Some Possible Relationships Between Strategy as Plan, Pattern, Position, Perspective

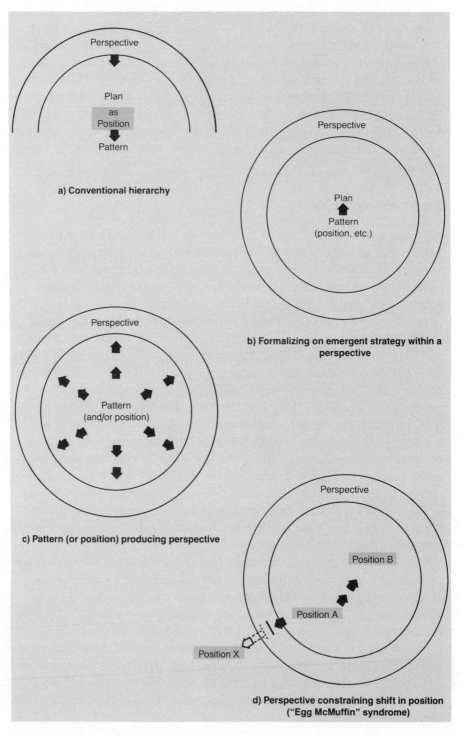

But a closer look at Honda's actual behavior suggests a very different story: it did not go to America with the main intention of selling small, family motorcycles at all; rather, the company seemed to fall into that market almost inadvertently.[43] But once it was clear to the Honda executives that they had wandered into such a lucrative strategic position, that presumably became their plan. In other words, their strategy emerged, step by step, but once recognized, was made deliberate. Honda, if you like, developed its intentions through its actions, another way of saying that pattern evoked plan. This is shown in Figure 2b.

Of course, an overall strategic perspective (Honda's way of doing things) seems to have underlaid all this, as shown in the figure as well. But we may still ask how that perspective arose in the first place. The answer seems to be that it did so in a similar way, through earlier experiences: the organization tried various things in its formative years and gradually consolidated a perspective around what worked.[44] In other words, organizations would appear to develop "character"—much as people develop personality—by interacting with the world as they find it through the use of their innate skills and natural propensities. Thus pattern can give rise to perspective too, as shown in Figure 2c. And so can position. Witness Perrow's discussion of the "wool men" and "silk men" of the textile trade, people who developed an almost religious dedication to the fibers they produced.[45]

No matter how they appear, however, there is reason to believe that while plans and positions may be dispensable, perspectives are immutable.[46] In other words, once they are established, perspectives become difficult to change. Indeed, a perspective may become so deeply ingrained in the behavior of an organization that the associated beliefs can become subconscious in the minds of its members. When that happens, perspective can come to look more like pattern than like plan—in other words, it can be found more in the consistency of behaviors than in the articulation of intentions.

Of course, if perspective is immutable, then change in plan and position is difficult unless compatible with the existing perspective. As shown in Figure 2d, the organization can shift easily from Position A to Position B but not to Position X. In this regard, it is interesting to take up the case of Egg McMuffin. Was this product when new—the American breakfast in a bun—a strategic change for the McDonald's fast food chain? Posed in MBA classes, this earth-shattering (or at least stomach-shattering) question inevitably evokes heated debate. Proponents (usually people sympathetic to fast food) argue that of course it was: it brought McDonald's into a new market, the breakfast one, extending the use of existing facilities. Opponents retort that this is nonsense, nothing changed but a few ingredients: this was the same old pap in a new package. Both sides are, of course, right—and wrong. It simply depends on how you define strategy. Position changed; perspective remained the same. Indeed—and this is the point—the position could be changed so easily because it was compatible with the existing perspective. Egg McMuffin is pure McDonald's, not only in product and package, but also in production and propagation. But imagine a change of position at McDonald's that would require a change of perspective—say, to introduce candlelight dining with personal service (your McDuckling à l'Orange cooked to order) to capture the late evening market. We needn't say more, except perhaps to label this the "Egg McMuffin syndrome."

The Need for Eclecticism in Definition

While various relationships exist among the different definitions, no one relationship, nor any single definition for that matter, takes precedence over the others. In some ways, these definitions compete (in that they can substitute for each other), but in perhaps more important ways, they complement. Not all plans become patterns nor are all patterns that develop planned; some ploys are less than positions, while other strategies are more than positions yet less than perspectives. Each definition adds important elements to our understanding of strategy, indeed encourages us to address fundamental questions about organizations in general.

As plan, strategy deals with how leaders try to establish direction for organizations, to set them on predetermined courses of action. Strategy as plan also raises the fundamental issue of cognition—how intentions are conceived in the human brain in the first place, indeed, what intentions really mean. Are we, for example, to take statements of intentions at face value? Do people always say what they mean, or mean what they say? Ostensible strategies as ploys can be stated just to fool competitors; sometimes, however, those who state them fool themselves. Thus, the road to hell in this field can be paved with those who take all stated intentions at face value. In studying strategy as plan, we must somehow get into the mind of the strategist, to find out what is really intended.

As ploy, strategy takes us into the realm of direct competition, where threats and feints and various other maneuvers are employed to gain advantage. This places the process of strategy formation in its most dynamic setting, with moves provoking countermoves and so on. Yet ironically, strategy itself is a concept rooted not in change but in stability—in set plans and established patterns. How then to reconcile the dynamic notions of strategy as ploy with the static ones of strategy as pattern and other forms of plan?

As pattern, strategy focusses on action, reminding us that the concept is an empty one if it does not take behavior into account. Strategy as pattern also introduces another important phenomenon in organizations, that of convergence, the achievement of consistency in behavior. How does this consistency form, where does it come from? Realized strategy is an important means of conceiving and describing the direction actually pursued by organizations, and when considered alongside strategy as plan, encourages us to consider the notion that strategies can emerge as well as be deliberately imposed.

As position, strategy encourages us to look at organizations in context, specifically in their competitive environments—how they find their positions and protect them in order to meet competition, avoid it, or subvert it. This enables us to think of organizations in ecological terms, as organisms in niches that struggle for survival in a world of hostility and uncertainty as well as symbiosis. How much choice do organizations have, how much room for maneuver?

And finally as perspective, strategy raises intriguing questions about intention and behavior in a collective context. If we define organization as collective action in the pursuit of common mission (a fancy way of saying that a group of people under a common label—whether an IBM or a United Nations or a Luigi's Body Shop—somehow find the means to cooperate in the production of specific goods and services), then strategy as perspective focusses our attention on the reflections and actions of the collectivity— how intentions diffuse through a group of people to become shared as norms and values, and how patterns of behavior become deeply ingrained in the group. Ultimately, it is this view of strategy that offers us the best hope of coming to grips with the most fascinating issue of all, that of the "organizational mind."

Thus, strategy is not just a notion of how to deal with an enemy or a set of competitors or a market, as it is treated in so much of the literature and in its popular usage. It also draws us into some of the most fundamental issues about organizations as instruments for collective perception and action.

To conclude, a good deal of the confusion in this field stems from contradictory and ill-defined uses of the term strategy, as we saw in the Egg McMuffin syndrome. By explicating and using five definitions, we may be able to remove some of this confusion, and thereby enrich our ability to understand and manage the processes by which strategies form.

References

1. P.F. Drucker, *Management: Tasks, Responsibilities, Practices* (New York, NY: Harper & Row, 1974), p. 104.
2. Moore, in fact, prefers not to associate the word strategy with the word plan per se: "The term *plan* is much too static for our purposes unless qualified. There is not enough of the idea of scheming or calculation with an end in view in it to satisfy us. Plans are used to build ships. Strategies are used to achieve ends among people. You simply do not deal strategically with inanimate objects." But Moore certainly supports the characteristics of intentionality. D.G. Moore, "Managerial Strategies," in W.L. Warner and N.H. Martin, eds., *Industrial Man: Businessmen and Business Organizations* (New York, NY: Harper & Row, 1959), pp. 220,226.
3. C. Von Clausewitz, *On War*, translated by M. Howard and P. Paret (Princeton, NJ: Princeton University Press, 1976), p. 177.

4. J. Von Newmann and O. Morgenstern, *Theory of Games and Economic Behavior* (Princeton, NJ: Princeton University Press, 1944), p. 79.
5. W.F. Glueck, *Business Policy and Strategic Management*, 3rd Edition (New York, NY: McGraw-Hill, 1980), p. 9.
6. *Random House Dictionary.*
7. M.E. Porter, *Competitive Strategy: Techniques for Analyzing Industries and Competitors* (New York, NY: The Free Press, 1980).
8. M.E. Porter, *Competitive Advantage: Creating and Sustaining Superior Performance* (New York, NY: The Free Press, 1985).
9. T.C. Schelling, *The Strategy of Conflict*, 2nd Edition (Cambridge, MA: Harvard University Press, 1980).
10. H. Mintzberg, "Research on Strategy-Making," *Proceedings after the 32nd Annual Meeting of the Academy of Management*, Minneapolis, 1972, pp. 90–94; M. Mintzberg, "Patterns in Strategy Formation," *Management Science*, 24/9 (1978):934–948; H. Mintzberg and J.A. Waters, "Of Strategies, Deliberate and Emergent," *Strategic Management Journal*, 6/3 (1985):257–272.
11. Evered discusses the Greek origins of the word and traces its entry into contemporary Western vocabulary through the military. R. Evered, "So What Is Strategy," *Long Range Planning*, 16/3 (1983):57–72.
12. As suggested in the results of a questionnaire by Ragab and Paterson; M. Ragab and W.E. Paterson, "An Exploratory Study of the Strategy Construct," Proceedings of the Administrative Sciences Association of Canada Conference, 1981. Two notable exceptions are Herbert Simon and Jerome Bruner and his colleagues; H.A. Simon, *Administrative Behavior*, 2nd Edition (New York, NY: Macmillan, 1957); J.S. Bruner, J.J. Goodnow, and G.A. Austin, *A Study of Thinking* (New York, NY: Wiley, 1956), pp. 54–55.
13. Quoted in J.B. Quinn, *Strategies for Change: Logical Incrementalism* (Homewood, IL: Richard D. Irwin, 1980), p. 35.
14. *Business Week*, October 31, 1983.
15. Via G. Majone, "The Uses of Policy Analysis," in *The Future and the Past: Essays on Programs*, Russell Sage Foundation Annual Report, 1976–1977, pp. 201–220.
16. A.D. Chandler, *Strategy and Structure: Chapters in the History of the Industrial Enterprise* (Cambridge, MA: M.I.T. Press, 1962), p. 13.
17. Von Clausewitz, op. cit., p. 128.
18. B. Franklin, *Poor Richard's Almanac* (New York, NY: Ballantine Books, 1977), p. 280.
19. R. P. Rumelt, "Evaluation of Strategy: Theory and Models," in D. E. Schendel and C. W. Hofer, eds., *Strategic Management: A New View of Business Policy and Planning* (Boston, MA: Little Brown, 1979), pp. 196–212.
20. We might note a similar problem with "policy," a word whose usage is terrible confused. In the military, the word has traditionally served one notch in the hierarchy above strategy, in business one notch below, and in public administration in general as a substitute. In the military, policy deals with the purposes for which wars are fought, which is supposed to be the responsibility of the politicians. In other words, the politicians make policy, the generals, strategy. But modern warfare has confused this usage (see Summers), so that today strategy in the military context has somehow come to be associated with the acquisition of nuclear weapons and their use against non-military targets. In business, while "policy" has been the label for the entire field of study of general management (at least until "strategic management" gained currency in the 1970s), its technical use was as a general rule to dictate decisions in a specific case, usually a standard and recurring situation, as in "Our policy is to require long-range forecasts every four months." Accordingly, management planning theorists, such as George Steiner, describe policies as deriving from strategies although some textbook

writers (such as Leontiades, Chang and Campo-Flores, and Peter Drucker) have used the two words in exactly the opposite way, as in the military. This reflects the fact that "policy" was the common word in the management literature before "strategy" replaced it in the 1960s (see, for example, Jamison, and Gross and Gross). But in the public sector today, the words "policy" and "policymaking" correspond roughly to "strategy" and "strategy making." H. G. Summers, *On Strategy: The Vietnam War in Context* (Carlisle Barracks, PA: Strategic Studies Institute, U.S. Army War College, 1981); G. A. Steiner, *Top Management Planning* (New York, NY: Macmillan, 1969), p. 264 ff; M. Leontiades, *Management Policy, Strategy and Plans* (Boston, MA: Little Brown, 1982), p. 4; Y.N.A. Chang and F. Compo-Flores, *Business Policy and Strategy* (Goodyear, 1980), p. 7; Drucker, op. cit., p. 104; C.L. Jamison, *Business Policy* (Englewood Cliffs, NJ: Prentice-Hall, 1953); A. Gross and W. Gross, eds., *Business Policy: Selected Readings and Editorial Commentaries* (New York, NY: Ronald Press, 1967).

21. C.W. Hofer and D. Schendel, *Strategy Formulation: Analytical Concepts* (St. Paul, MN: West Publishing, 1978), p. 4.
22. E.H. Bowman, "Epistomology, Corporate Strategy, and Academe," *Sloan Management Review*, 15/2 (1974):47.
23. J.D. Thompson, *Organizations in Action* (New York, NY: McGraw-Hill, 1967).
24. T.J. McNichols, *Policy-Making and Executive Action* (New York, NY: McGraw-Hill, 1983), p. 257.
25. Rumelt, op. cit., p. 4.
26. R. P. Rumelt, "The Evaluation of Business Strategy," in W.F. Glueck, *Business Policy and Strategic Management*, 3rd Edition (New York, NY: McGraw-Hill, 1980), p. 361.
27. E.g., Porter, op. cit., (1980, 1985), except for his chapters noted earlier, which tend to have a 2-person competitive focus.
28. Expressed at the Strategic Management Society Conference, Paris, October 1982.
29. W.G. Astley and C.J. Fombrun, "Collective Strategy: Social Ecology of Organizational Environments," *Academy of Management Review*, 8/4 (1983):576–587.
30. Ibid., p. 577.
31. P. Selznick, *Leadership in Administration: A Sociological Interpretation* (New York, NY: Harper & Row, 1957), p. 47. A subsequent paper by the author (in process) on the "design school" of strategy formation shows the link of Selznick's early work to the writings of Kenneth Andrews in the Harvard policy textbook. K.R. Andrews, *The Concept of Corporate Strategy*, Revised Edition (Homewood, IL: Dow Jones-Irwin, 1987).
32. J. Bieri, "Cognitive Structures in Personality," in H.M. Schroder and P. Suedfeld, eds., *Personality: Theory and Information Processing* (New York, NY: Ronald Press, 1971), p. 178. By the same token, Bieri (p. 179) uses the word "strategy" in the context of psychology.
33. Drucker, op. cit.
34. B.B. Tregoe and J.W. Zimmerman, *Top Management Strategy* (New York, NY: Simon & Schuster, 1980).
35. T.S. Kuhn, *The Structure of Scientific Revolution*, 2nd Edition (Chicago, IL: University of Chicago Press, 1970).
36. My own translation of "un reve ou un bouquet de reves en quete de realite." L. Lapierre, "Le changement strategique: Un reve en quete de reel," Ph.D. Management Policy course paper, McGill University, Canada, 1980.
37. Summer, op. cit., p. 18.
38. G. Majone, op. cit.
39. B. Hedberg and S.A. Jonsson, "Strategy Formulation as a Discontinuous Process," *International Studies of Management and Organization*, 7/2 (1977):90.
40. Tregoe and Zimmerman, op. cit., p. 17.
41. Boston consulting Group, *Strategy Alternatives for the British Motorcycle Industry* (London: Her Majesty's Stationery Office, 1975).

42. E.g., H.I. Ansoff, *Corporate Strategy* (New York, NY: McGraw-Hill, 1965); Andrews, op. cit.; Steiner, op. cit.; D.E. Schendel and C.H. Hofer, eds., *Strategic Management: A New View of Business Policy and Planning* (Boston, MA: Little Brown, 1979), p. 15.
43. R.T. Pascale, "Perspectives on Strategy: The Real Story Behind Honda's Success," *California Management Review*, 26/3 (Spring 1984):47–72.
44. J.B. Quinn, "Honda Motor Company Case," in J.B. Quinn, H. Mintzberg, and B.G. James, *The Strategy Process: Concepts, Contexts, Cases* (Englewood Cliffs, NJ: Prentice-Hall, 1988).
45. C. Perrow, *Organizational Analysis: A Sociological View* (Belmont, CA: Wadsworth, 1970), p. 161.
46. E.g., N. Brunsson, "The Irrationality of Action and Action Rationality: Decisions, Ideologies, and Organizational Actions," *Journal of Management Studies*, 19/1 (1982):29–44.

Chapter 3

The Strategy Concept II: Another Look at Why Organizations Need Strategies

Henry Mintzberg

I **n the preceding chapter, I proposed five definitions of strategy —as a plan, ploy, pattern, position, and perspective. Drawing on these, I wish to investigate here the question of why organizations really do need strategies. In discussing some of the conventional reasons as well as other ones—to set direction,** focus effort, define the organization, provide consistency—I will consider how these may suggest not only why organizations *do* need strategies, but also why they *don't*.

Setting Direction

Most commentators, focussing on the notions of strategy as deliberate plan and market position, argue that *organizations need strategy to set direction for themselves and to outsmart competitors, or at least enable themselves to maneuver through threatening environments.* In its boldest (and baldest) form: "the main role of strategy is to evolve a trajectory or flight path toward that bull's eye."[1] If its strategy is good, such commentators argue, then the organization can make various mistakes, indeed can sometimes even start from a weaker position, and still come out on top. Chandler quotes one of the men responsible for Sears Roebuck's great success: "Business is like war in one respect—if its grand strategy is correct . . . any number of tactical errors can be made and yet the enterprise proves successful."[2] In a similar vein, Tilles explains that:

> When Hannibal inflected the humiliating defeat on the Roman army at Cannae in 216 B.C., he led a ragged band against soldiers who were in possession of superior arms, better training, and competent 'noncoms.' His strategy, however, was so superior that all of those advantages proved to be relatively insignificant.[3]

The assumption here is that the competitor with the better strategy will win, or, as a corollary, that the competitor with a clear strategy will beat the one that has none. Strategy, it is suggested, counts for more than operations: what really matters is *thinking* it through; *seeing* it through, while hardly incidental, is nonetheless secondary. "Doing the right thing" beats "doing things right" is the expression for such strategic thinking, or to take the favorite example of the opposite, "rearranging the deck chairs on the Titanic."

Sound strategic thinking can certainly explain a good deal of success, in fact, more success than it should, since it is always easy, after the fact, to impute a brilliant strategy (and, behind it, a brilliant strategist) to every great victory. But no shortage of failure can probably be attributed to organizations that got their strategy right while messing up their operations. Indeed, an overdose of strategic thinking can impede effectiveness in the operations, which is exactly what happened on the Titanic. The ship did not go down because they were rearranging the deck chairs at all, but for exactly the opposite reason: they were so busy glorying in the strategy of it all—that boat as a brilliant conception—that they neglected to look out for icebergs.

As for the assumption that any strategy is always better than none, consider an oil company executive in 1973, just as the price of oil went up by a factor of four. What strategy (as plan) should he have pursued when his whole world was suddenly upset. Setting oneself on a predetermined course in unknown waters is the perfect way to sail straight into an iceberg. Sometimes it is better to move slowly, a little bit at a time, looking not too far ahead but very carefully, so that behavior can be shifted on a moment's notice.

The point is not that organizations don't need direction, it is that they don't need homilies. It stands to reason that it is better to have a good strategy, all things being equal. But all things are never equal. The Titanic experience shows how a good strategy can blind an organization to the need to manage its operations. Besides, it is not always clear what a good strategy is, or indeed if it is not better at times to proceed without what amounts to the straitjacket of a clear intended strategy.

Focussing Effort

A second major claim, looking inside the organization, is that *strategy is needed to focus effort and promote coordination of activity.* Without strategy, an organization is a collection of individuals, each going his or her own way, or else looking for something to do. The essence of organization is *collective action*, and one thing that knits individual actors together is strategy—again, through providing a sense of direction. Alfred Sloan notes in his memoirs a justification of the consolidated product line strategy developed at General Motors under his leadership: "some kind of rational policy was called for . . . it was necessary to know what one was trying to do," especially with regard to duplication across certain product lines.[4] Of course, by so focussing effort and directing the attention of each part within the integrated whole, the organization runs the risk of being unable to change its strategy when it has to.

Defining the Organization

Third, *strategy is needed to define the organization*. Strategy serves not only to direct the attention of the people working within an organization, but also to give the organization meaning for them as well as for outsiders. As plan or pattern, but especially as position or perspective, its strategy defines the organization, providing people with a shorthand way to understand it and to differentiate it from others. Christensen et al. discuss "the power of strategy as a simplifying concept" that enables certain outsiders (they are referring here to independent directors, but the point applies to any interested outsider) "to *know* the business (in a sense) without being *in* the business."[5] Of course, that "little knowledge" can be "a dangerous thing." But there is no denying that strategy does provide a convenient way to understand an organization.

In the early 1980s, the business press was very enthusiastic about General Electric. A reading of the reports of journalists and financial analysts suggests that what really impressed them was not what General Electric had done up to that point but that its new chief executive had articulated a clear, intended strategy for the firm. Thus Kidder, Peabody opened a December 21, 1983 newsletter with the statement: "General Electric is in the process of becoming a somewhat simpler company to understand," the result of the CEO's statement that it would focus on three major segments—core businesses, high technology, and services. Later they explained that "one of the main reasons we have been recommending General Electric for the past three years is the dynamic, creative, motivational leadership that the youthful Jack Welch . . . has provided . . . . His energy, enthusiasm, and ability to articulate a tight and viable corporate strategy are very impressive." No analyst can ever hope to understand much about a company so diversified and complex as General Electric, hence a clear, articulated strategy becomes a surrogate for that understanding.

The important question is whether a simplified strategy for such a complex system helps or hinders its performance—and the question is not meant to be rhetorical. On one hand, such a strategy cannot help but violate the immense complexity of the system, encouraging various dysfunctional pressures from outsiders (directors, for example, who may try to act on their "little knowledge") or even from insiders (chief executives, for example, who try to exercise control over divisions remote form their understanding by putting them into the simplistic categories of "dog" or "cash cow"). On the other hand, the enthusiasm generated by a clear strategy—a clear sense of mission—can produce a host of positive benefits. Those stock analysts not only helped to raise General Electric's stock price, they also helped to fire up the enthusiasm of the company's suppliers and customers, as well as the employees themselves, thereby promoting commitment which can improve performance. Thus, strategy may be of help, not only technically, through the coordination of work, but also emotionally, through the development of beliefs.

Imagine an organization without a name. We would not even be able to discuss it. For all purposes—practical and otherwise—it would not exist. Now imagine an organization with a name but with no strategy, in any sense—no position, no perspective, no plan (or ploy), not even any pattern consistent in its behaviors. How would we describe it or deal with it? An organization without a strategy would be like an individual without a personality—unknown, and unknowable. Of course, we cannot imagine such an organization. But some do come close. Just as we all know bland people with hardly any personality, so too do we know organizations with hardly any sense of strategy (which Rhenman labels "marginal organizations"[6]).

Most people think of such organizations as purely opportunistic, flitting from one opportunity to another,[7] or else as lethargic, with little energy to do anything but allow inertia to take its course (which may suggest strategy as pattern but not as plan). But we need not be so negative about this. Sometimes, lack of strategy is temporary and even necessary. It may, for example, simply represent a stage in the transition from an outdated strategy to a new, more viable one. Or it may reflect the fact that an environment has turned so dynamic that it would be folly to settle on any consistency for a time (as in the oil companies in 1973).

In one study,[8] a film company that began with a very clear direction lost it over time. It never really had formal plans; at best there existed broad leadership intentions in the earliest years. But it did have a very clear position and a very distinct perspective, as well as rather focussed patterns, the latter at least at certain periods in its history. But over time, the position eroded, the perspective clouded, and the patterns multiplied, so that diffusion replaced definition. The insiders become increasingly frustrated, coming to treat their organization more like a shell under which they worked than a system of which they were an integral part. As for the outside influences, lacking any convenient means to define the organization, they attacked it increasingly for irrelevance. Ironically, the organization turned out a number of brilliant films throughout all this, but—contrary to General Electric yet reinforcing the same conclusion—what it did do proved less important than what it did not exhibit, namely, strategy as a clear sense of direction.

Providing Consistency

A return to the notion of strategy as a "simplifying concept" may provide the clearest reason as to why organizations seem to need strategies. *Strategy is needed to reduce uncertainty and provide consistency (however arbitrary*

*that may be), in order to aid cognition, to satisfy intrinsic needs for order,
and to promote efficiency under conditions of stability (by concentrating
resources and exploiting past learning).*

Psychologist William James once described the experiences of the infant
as a "blooming, buzzing confusion." According to Ornstein, who so quotes
him, that is due to "the lack of a suitable categorizing scheme in which to
sort experiences consistently."[9] An organization without a strategy experiences the same confusion; its collective cognition can become overloaded,
its members having no way to deal with experiences consistently. Thus,
strategy is a categorizing scheme by which incoming stimuli can be ordered
and dispatched.

In this sense, a strategy is like a theory, indeed, it *is* a theory (as in
Drucker's "theory of the business"[10])—a cognitive structure (and filter) to
simplify and explain the world, and thereby to facilitate action. Rumelt
captures the notion well with the comment that "the function of strategy is
not to 'solve a problem,' but to so structure a situation that the emergent
problems are solvable."[11] Or, as Spender puts it (and so specifies how ambi-
tious is research on the process of strategy making): "Because strategy-
making is a type of theory building, a theory of strategy-making is a theory
of theory-building."[12]

But, like every theory, strategy is a simplification that necessarily dis-
torts the reality. Strategies and theories are not reality themselves, only
representations (that is, abstractions) of reality in the minds of people.
Thus, every strategy must misrepresent and mistreat at least some stimuli;
that is the price of having a strategy. Good strategies, like good theories,
simply minimize the amount of distortion.

"Strategy," notes James Brian Quinn, "deals . . . with the unknowable."[13]
But it might perhaps be more accurate to write that strategy assumes the
unknowable can be made knowable, or at least controllable. As such, it is
important to emphasize that strategy is a concept rooted in *stability*.[14] No
one should be fooled by all the attention to change and flexibility. When
Miller and Friesen write that "strategy is essentially a dynamic concept. It
describes a modus operandi more than a posture, a process more than a
state,"[15] they are not talking about strategy at all but about the process of
making strategy. Strategy is not about adaptability in behavior but about
regularity in behavior, not about discontinuity but about consistency. Organizations have strategies to reduce uncertainty, to block out the unexpected,
and, as shown here, to *set* direction, *focus* effort, *define* the organization.
Strategy is a force that *resists* change, not encourages it.

Why then do organizations seem to have such an overwhelming need for
consistency? In other words, why the obsession with strategy? To some
extent, this is a human need per se. Consistency provides us with a sense
of being in control (and nowhere is this better illustrated than in the prescriptive literature of strategic management, although those of us who feel
compelled to study strategy as pattern in behavior may be accused of the

same thing). That is presumably why some psychologists have found that people claim to discover patterns even in streams of random numbers.[16] Moore makes this point well: strategy is "a relief from the anxiety created by complexity, unpredictability, and incomplete knowledge. As such, it has an element of compulsion about it."[17]

But there is more to the need for consistency than that. Above all, consistency is an efficient response to an environment that is stable, or at least a niche that remains lucrative.

For one thing, strategy enables the organization to concentrate its resources and exploit its opportunities and its own existing skills and knowledge to the very fullest. Strategies reflect the results of organizational learning, the patterns that have formed around those initiatives that have worked best. They help to ensure that these remain fully exploited.

Moreover, once established, strategies reduce the need to keep learning in a broad sense.[18] In this respect, strategy works for an organization much like instinct works for an animal: it facilitates fast, almost automatic response to known stimuli. To be efficient, at least in a stable environment, means to get on with things without the need to think them through each time. As Jonsson notes about "myth," his equivalent to what we call strategy as perspective:

> The myth provides the organization with a stable basis for action. It eliminates uncertainty about what has gone wrong, and it substitutes certainty: we can do it, it is up to us . . . the riskiness disappears when you 'know' what has to be done. If there is much at stake and you are uncertain as to what is wrong, action is inhibited. If you are certain about what should be done, action is precipitated.[19]

To rethink everything all the time, as Jonsson implies, is unproductive. The person who gets up every morning and asks, "Do I really want to remain married?" or even, "I wonder if it is better today to wash before I brush my teeth," will eventually drive themselves crazy, or at least work themselves into inaction. The same will be true of the organization that is constantly putting its strategies into question. That will impede its ability to get on with things. (A colleague makes this point best with his proposed epitaph: "Here lies RR: he kept his options open.")

We function best when we can take some things for granted, at least for a time. And that is a major role of strategy in organizations: it resolves the big issues so that people can get on with the little details—targeting and serving customers instead of debating which markets are best, buying and operating machines instead of wondering about different technologies, rearranging deck chairs and looking for icebergs. This applies not only at the bottom of the hierarchy, but all along it, right to the very top. Most of the time, the chief executive, too, must get on with managing the organization in a given context; he cannot continually put that context into question.

There is a tendency to picture the chief executive as a strategist, conceiving the big ideas while everyone else gets on with the little details. But his job is not like that at all. A great deal of it has to do with its own little de-tails—reinforcing the existing perspective ("culture" is the currently popu-lar word now) through all kinds of mundane figurehead duties, maintaining the flow of information by developing contacts and disseminating the re-sulting information, negotiating agreements to reinforce existing positions, and so on.[20]

The problem with all this, of course, is that eventually situations change, environments destabilize, niches disappear. Then all that is constructive and efficient about an established strategy becomes a liability. That is why even though the concept of strategy is rooted in stability, so much of the study of strategy making focusses on change. But while prescription for strategic change in the literature may come easy, management of the change itself, in practice, especially when it involves perspective, comes hard. The very encouragement of strategy to get on with it—its very role in pro-tecting the organization against distraction[21]—impedes the organization's capacity to respond to change in the environment. As Kuhn notes, in dis-cussing the paradigms of communities of scholars, "retooling is expen-sive."[22] This is especially true when it is not just machines that have to be retooled, but human minds as well. Strategy, as mental set, can blind the organization to its own outdatedness. Thus we conclude that strategies are to organizations what blinders are to horses: they keep them going in a straight line, but impede the use of peripheral vision.

And this leads to our final conclusion, which is that strategies (and the strategic management process) can be vital to organizations, both by their presence *and* by their absence.

References

1. B. Yavitz and W.H. Newman, *Strategy in Action: The Execution, Politics, and Payoff of Business Planning* (New York, NY: The Free Press, 1982), p.7.
2. A.D. Chandler, *Strategy and Structure: Chapters in the History of the Industrial Enter-prise* (Cambridge, MA: M.I.T. Press, 1962), p. 235.
3. S. Tilles, "How to Evaluate Corporate Strategy," *Harvard Business Review* (July/August 1963), p. 111.
4. A.P. Sloan, *My Years at General Motors* (New York, NY: Doubleday, 1963), p. 267.
5. C.R. Christensen, D.R. Andrews, J.L. Bower, R.G. Hamermesh, and M.E. Porter, *Business Policy: Text and Cases*, 5th Edition (Homewood, IL: Richard D. Irwin, 1982), p. 834.
6. E. Rhenman, *Organization Theory for Long-Range Planning* (New York, NY: Wiley, 1973).
7. H.I. Ansoff, *Corporate Strategy* (New York, NY: McGraw-Hill, 1965), p. 113.
8. H. Mintzberg and A. McHugh, "Strategy Formation in an Adhocracy," *Administrative Science Quarterly*, 30 (June 1985):160–197.
9. R.F. Ornstein, *The Psychology of Consciousness* (New York, NY: Freeman, 1972), p. 74.
10. P.F. Drucker, *Management: Tasks, Responsibilities, Practices* (New York, NY: Harper and Row, 1974).

11. R.P. Rumelt, "Evaluation of Strategy: Theory and Models," in D.E. Schendel and W.C. Hofer, eds., *Strategic Management: A New View of Business Policy and Planning* (Boston, MA: Little Brown, 1979), p. 199.
12. J.C. Spender, "Commentary," in D.E. Schendel and C.W. Hofer, eds., *Strategic Management: A New View of Business Policy and Planning* (Boston, MA: Little Brown, 1979), p. 396.
13. J.B. Quinn, *Strategies for Change: Logical Incrementalism* (Homewood, IL: Richard D. Irwin, 1980), p. 163.
14. D.J. Teece, "Economic Analysis and Strategic Management," *California Management Review,* 26/3 (Spring 1984):88; R.E. Caves, "Economic Analysis and the Quest for Competitive Advantage," *AEA Papers and Proceedings,* 74/2 (May 1984):127–128.
15. D. Miller and P.H. Friesen, "The Longitudinal Analysis of Organizations: A Methodological Perspective," *Management Science,* 28/9 (1982):1020.
16. R.N. Taylor, "Psychological Aspects of Planning," *Long Range Planning,* 9/2 (1976):70.
17. D.G. Moore, *Managerial Strategies and Organization Dynamics in Sears Retailing,* Ph.D. Thesis, University of Chicago, 1954, p.34.
18. J.S. Bruner, J.J. Goodnow, and G.A. Austin, *A Study of Thinking* (New York, NY: Wiley, 1956), p. 12.
19. S.A. Jonsson and R.A. Lundin, "Myths and Wishful Thinking as Management Tools," in P.C. Nystrom and W.H. Starbuck, eds., *Perspective Models of Organization* (New York, NY: North Holland Publishing, 1977), p. 43.
20. H. Mintzberg, *The Nature of Managerial Work* (New York, NY: Harper and Row, 1973).
21. Christensen et al., op. cit.
22. T.S. Kuhn, *The Structure of Scientific Revolutions,* 2nd Edition (Chicago, IL: University of Chicago Press, 1970), p. 76.

Chapter 4

Information Technology, Organization, and the Response to Strategic Challenges

John Child

T*he information processing requirements of enterprises are expanding as their competitive environments become more dynamic and volatile. This strains management's organizational capabilities, a problem which the adoption of more complex structures such as the matrix has recognized but not often* resolved. Advances in information technology (IT), however, now hold out the prospect of increasing the efficiency and scope of information processing within organizations and so easing the problem directly. IT also facilitates the external contracting of activities, which spreads the risks of operating in turbulent environments and simplifies the task of managing the remaining core enterprise. There are several ways of organizing external transactions, all of which are today becoming increasingly significant.

This chapter explores the contribution of IT towards the different modes of organizing transactions that are being adopted within the contemporary strategic context of mature economies. Most evidence and illustration is drawn from Western Europe, though the analysis applies to North America and other industrial economies as well. Competitive conditions are drawing forth both advances in IT and organizational adaptations which benefit from the advances in technology. Contrary to some popular views, however, IT is not the determinant of organization, though it certainly extends the range of possibilities. Indeed, there are historical precedents for most of the organizing modes discussed here which long pre-date the new technologies.

Response to Strategic Challenges

There are three novel strategic challenges which large firms in particular face under present competitive conditions.[1] These challenges both heighten information-processing demands directly as well as encourage changes in the way economic transactions are organized—changes which, in turn, also present new informational requirements.

- The first strategic challenge stems from *demand risk*. This is the risk of sharply fluctuating demand or even the collapse of markets. It is associated with the threat of severe recession—already experienced twice since 1973—coupled with intensifying world competition and the entry of newly industrializing nations. It is exacerbated by rapid changes in taste and by advances in product specifications. Fluctuations in demand require firms to be flexible and able to adapt. This necessarily adds to their information-processing and organizational burden in terms of the speed and cohesion of response they must now achieve.[2] If the search for additional flexibility leads large enterprises towards a looser coupling of their major areas of activity, then this adaptation will in turn modify the form of information processing appropriate for coordination and control.

- The second strategic challenge derives from an *innovation risk*, the failure to match competitors' innovations in a context of accelerating technological change. Firms need to "de-mature" (as Abernathy et al. put it)[3] and retrieve the capacity to innovate, particularly in the design of their products. Most commentators agree that innovative capability depends on effective information processing in a number of aspects: including access to sources of concepts and ideas; the integration of internal specialist contributions to the development and commercialization of those concepts; and the ability to achieve sufficient operational flexibility to support new and evolving product specifications.[4] The organizational contribution here turns on the integration of inputs to innovation from a range of sources (some external to the enterprise) and the facilitation of speedy implementation attuned to commercial needs.

- The third strategic challenge derives from an *inefficiency risk*, the failure to match competitors' unit costs. This generates the need to increase control over operations and, therefore, to improve operational information so that inefficiencies and associated costs (such as inventory) may be reduced to a minimum. It encourages examination of contracting-out as a possibly cheaper option. The achievement of greater control and coordination of external contracting creates extra information-processing demands, particularly if they have to be combined with increased flexibility to meet demand risk.

Many firms in mature economies are responding to these strategic challenges by modifying the way they organize transactions. They are tending to slim down and simplify their constituent units, sometimes by uncoupling these into separate activity areas and at other times by sourcing more goods and services externally rather than through encompassing the whole productive process within their organizational boundaries. Consequently, there is a shift away from hierarchically coordinated transactions and towards

market-based transactions; first, in terms of an increased use of internal
trading and quasi-market resource allocation between more loosely-coupled
units and, second, in terms of a resort to the external marketplace. The
information-processing implications of this shift derive from the mode of
organizing transactions that is adopted.

Alternative Modes of Organizing Transactions

Transactions consist of the material and contractual exchange of goods and
services across technologically separable interfaces. Economists such as
Alfred Marshall[5] recognized that the hierarchically managed firm was an
alternative system for organizing transactions to the marketplace of classical theory. Williamson's more recent analysis, based on the costs and risks
involved in transactions, identifies circumstances under which the balance
of advantage shifts between the integrated hierarchical firm and the market
mechanism.[6] He argues that the integrated firm has the advantage for organizing transactions which involve recurrent exchange, incur high uncertainty about the conditions attaching to or surrounding them, and necessi-
tate investments that are specific to those transactions such as dedicated
equipment or specially trained staff.

Williamson now recognizes that, in practice, the modes by which transactions may be organized fall between the two extremes of the wholly integrated firm and the marketplace. In *The Economic Institutions of Capitalism*, he identifies five organizational modes which fall between the
extremes and can be broadly categorized as forms of either periodic or continuous contracting.[7] Williamson has, through these extensions, aligned his
analysis much closer to contemporary realities, although he was by no
means the first economist to posit a range of transactional modes.
Richardson, for example, wrote of "a continuum passing from transactions,
such as those on organized commodity markets, where the co-operative
element is minimal, through intermediate areas in which there are linkages
of traditional connection and goodwill, and finally to those complex and
inter-locking clusters, groups and alliances which represent co-operation
fully and formally developed."[8]

One of the important features of Williamson's approach (for present purposes) lies in its identification, as consequential for the relative efficiency
of different organizational modes, of task-related technological attributes
(such as asset-specificity) and of the coordination needs which arise within
the productive chain. The significance of IT lies in the way that it can both
lessen asset-specificity by introducing elements of programmable flexibility
(as with Flexible Manufacturing and many office systems) and, secondly,
provide a greatly improved basis for coordinating and controlling market
or quasi-market transactions with external parties. These contributions may
be expected to reduce the constraints upon choosing modes of organizing

transactions that are not coordinated through hierarchical supervision and that are today gaining favor in face of the strategic challenges noted.

During the 1980s, an increasing number of U.K. enterprises have decided to secure—from external sources—components and services which were previously provided in-house. Although there appears to be no reliable statistical information on the trend as a whole, it has emerged consistently from company case studies.[9] In the field of employment, there has been a parallel move towards the greater use of self-employed and agency-employed labor, while homeworking is also on the increase.[10]

Examples of the putting-out to external agents of activities previously undertaken internally can be found in many industries. These include the outsourcing of electronic components that were formerly produced in-house at a time when their technical specification was less advanced and their conditions of manufacture less exacting. Some food companies have given up the production and printing of their own packaging materials—a move stimulated by the growing technical sophistication of this process, by the fact that it does not draw upon a core competence, and (in Britain) by the militant stance adopted by the printing unions which organized workers in this field. Within the construction industry, it has long been the norm for projects to be executed by general contractors who retain the services of specialist subcontractors. This arrangement represents an adaption to a set of transactional conditions that Eccles has analyzed in detail.[11] These include: the relatively loosely coupled nature of specialist inputs to the task; the uniqueness of the combination of inputs required in each project; the risk of non-productive labor and equipment due to adverse weather; and the important human capital investments in skilled-trade areas which can provide specialist contractors with production economies.

In retailing, many department stores have increased the number of independent specialist up-market boutiques operating concessions under their roof. This has been done largely in an attempt to recapture the fashion and leisure trade they had been losing. However, this policy faces limits in terms of the transaction costs associated with matching store-owner and concessionaire needs (with regard to the range of products stocked) as well as the tension between the concessionaire's need for autonomy and the owner's need for overall coordination of the store. In clothing, sales have become increasingly geared both to fashion design and to a short style-life that requires a flexible production system. Designer-producers, such as Benetton, that have achieved remarkable growth owe their success not only to a sensitivity to consumer taste (including an ability to mold this), but also to the spreading of the risks of their marketing operation over a wide range of sub-contract producers who are small domestically based firms. Risk is reduced both by the ability of this production network to adjust rapidly to changes in product design and by the low-cost nature of the production itself.[12]

The external contracting of ancillary services (such as plant repair and maintenance, transport and cleaning) has become particularly common. This is usually motivated by the cost advantages to be obtained from a substantial reduction in the enterprise's labor establishment, the keen pricing which pertains in the market, and the economies and/or concentrated expertise secured by external specialists. In 1980, for instance, the British Steel Corporation decided to contract out all modernization and maintenance work previously carried out by its own employees at its Port Talbot plant in South Wales. The switch to external contracting had become a BSC corporate policy, seemingly prompted by the need to cut total employment in line with the government's cash limits for state enterprises as well as by the belief that securing services from the market would be more cost-effective.[13]

The net benefits of external contracting have, however, been the subject of controversy in cases where the quality of externally provided services has a particularly close bearing upon the organization's operational effectiveness and where there are difficulties of control because performance specifications are not wholly precise. In such instances the risk of and from substandard externally performed work is greater. British Steel Corporation employees, for instance, complained that shoddy maintenance work by subcontractors reduced production. There has also been considerable tension between hospitals and external laundry and cleaning contractors over the question of standards.[14] The control of subcontracting standards and the coordination of contracted activities with the internal production process is a managerial cost that improvements in the quality of relevant information ought to reduce significantly.

These processes of externalization have been variously called "spinning off,"[15] "distancing,"[16] and "fragmentation."[17] As the National Economic Development Office comments, an overall picture of the trend is still clouded by shorter-term adjustments such as the precautionary effect of contracting out at the onset of growth out of recession.[18] Nevertheless, greater recourse to market and quasi-market transactions is likely to be a continuing feature—and not merely a passing fashion reflecting inter alia the Japanese use of subcontracting—because it offers identifiable advantages in the modern economy.

Under conditions of *demand risk*, it can be dangerous for an enterprise to lock itself into the boundaries of a particular industry through vertical integration, despite the cost or supply advantages which this may offer. If a firm commits itself too heavily and comprehensively to an industry, it becomes vulnerable to that market's possible collapse. Subcontracting and cooperative agreements become attractive alternatives since they enable the firm to gain access to skills and capacities without anchoring itself too firmly to one strategic territory.[19] In effect, externalization is a policy for reducing the burden of risk under conditions of uncertainty while still maintaining a significant presence in the industry.

Another aspect of demand risk stems from the growing competitive significance of sensitivity to changing consumer taste (as with fashion clothing) or of customization (as with many products ranging from automobiles to computer software). This places a higher premium on the ability to adjust production flexibly and correspondingly makes heavy investment in fixed plant more vulnerable. As noted, the externalization of production to a network of small contractors offers one response to this need for flexibility and a low commitment to specific assets. Williamson's analysis would support the proposition that as a firm reduces its asset specificity, or indeed its fixed asset base in general, so it lessens the need to manage complementary specific activities and their labor inputs directly. Furthermore, high demand-risk conditions render a high asset-specificity policy less tenable in any case.

Increasing demand risk has stimulated technical developments aimed at lowering asset specificity. Advanced Manufacturing Technology (AMT) is characterized by a considerably higher degree of programmable flexibility. This is aimed at securing economies of scope whereby it is now more feasible and less costly to switch production, as demand requires, across a wider range of product specifications. Within the chain of production, this provides the principal or final producer with greater assurance that it can secure required inputs with relatively short lead-times because those suppliers now enjoy greater production flexibility. Looseness of coupling within a production system (as in construction) and a capability for flexible response among suppliers reduce the risk of shortages should the principal rely upon external contracting rather than in-house production. IT should lessen this risk still further insofar as shortages can be avoided by the wide dissemination of precise requirements over a wide range of potential suppliers.

The conditions for access to overseas markets are set by governmental policies either inside or outside the framework of international agreements. It is quite common today for governments to impose—as a condition for entry into their national markets, either via trade or via setting up manufacture—the condition that a significant amount of work should be subcontracted to local producers. Thorelli cites the example of General Electric's bid to provide jet engines for Sweden's new JAS fighter. The bid was accepted only on condition that GE gave important subcontracts to local manufacturers.[20] A similar agreement was reached with the U.K. government for the supply of Boeing AWACS aircraft. This is a further instance of how the conditions of access to contemporary markets encourages the widening of contracting networks.

Innovation risk presents the dangers of falling behind in technical development because it has become impossible to concentrate sufficient expertise and attention in all relevant areas and/or because the expense of the necessary research becomes prohibitive. It may be advantageous to buy in from specialist firms, especially for items requiring advanced R&D. This

concentrates the enterprise's resources on its areas of distinctive competence, leaving other activities to suppliers who enjoy an advantage in them.
The relative costs of resorting to the market should also be favorable when
outside suppliers enjoy economies of scale, lower labor costs, or superior
buying power by virtue of their specialization. With this reasoning in mind,
Rank-Xerox (a manufacturer of high-technology products) decided to cease
in-house production of certain components requiring heavy R&D support
and chose instead to secure them from specialist producers. This move (in
the late 1970s) was prompted by a specific conjunction of factors: its own
patents were running out, technology was changing from electro-mechani-
cal to electronic, and its risk profile was being accentuated by Japanese
competition.

The question of costs has already emerged as an incentive to engage in
external contracting, and it is of course particularly germane to *inefficiency
risk*. The costs of managing external transactions have been declining due
to a combination of market and technological factors. On the market side,
competitive pressures have increased suppliers' and contractors' willingness to accept the quality standards and delivery requirements of principal
producers. This closer cooperation reduces the costs of managing contractual relations themselves, since it significantly increases levels of certainty.
On the technical side, IT systems can assist the management of external
contractual relations by supporting the precise, detailed exchange of coded
data (such as part specifications) and the speedy transmission of data.
Therefore, the reduction in the costs of management is another factor which
encourages externalization.

Externalization has, finally, been regarded as an opportunity to slim
down and simplify the remaining core organization, and in so doing facilitate the development of a cohesive corporate culture.[21] It is always more
difficult for employees to identify with a larger and more diversified organization. The strength of their identification is likely to bear upon their willingness to offer commitment and flexibility to meet more challenging competitive conditions.

Over the past hundred years of its development, the integrated firm has
been perceived to offer certain advantages for the efficient control and
coordination of the processes of procurement, production, and distribution.[22] Moves towards externalization cannot overlook the requirement for
adequate control and coordination of transactions reflected in this historical
evolution. It is not surprising, therefore, that use is often made of organizational modes which overlay market-contracting relations with various inte-
grative arrangements. It is possible, in fact, to identify a range of organizational modes between the integrated hierarchy and the "pure" market, all
of which are in use today. Figure 1 indicates the forms of control and coordination involved and notes common examples of each.

Figure 1. Modes of Organizing Transactions in Productive Systems

Organizing Mode	Control & Coordination	Common Examples
integrated hierarchy	direct authority relations	single product firm
semi-hierarchy	arms-length control & periodic review	multi-divisional firm; holding company
co-contracting	arms-length control but the organization also mediates between co-contractors	mutual organization; joint ventures
coordinated contracting	use of agreed specifications & deadlines; long-standing trust relations	contractors and subcontractors
coordinated revenue links	formal financial agreements; monitoring of service standards with franchising	licensing, franchising
spot network	limited to the terms of the contract	market transacting between independent traders

- The *integrated hierarchical mode* of organizing transactions is most likely to be found in a unitary firm engaged in one area of activity, often of a traditional nature and on a relatively small scale. Examples include medium-size, non-diversified engineering firms (in locations such as northern Ohio and the English Midlands) as well as many retailing companies. These firms are usually quite centralized and they rely heavily upon hierarchical authority for control and coordination. This may involve a relatively personalized form of direct supervision, exercised according to the supervisor's preferred style or local custom and practice rather than according to any code of rules or procedures. The unitary firm undertakes most, if not all, of the activities contributory to its system of production. Larger unitary firms tend to be vertically integrated, particularly those which process raw materials through to finished products (such as aluminum and paper). Firms in this category, then, tend to operate through a relatively non-formalized management system and the scope of their informational requirements may be quite localized.
- The *semi-hierarchical mode* of organization is exemplified by the multi-divisional firm, the parent-subsidiary configuration, and the holding company. Most multinational corporations that are diversified on the basis of related product markets or technologies adopt the multi-divisional form. Examples include the major American and British companies in chemicals, electricals, foods, and (in the U.S.) automobiles; examples of large holding companies include Hanson Trust and ITT. The

multi-divisional corporation often places transactions between the corporate and divisional levels, and between divisions themselves, onto a
quasi-market basis in terms of expected rate of return on capital funding
and transfer prices. Its control and coordinative arrangements, on the
other hand, are likely to remain quite hierarchically managed. The holding company arrangement tends to be dispersed over a wider range of
subsidiaries which are less inter-related in their product markets or technologies. The informational requirements they generate for managerial
purposes are therefore more diffused, but tend to be codified only in
respect to a limited number of control and coordination criteria. These
criteria are usually financial, and they effectively place subsidiary companies in a semi-independent market relationship with their parent.
Buhner suggests that the more loosely coupled holding mode, with subsidiaries enjoying a high level of strategic independence, may be well
suited to take advantage of entrepreneurial opportunities in new technological areas.[23]

- The *co-contracting mode* of organizing transactions has been identified
by Koenig and Thietart[24] within the European aerospace industry, a successful example being Airbus Industrie. They call this a "mutual organization" formed by a set of independent co-contractors engaging in a recurring relationship, in which the parties are both principals and agents.
The European aerospace industry exhibits characteristics that point to
the rationality of establishing a single integrated company, including
high asset-specificity for airframe production, high economies of scale,
scarcity of resources, and markets too small for each producer. Political
and cultural obstacles, however, stand in the way of merger into one
European firm, and so the mutual organization has emerged as a form of
contractual cooperation without merger. This allows the risks of the large
R & D investments to be shared, expertise to be pooled, and economies
of scale to be reaped. The organization's key management positions are
pre-allocated to incumbents from each partner country and its policy
emerges from negotiation between the partners. Operationally, the
mutual organization's management controls and coordinates the agreed
division of labor between the partners' factories. Joint ventures also
come into the co-contracting category. The joint venture partners share
know-how—including management expertise—and they may jointly
commit equity as well. An example of the latter is the joint venture between the American Motors Corporation and the Beijing Jeep Corporation in China.

- The *coordinated contracting mode*, or "quasi-firm" as Eccles has called
it,[25] relates a prime contractor or producer as principal with a set of subcontractors as agents in a recurring relationship which may persist over
many years. One example is provided by the construction industry.[26]
Another well-known instance is found in the relations between large

Japanese automobile and electronic goods assemblers and their component suppliers.[27] Benetton, the fashion designer-retailer, also operates in this mode. The use of agreed performance specifications and delivery schedules for supplier inputs is an important requirement for the successful operation of coordinated contracting. The network of communication involved may be international in scope and quite complex in the case of a sophisticated product. Many coordinated contracting arrangements are of long-term duration, and the management of their transactions may therefore be able to rely on a significant degree of mutual confidence and trust. Lorenz, for example, stresses the significance of trust and the handling of contingencies through personal contact in the case of sub-contracting among small and medium-size French engineering firms.[28]

- The category of *coordinated revenue links* refers primarily to licensing and franchising. Management of licensing transactions is likely to be straightforward, concentrating on adherence to the financial and territorial terms of the contract. In the case of franchising (of which there are many examples in service activities such as fast-food, fashion retailing, and laundrettes), the management of transactions between franchise operators and franchisees will normally involve a close specification by the former of the service or product as well as a careful monitoring of operating standards. The franchise operator's good name is the main asset underwriting the relationship, and its attempts to maintain control can conflict with the entrepreneurial aspirations of the franchisee. The extent of the total franchise contractual network can be extremely wide, as in the case of familiar examples such as Kentucky Fried Chicken.

- Finally, the *spot network* refers to non-recurring contracting between independent firms or parties. This involves a resort to the market for short-term opportunistic ends. The burden of control and coordination is limited to the terms of the contract. Contracts tend to be precisely defined (highly formalized) in terms of clearly understood categories, this being a vital requirement for market trading conducted at a distance in time or space from the items which are being traded. Examples of spot market transactions include those contracted in stock markets and international commodity markets. It is clear that the spread of information networking involved in such markets can be very wide indeed.

This sixfold categorization of ways in which transactions are organized is neither exclusive nor exhaustive. It does, nevertheless, point to several of the channels down which the trend towards externalization is moving. Particularly significant for the present purposes is the way that each of these organizing modes presents different information-processing requirements, such as the degree to which transactions are formalized and the scope of transactional networks which are likely to be involved. Information technology can make a significant contribution to these organizational developments.

The Contribution of Information Technology

Information technology refers to the technologies and applications which combine the data-processing and storage powers of computers with the distance-transmission capabilities of telecommunications. The power, capacity, accuracy, and reliability of these technologies has increased enormously in relation to the constraints of capital cost, bulk, and energy consumption. The economics of mass information processing and transmission have therefore become increasingly favorable. Also, considerable efforts have been expended to make IT systems user-friendly.

The organizational possibilities of IT, however, do not just derive from its increasingly favorable economics and ease of use. They stem more particularly from the forms in which it permits information to be held and the way these forms lift restrictions on its temporal and spatial access. Boisot distinguishes these two dimension by referring to the *codification* and *diffusion* of information.[29] Codification refers to the social equivalent of the structuring of information by individuals, namely, a coding process in which both information compression and specificity are achieved. Codification is therefore part and parcel of formalization. Diffusion refers to the extent of information sharing within a given population and is therefore directly related to the scope of a communications or transactions network.

The data-processing applications of IT involve the manipulation of codified information, both in the form of binary arithmetic and at a higher level in the form of structures such as files, spreadsheets, and the scaled parameters included in control programs. This facet of IT facilitates the rationalization of information and its expression in very precise form. The capacity to store and process large amounts of such data is being progressively enlarged. As Boisot points out, the codification of information also assists its speedy and extensive diffusion. In addition, the modern communications facilities now available to IT allow for choice between codified and impersonal modes of information processing and transmission as opposed to uncodified and more personal modes. The former category includes on-line input and output access via keyboards to computer-based data files. By contrast, the latter includes advanced telephone systems, video conferencing, and facsimile. Although certain of these latter information diffusion technologies rely on conversion to coded digital data, the service they offer permits naturalistic and relatively uncoded communication over long distances. Moreover, the addition of electronic storage facilities releases personalized communications from the constraints of synchronization, which are evident, for instance, with the telephone.

IT has, in short, changed the economic cost-benefit balance in favor of greatly enlarging the information-processing capabilities of organizations. Additionally, it has expanded the options for the codification and diffusion of information. The availability of these options makes a significant contribution towards the viability of externalizing transactions. Each of the six organizing modes tends to present a somewhat different configuration of information-processing requirements in terms of codification and diffusion. Figure 2 portrays the approximate correspondence between organizational mode and information-processing requirements in a schematic fashion.

The unitary firm with an integrated hierarchy is likely to present the least demand for either information codification or diffusion, particularly if it is small, confined to a simple product portfolio, and does not form part of a wider, closely coordinated contracting network. Given these conditions, it should be able to envelope all its activities within a compact organization. This will often be managed through close personal contact and supported by a strong organizational culture which draws upon tradition and the standing of family or entrepreneurial leadership.

If, however, it is to take advantage of opportunities for growth (particularly those obtained through product innovation and diversification), the unitary firm will benefit from a move towards more arms-length semi-hierarchical management. Initially, this may take the form of delegation down a unitary hierarchy, requiring an increase of information codification both in the form of rules for exception reporting and in the format of reporting-back itself. Subsequently, a sharper discontinuity within the hierarchy and a widening of the organizational base will probably prove advantageous, taking the form of a corporate and divisional structure or head office and subsidiaries.[30] With this transformation into a "semi-hierarchy," the enterprise will have to extend its codification, especially of rules for subsidiary units' accountability and of the data that are transmitted under such rules. Codification will quite likely be extended in other respects as well, such as rules for the maintenance of common terms of trading and consistent employment policies among the divisions or subsidiaries. As the range of divisions and subsidiaries spreads and they develop their own distinctive competencies, so they may increasingly relate to each other and to the center on a quasi- or full-market basis in terms of transfer prices, competitive internal contracting, and so forth. When this happens, the informational requirements of the corporation become more widely diffused into external market arenas, so that, for instance, transfer prices may be checked in relation to the external market prices they shadow. A holding company's subsidiaries may trade on a wholly market basis in unrelated industries.

Volkswagen AG is an example of a geographically diversified semi-hierarchy which uses an international satellite network (INTELSAT) to link its operations in Germany, Brazil, and Canada, greatly speeding up data transfer. It also uses a satellite and submarine cable network (GEISCO) for product-related services and communication. The company has found that these IT-based links increase its ability to take advantage of the economies afforded by international dispersion while at the same time maintaining uniformity between the different affiliated companies within the Volkswagen Group.[31]

Figure 2. Information Processing Requirements of Organizing Modes

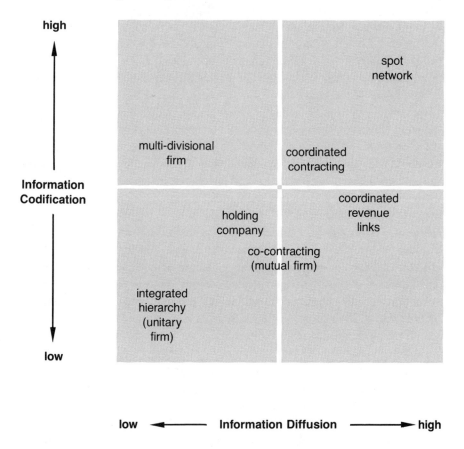

As the modes of organizing transactions incorporate a stronger market element, so the need for access to diffused information increases. The perfect market of classical economics requires that there are no limits to the availability of information of alternative suppliers, customers, and prices—and this model serves to make the point very clearly. The remaining organizing modes vary in their reliance on wide-ranging market information and particularly in the frequency of their recourse to it. The co-contracting mode requires access to information on potential partners in the market—so as to enable each to weigh-up opportunity costs—prior to its formation and from time to time when a partner is considering whether or not to remain within the mutual arrangement or to attempt a renegotiation of its terms. During the life of the co-contracting arrangement, however, its internal operations will proceed on the basis of a mutually determined division of labor rather than through market-type contracting. The degree to which these operations rely upon information codification will probably depend on the technological level of its products and processes as well as on cultural predilection (thus a European mutual organization like Airbus Industrie is likely to operate with a lower level of codification than would a North American equivalent).[32]

The coordinated contracting mode typically involves a long-term relationship between the principal and subcontractors. For example, many contracts between Japanese automobile manufacturers and their component suppliers are of ten years' duration. The principal resorts to the market in searching out contract partners and in checking suppliers' relative performances. However, the operation of the arrangement itself may rely primarily upon trust and mutual cooperation. In fact, it is not unusual for a number of features usually associated with the hierarchical mode to develop within coordinated contracting. Thus, Marks and Spencer (the retailing chain) not only lays down quality standards for its suppliers, but also assists them with process innovations to improve both quality and price competitiveness.[33] Automobile assemblers are increasingly introducing their quality procedures into their suppliers in order to effect improvements at source, and this can involve the suppliers in considerable equipment expenditures. The adoption of "just-in-time" production systems imposes very precise scheduling requirements on suppliers; and in Japan many have located their plants close to their large customer in order to minimize the risk of delay due to transportation system failures.

Although coordinated contracting is market-based and thus implies reference to a wide range of information sources, the level of information diffusion is bounded since communication is focussed onto a limited range of partners and operational issues. The tightness of integration and control (which characterizes this system at its most highly developed, particularly in the Japanese form which Kaplinsky has described as "systemofacture")[34] does however entail a high degree of codification of operational information. At the senior managerial level, however, relations tend to be less formal and to rely instead on long-standing personal relationships and the mutual assurance (or at least knowledge) these engender.

Coordinated revenue links and spot contracting require for their efficient operation the most extensive access to market information of all the modes of organizing transactions. The means have to be found of diffusing information widely, and the more this is possible the more such modes become attractive on efficiency grounds. The foreign exchange market provides a good example of a spot contracting arena. The introduction of internationally networked IT systems into exchange markets has considerably increased their efficiency since it is now possible for dealers and their clients to call up rates around the world in real-time and thereby secure the best deal available. The making of effective coordinated revenue links also requires a wide diffusion of information about, for instance, potential licensees and factors such as the degree of political risk attaching to each licensee's location (e.g., the risk of appropriation and default on contract).

Coordinated revenue links tend to require less codification of information than do spot market transactions, and they tend to incorporate elements of personal contact and informal evaluation. Spot transactions are often completely impersonal and rely on a high degree of information codification in the form of prices, precise specifications of goods or services purchased (such as grades of commodities), and delivery conditions.

IT offers a significant contribution towards meeting contemporary strategic challenges because it extends the choice of viable transaction modes. In particular, IT facilitates moves away from purely or wholly internal transacting and towards the various forms of externalization. It does this through its ability both to process huge amounts of codified data and to diffuse information widely and largely free of time and space constraints. As noted, information codification and diffusion demands vary between each of the modes of organizing transactions; and, in practice, a corporation could employ several modes at the same time. The appropriate combination of computing and communications facilities will depend on the balance between codification and diffusion requirements presented by the choice of transaction-organizing modes (as suggested in Figure 2).

Probably the most significant area of change at the present time lies in the development of coordinated contracting arrangements by previously integrated firms. Here the key managerial requirement is to apply the same degree (though *not* kind) of control and coordination to transactions within a chain or network of firms as could be applied within the one integrated firm. The investment risks of a productive system are in this way externalized and spread over a number of separately owned firms. The productive system itself must still be integrated—indeed, the degree of its integration will increase the more that "just-in-time" and similar operating philosophies are adopted.

Developments in IT can, through the way they permit codified data to be transmitted accurately and immediately over distances, facilitate this management of interdependent transactions across the boundaries of firms. One example is the combination of IT with CAD systems. Such systems permit the specification of components to be expressed in a standardized set of codes, namely, geometric coordinates. Once this codification has been achieved—and agreed—material or parts specifications can be transmitted with total precision directly to the control program of a supplier's or subcontractor's CNC equipment. Moreover, an IT linkage between suppliers or contractors and customer firms can provide the basis for systems that permit the customer firm to monitor performance in terms of quality, scheduling, cost, and other criteria.

Another area of work which illustrates how IT facilitates coordinated contracting is software development. A particular example is provided by a U.K. firm which designs and develops children's educational software to a customer's specification. The firm consists only of a small marketing, design, programming, and secretarial group. Once the story has been designed (by a subcontractor), the specifications for the individual programs are worked-out in-house and then are passed to external programmers who develop the fairly routine and simple sub-programs for a fee. These programs subsequently have to be joined together and tested. The company concluded that this process would be more effectively integrated and speeded up if it provided a telecommunications link to the microcomputers used by the contract programmers, who would then be able to enter their programs directly into the company's central computer. In this way, operational effectiveness was increased by the closer coupling offered by IT, but the economic benefits of the contractual relationship (payments at lower rates and only for work required) were retained.

Conclusion

Information technology can support the organization of transactions. In particular IT can facilitate the process of their externalization, which has been encouraged by strategic challenges. IT-based systems and software have effectively become an integral element of organizational design. Such systems have the capacity to handle codified information and to diffuse it across barriers of space and time. The ability to reprogram software offers considerable flexibility in the face of changing requirements and other uncertainties. These characteristics lessen the technical constraints on the choice of arrangements for organizing transactions. They diminish the need to place integrated operational systems under one organizational roof. They extend Peters and Waterman's precept of "simultaneous loose-tight coupling"[35] to the organization of contractual relations within wide transactional nets, and they enable the benefits of externalization to be secured with considerably less risk of losing operational control.

This mutuality of IT and organization remains in a formative stage and we have not yet proceeded very far along the learning curve in this area. There is no doubt, however, that it calls for a reorientation of organizational analysis. The key conceptual requirement is to redefine organization to embrace a portfolio of organizing modes for integrating and controlling a production or service-providing *system* which may exhibit flexibility in regard to its constituent contributors and to the contractual arrangements between them. The key theoretical need is to account for the various organizing modes, including the IT systems incorporated in them. Reference must be made to the strategic and economic conditions bearing upon a particular productive system, and this generally means referring to the industry or sector in which it is located.

While an awareness of the policy options for IT and organization depends upon conceptual and theoretical progress, there are problems in the realization of the potentialities. The most evident problem is that organizational and technological change is a social process. In many countries, the introduction of new technologies has so far been accompanied by an organizational conservatism in realizing their full potential.[36] This is not surprising, in view of the psychological stake most organizational members have in the maintenance of familiar structures and working arrangements. For many, this is complemented by a material stake in careers and jobs which they perceive to be at risk from organizational change, not the least being the external contracting of activities previously performed in-house. Studies conducted within the U.K. also point to a low level of IT appreciation among managers and to their reluctance to adjust their mode of working to take advantage of the additional services which the new technology offers.[37]

In Europe, with its weight of tradition, organizational conservatism is particularly entrenched. It exists in the U.S. as well. Kaplan, for instance, has pointed out that cost-accounting and management-control practices in the U.S. lag behind the new capabilities for flexibility and short product-launch times now offered by computer-controlled production systems.[38] Although the phenomenon of organizational conservatism lies beyond the scope of this chapter, its persistence is clearly germane to the rate at which the developments discussed here will proceed.

References

1. J. Shutt and R. Whittington, "Fragmentation Strategies and the Rise of Small Units," *Regional Studies,* 21 (1987):13-23.
2. R.M. Kanter, *The Change Masters* (London: Allen and Unwin, 1983).
3. W.J. Abernathy, K.B. Clark, and A.M. Kantrow, *Industrial Renaissance* (New York, NY: Basic Books, 1983).
4. C. Freeman, *The Economics of Industrial Innovation* (London: Pinter, 2nd Edition, 1982).
5. A. Marshall, *Industry and Trade* (London: Macmillan, 1923).
6. O.E. Williamson, *Markets and Hierarchies* (New York, NY: Free Press, 1975); O.E. Wiliamson, "Transaction-Cost Economics: The Governance of Contractual Relations," *Journal of Law and Economics,* 22 (1979):233-263.
7. O.E. Williamson, *The Economic Institutions of Capitalism* (New York, NY: Free Press, 1985).
8. G.B. Richardson, "The Organisation of Industry," *Economic Journal,* 82 (1972): 887.
9. D. Clutterbuck, "The Subcontracting Boom," *The Times,* November 10, 1983; Institute of Manpower Studies (IMS), *New Forms of Working Organization* (Brighton, England: IMS, 1985); National Economic Development Office (NEDO), *Changing Working Patterns* (London: NEDO, 1986).
10. C. Hakim, "Homework and Outwork: National Estimates from Two Surveys," *Employment Gazette,* 92 (1984):7-12; U. Huws, *The New Homeworkers* (London: Low Pay Unit, 1984).
11. R.G. Eccles, "The Quasi-firm in the Construction Industry," *Journal of Economic Behavior and Organizations,* 2 (1981):335-357.
12. R. Loveridge, "International Retailing Study," unpublished report, Microelectronics in the Service Sector Project, Work Organization Research Centre, Aston University, 1986.
13. R. Fevre, "Contract Work in the Recession," in K. Purcell et al., eds., *The Changing Experience of Employment* (London: Macmillan, 1986).

14. Cf. Labour Research Department, "Privatisation: NHS and Laundries," *Labour Research,* 73 (1984):113-115.
15. British Institute of Management (BIM), *Managing New Patterns of Work* (London: BIM, 1985).
16. NEDO, op. cit.
17. Shutt and Whittington, op. cit.
18. NEDO, op. cit., p. 54.
19. M. Delapierre, "Technology Bunching and Industrial Strategies," in K. Urabe and J. Child, eds., *Innovation and Management* (New York, NY: De Gruyter, forthcoming 1988).
20. H.B. Thorelli, "Networks: Between Markets and Hierarchies," *Strategic Management Journal,* 7 (1986):37-51.
21. E.g., Sir A. Cadbury, "Cadbury Schweppes: More than Chocolate and Tonic," *Harvard Business Review* (January/February), pp. 134-144.
22. Cf., A.D. Chandler, *The Visible Hand* (Cambridge, MA: Harvard University Press, 1977).
23. R. Buhner, "Management-Holding," *Die Betriebswirtschaft,* 47 (1987):40-49.
24. C. Koenig and R-A. Thietart, "Managers, Engineers and Politicians: The Emergence of the Mutual Organization in the European Aerospace Industry," paper given to the "Workshop on Business Strategy and Technological Innovation," Work Organization Research Centre, Aston University, January 1987.
25. Eccles, op. cit.
26. A. McKinlay, "Construction, Contracting and Business Strategy," *Work Organization Research Centre Working Paper Series,* No. 9, February 1984.
27. C.J. McMillan, *The Japanese Industrial System* (New York, NY: De Gruyter, 1984).
28. E.H. Lorenz, "Neither Friends nor Strangers: Informal Networks of Subcontracting in French Industry," paper given to Seminar on Trust, King's College, Cambridge, England, 1987.
29. M.H. Boisot, "Markets and Hierarchies in a Cultural Perspective," *Organization Studies,* 7 (1986):135-158.
30. L. Donaldson, *In Defence of Organization Theory* (Cambridge: Cambridge University Press, 1985).
31. R.E. Mansell, "The Economics Framework," Block 3, Unit 4 in DT200, *Introduction to Information Technology* (Milton Keynes: Open University, forthcoming 1987).
32. Cf., J.H.K. Inkson, J.P. Schwitter, D.C. Pheysey, and D.J. Hickson, "A Comparison of Organization Structure and Managerial Roles: Ohio, USA and the Midlands, England," *Journal of Management Studies,* 7 (1970):347-363.
33. P. Braham, "Marks and Spencer: A Technological Approach to Retailing," in E. Rhodes and D. Wield, eds., *Implementing New Technologies* (Oxford: Blackwell, 1985).
34. R. Kaplinsky, "Electronics-Based Automation Technologies and the Onset of Systemofacture," seminar given to the Work Organization Research Centre, Aston University, November 28, 1984.
35. T.G. Peters and R.H. Waterman, *In Search of Excellence* (New York, NY: Harper and Row, 1982).
36. J. Child, H-D. Ganter, and A. Kieser, "Technological Innovation and Organizational Conservatism," in J.M. Pennings and A. Buitendam, eds., *New Technology as Organizational Innovation* (Cambridge, MA: Ballinger, 1987).
37. P. Behr, "Why the New Age is Late in Dawning," *The Times,* July 29, 1986, p. 26; EOSYS, *Top Executives and Information Technology: Disappointed Expectations* (Slough, England: EOSYS Limited, 1986).
38. R.S. Kaplan, "Accounting Lag: The Obsolescence of Cost Accounting Systems," in K.B. Clark, R.H. Hayes, and C. Lorenz, eds., *The Uneasy Alliance: Managing the Productivity-Technology Dilemma* (Boston, MA: Harvard Business School Press, 1985).

Chapter 5

Stratocracy in High-Technology Firms

Homa Bahrami & Stuart Evans

Organizational innovations have made significant contributions to the performance and efficiency of the modern business enterprise. Economists consider the use of organization to be among man's greatest innovations. The ecological perspective views organizational form as the major determinant of a firm's long-term survival chances. Moreover, historians explain the rise of the modern business enterprise as an *organizational* response to fundamental changes in processes of production and distribution made possible by technological inventions and new sources of energy.[1]

Historically, major innovations have appeared in "waves" during periods of technological upheaval as a response to new environmental opportunities and deficiencies of existing organizational forms. This is exemplified by the development of the managerial hierarchy and its major variants. The functional structure first emerged in the newly formed railroads during the 1860s as a way of monitoring and coordinating different activities of the large-scale enterprise. The multidivisional structure was pioneered by General Motors and DuPont in the 1920s in order to manage business diversity and balance the requirements of short-term operational and long-term strategic activities.[2]

This chapter describes an organizational innovation pioneered by high-technology firms in California's "Silicon Valley." We term this innovation "stratocracy" and suggest that it provides the organizational capability to focus on short-lived opportunities, and the flexibility to maneuver in capricious settings. The chapter examines the environment of high-technology firms, describes their structural characteristics, and discusses the concept of stratocracy.

Research Approach

This chapter is based on a two-phased research study conducted over a period of three and a half years. The first phase involved a cross-sectional survey of 15 firms operating in diverse technological arenas, encompassing computers, peripherals, telecommunications, semiconductors, and instrumentation. This took the form of an exploratory study which focused on organizational and strategic features of high-technology firms and characteristics of their external infrastructure.

In the second phase, a longitudinal study of two firms in telecommunications and computer peripheral sectors was undertaken in parallel over a period of two years. Sources of information included attendance at company meetings, as well as structured and unstructured interviews with founders, board members, corporate officers, senior executives, and line managers. This was augmented by archival research through published data and internal documents.

The research process is best described as a combination of the grounded theorizing approach, involving "intertwined, iterative processes of data collection, conceptualization, article writing, revision and further elaboration,"[3] and the "direct," inductive approach, with an emphasis on description, reliance on simple methodologies for collecting "valid" data, and an attempt to "synthesize diverse elements" into an integrated description and explanation of the organizational regimes of high-technology firms.[4]

The High-Technology Arena

Technology ventures are generally associated with the commercial development of a novel idea resulting in a new product, process, or service, spawned by scientific breakthroughs. The term "technology" refers to the systematic application of scientific knowledge in a device, process, or concept, with commercial, competitive, or socially desirable value. High-technology firms commercialize inventions described in patents; spend a major portion of their budgets on research and development activities; are staffed by scientific and engineering personnel; and sell novel products, often to new market segments.[5]

Environmental Context—The high-technology arena is characterized by strategic, technological, and operational uncertainty which affects growth rates, competitive positions, and industry boundaries. Successful firms experience exponential rates of growth and have to adjust to imperatives of different stages of evolution in rapid succession. A successful start-up can increase its revenues to hundreds of millions of dollars and expand its workforce from a handful of people to several thousand within five years. This necessitates an effective transition from an entrepreneurial start-up to a large and complex enterprise in a short period of time.

A continuous stream of innovations transforms competitive boundaries and reduces product and process life cycles. For example, the success of digital telephone switching systems in the 1970s helped transform the telecommunications sector from a conservative industry into a vibrant competitive arena by enabling computer firms to enter the field. Disk drives exemplify the short life cycles associated with many technology products. In just three years, between 1982–85, three generations of floppy and Winchester disk drives were introduced in rapid succession.

Since the most crucial capability in high-technology industries is knowledge—which resides in people— spinoffs from established firms and movement of key personnel between firms can rapidly transform industry dynamics. The incidence and frequency of spinoffs in high-technology sectors is due to several factors. These include the presence of concentrated pools of experts, abundant opportunities in growing markets, and the potentially lucrative financial rewards of holding equity in a new start-up.

Furthermore, an intricate external infrastructure, in environments such as Silicon Valley, enables new firms to quickly capitalize on their ideas and capabilities. Close proximity to major technological universities provides access to state-of-the art expertise and a reservoir of talented new recruits. Availability of venture capital makes it possible to fund a new project in a short period of time. Access to a sophisticated network of legal, financial, market research, public relations, executive search, product design, and subcontracting services enables firms to use experts on a variable basis at critical junctures. Finally, California's "frontier" spirit provides a conducive home for pioneering and non-conformist entrepreneurs.[6]

Organizational Imperatives—Since technologies, markets, and competitive boundaries are in a state of flux, high-technology firms are faced with unique organizational challenges. They have to focus their resources on emerging technological innovations and short-lived market opportunities. They need to be fast on their feet and act quickly as new developments unfold. They have to be flexible and accommodate impermanent tasks. Moreover, even as they grow, they have to retain the spirit of entrepreneurship in order to sustain the flow of innovative ideas. In short, they have to be organized for focused action, swift response, impermanent tasks, and innovative capability.[7]

Traditional bureaucratic structures provide the means for performing and administering standard, durable tasks in stable environments. As Mintzberg argues:

> It stands to reason that in a stable environment, the organization takes on the form of a protected . . . system . . . which can predict its future conditions and . . . clearly standardize its activities, establish rules, formalize work, plan actions and standardize skill.[8]

However, they do not address the imperatives confronting high-technology firms. Indeed, the relative absence of innovative capability in established firms is partly attributed to their entrenched bureaucratic structures, which stifle creativity and impede effective implementation of new ideas.[9]

Contemporary high-technology firms are not subjected to problems of structural inertia, because they are not constrained by prior experiences, entrenched values, and established structures.[10] Many of their founders are former executives and scientists of established concerns, or young entrepreneurs from universities and research institutes. The first group have direct experience of the deficiencies of large bureaucratic structures; the second group have few preconceived notions about organization and administration. Their organizational experiments are driven by their anti-bureaucratic sentiments and the imperatives confronting them.

Structural Characteristics of High-Technology Firms

The overriding organizational objective is to design structures which emphasize fluidity and flexibility, while retaining cohesion across interdependent functional and technological activities. Experimentation has led to the development of specific structural features which have become standard practice among many high-technology firms.

Multiple Roles, Temporary Assignments—In contrast to the specialized orientation of bureaucracies, individuals in high-technology firms fulfill different roles and are rotated through various assignments in rapid succession, depending on the firm's priorities. For example, the chief financial officer of one of the surveyed firms took charge of an operating unit when its activities had to be streamlined and later took over the sales function when negotiations were under way with a joint venture partner.

This continuous rotation through different assignments serves a useful purpose for both the individual and organization. The individual can develop new skills through exposure to different experiences; the organization has the versatility to deal with new imperatives as they arise and to maintain fluid boundaries between different functions and activities. The structure is thus designed to leverage the capabilities of individuals, rather than to fulfill predetermined roles through stable positions in the hierarchy.

Project Teams and Task Forces—Since high-technology firms operate in knowledge-intensive industries, special blends of expertise are brought together for undertaking different activities. For example, the development of computerized telephone switching systems requires a blend of expertise in computer hardware, software, and telephony. The development of disk-drive controllers demands specialized skills encompassing integrated-circuit design, knowledge of disk drives, system software, and host-system adapters. This emphasis on grouping of complementary capabilities is reflected in the composition of the founding teams of many start-up firms, and it is a key criterion for assessing the potential viability of a new venture.

Experts are typically assembled in ad-hoc task forces and project teams, which represent a flexible structural arrangement since they can be disbanded after their mission has been accomplished. They also provide an effective way of generating commitment and facilitating the implementation of decisions, especially when addressing issues which transcend several technologies or functional activities.

Coordination Mechanism—High-technology firms rely on communication for co-ordination purposes because of the frequency of adjustments which typically have to be made to existing strategies and programs. This emphasis is underscored in the amount of time that is spent in group and "one-on-one" meetings. Even formal activities, such as planning and strategy sessions, are largely used as communication and discussion forums.

Many firms use electronic mail and computerized voice-messaging systems to speed up the flow of information within the organization. These provide the means for updating information quickly and are an effective way of communicating information to large numbers of people in a short period of time.[11] Some of the larger companies use video conferencing systems for activities, such as new product launches, that transcend geographically-dispersed sales offices and operating units.

Informal interactions through sporting events, social activities, and periodic retreats augment the formal modes of communication. These provide additional opportunities for discussing business concerns without organizational constraints, foster a spirit of community, and forge interpersonal relationships outside the formal work setting.

Role of Staff—Staff functions are kept to a minimum in high-technology firms, since co-ordination is achieved through communication rather than standardization of processes, outputs, and skills. Moreover, a sophisticated external infrastructure provides variable access to specialized expertise, thus avoiding the high cost and inflexibility of internal staff departments.

Those staff functions that do exist are expected to support line groups, rather than perform self-contained tasks or act as intermediaries. Recruitment of new personnel is a good case in point. Although the personnel staff may co-ordinate the activity by advertising, organizing recruiting campaigns, and contacting executive search firms, it is the line managers, typically, who make the actual hiring decisions.

Many of the larger firms use staff functions, such as strategic planning, as temporary assignments for line managers in order to give them a broad perspective on the firm's operations. This emphasis on frequent rotation maintains fluid boundaries between staff and line functions and prevents the formation of rigid organizational "turfs."

Hierarchical Configuration—High-technology firms need an organizational structure which enables them to think, plan, and act quickly as new developments unfold. This is achieved by configuring the hierarchy so that the strategic apex is aligned with the operating core.[12] By shortening lines of command and communication, reducing spans of control, and eliminating intermediaries, the firm is positioned to *formulate* and *implement* decisions quickly. This alignment is facilitated by the operational orientation of strategists, minimal use of intermediaries, reliance on hybrid structures, extensive communication, and informal modes of interaction.

This arrangement affects the hierarchical configuration of the firm. In contrast to the traditional organizational architecture, the pyramid, where the apex is detached from the operating core by the middle segment, high-technology firms are organized so that the strategic apex is directly coupled to the operating core, as illustrated in Figure 1.

This configuration differs from the pyramidal hierarchy along two dimensions. While the pyramid is a combination of line and staff, successful technology firms deploy a line hierarchy, with staff functions in support roles. Second, whereas authority is the mainstay of the pyramid, power in these firms is exercised through influence. This is largely based on interpersonal relationships which are forged amongst members over time, as well as individuals' reputations, perceived capabilities, and previous accomplishments.

Grouping Activities—Due to short product life cycles, many technology firms typically diversify into related businesses relatively early in their life cycle. This poses a critical challenge: that of devising structures which can innovate by providing an entrepreneurial atmosphere through small, "stand alone" divisions, while assuring integration across an interdependent product portfolio. As a senior executive of one of the surveyed companies observed:

> "We like the idea of small, entrepreneurial units, but realize that we are in one business and our products have to play together . . . there is a major element of success that depends on co-operation between the units."

In order to address the co-ordination needs of their interdependent businesses, some of the larger firms rely on variants of the "hybrid" structure.[13] One variation is in the form of a divisional sub-structure within a functional superstructure. The divisional substructure enables line units to have autonomy, focus, and an entrepreneurial atmosphere. The functional superstructure provides strategic cohesion through the co-ordination of divisional strategies at the apex. Such a structure aligns the apex (the functional executives) and the core (divisional general managers) and makes it easier to devise and implement strategies quickly.

However, the hybrid structure does not represent a permanent structural arrangement. As a result of frequent changes in strategy and direction, reorganizations are the norm in many technology firms. These are used to

Figure 1. The "Aligned" Hierarchy

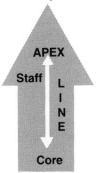

dismantle existing structures when specific tasks have been accomplished and to re-group organizational resources when new activities need to be undertaken.

Organizational Control—In contrast to bureaucracies, high-technology firms do not typically control activities by means of standard rules and procedures. Since tasks change frequently, it would either be impossible or too costly to anticipate every possible contingency and devise an appropriate rule accordingly.

As in clans and organic structures, high-technology firms deploy cultural norms as implicit rules of conduct to provide a uniform, yet broad, method of control.[14] These provide an overarching framework within which members can operate and provide guiding principles and rules of thumb for dealing with unforeseen contingencies as they arise.[15] These norms are communicated and reinforced through the process of socialization and performance evaluation. Moreover, the convergence of ownership interests and managerial control provides an additional means of control, since the employees' financial incentives are closely coupled with the firm's performance as a whole.

Decision Making—Decision-making procedures of high-technology companies have two distinctive features. First, they are set up to be simultaneously centralized and decentralized. Second, they emphasize the importance of pathfinding and implementation, rather than problem solving through extensive analysis.[16] They are centralized in that the apex is responsible for charting the broad strategic direction and defining the cultural norms. They are decentralized in that line managers participate extensively in the strategy-formation process and have considerable autonomy in dealing with new developments as they unfold. This dual emphasis is achieved through the alignment of apex and core, minimal use of staff, and bilateral channels of communication.

Moreover, many high-technology firms have neither the time nor accurate and timely information to engage in extensive analyses for decision-making purposes. Instead they focus on frequent revisions of strategies, re-assessment of priorities, and rapid implementation of decisions before they become irrelevant or out of date. As the senior executive of one of the surveyed companies commented:

> "Our decisions are not based on elaborate plans or sophisticated analyses of different options but on a few simple bedrock principles and many informal discussions."

This orientation is often reflected in their planning processes which place considerable emphasis on updating strategies by establishing systematic forums for discussion, rather than on extensive forecasts of future conditions.

Reward Systems—In the surveyed companies, reward systems had two distinctive features. First, they were designed to align the interests of the individual with that of the firm as a whole. This is evident in the widespread use of stock option programs which are generally granted not only to senior executives but to all employees. Second, compared with traditional organizations, they have a broad conception of incentives which go beyond rudimentary, monetary rewards. Some attributed this to the need to motivate a professional, expectant, and mobile work force; others emphasized the importance of rewarding employees in ways that would also help develop their capabilities. The innovative non-financial rewards include paid sabbatical leaves, internal management development programs and external educational opportunities, flexible working conditions and pleasant work settings (including sports and recreation facilities), and spontaneous rewards in recognition of outstanding performance.

In summary, there are various structural mechanisms used by high-technology firms to provide focus, flexibility, and responsiveness. While some features address only a single imperative, others span all three. Frequent job rotations, for example, provide flexibility by maintaining fluid departmental boundaries and staff/line distinctions; the aligned hierarchical configuration improves focus, flexibility, and responsiveness in parallel. However, it is the confluence of all the features which provides the capability for addressing the different imperatives confronting high-technology firms.

Distinguishing Structural Features

Some of these structural features are consistent with findings of previous studies. In this regard, organic forms, adhocracies, and entrepreneurial or "simple" structures are pertinent. Organic forms—as indicated in Figure 2 —align individual and organizational goals, control behavior through cultural norms or "rules of conduct," and facilitate lateral communication.

Figure 2. Contrasting Structural Regimes

Organizational Features	Structural Regime			
	Bureaucracy	Adhocracy	Organic	High Technology
Job Design	Specialization	Horizontal Specialization	Contributive	Multiple Roles
Departmentalization	Formal Boundaries	Fluid	Fluid	Fluid
Coordination Mechanism	Standardization	Mutual Adjustment	Mutual Adjustment	Mutual Adjustment
Role of Staff	Work Standardization	Undifferentiated	Blurred	Support
Hierarchical Disposition	Pyramid	Dynamic	Stratified	Aligned
Grouping Arrangement	Functional	Functional & Market	Network	Hybrid
Decision Making	Top Down	Selective Decentralization	Consultative	Centralized & Decentralized
Control System	Formal Rules	Action Plans	Informal Norms	Cultural
Reward Criteria	Span of Control/ Seniority	Expertise	Expertise	Accomplishments/ Expertise

Moreover, they de-emphasize formal job definitions and specialized roles within a clearly defined hierarchy. Adhocracies distribute decision-making authority, use multi-disciplinary task forces, and rely on mutual adjustment and liaison devices for co-ordination. The simple structure involves a loose division of labor, minimal use of staff, and cultural means of control.[17]

There are nonetheless substantive differences between these structural arrangements and our observations of those extant in high-technology firms. These may, in part, be explained by the different imperatives each regime is designed to address. Organic structures represent organizational arrangements geared for innovation and designed to deal with a continuous stream of novel tasks:

> The core of all the studies . . . is the description of what happens when new and unfamiliar tasks are put upon . . . organizations . . . such firms, in so far as they are successful, have either spontaneously or deliberately worked out a kind of management system which will facilitate non-programmed decision-making.[18]

Similarly, adhocracies are designed for "sophisticated innovation" and the development of "unique" outputs, typically at the margin of a larger concern. Therefore, both regimes place considerable emphasis on structural arrangements which maintain fluid boundaries and provide the capability for undertaking temporary assignments. The emphasis is on flexibility and innovative capability, rather than on focus or responsiveness:

> Adhocracies . . . cater to impulse, to peripheral patterns tolerated or simply lost within the system. That provides their great strength—their ability to innovate—but it also gives rise to the problem of achieving focused direction.[19]

A critical difference between the environmental contexts of these regimes and that of high-technology firms is the latter's ephemeral nature. Failure to introduce new or upgrade existing products, respond to new competitive dynamics, and exploit short-lived market opportunities can quickly eradicate an incumbent pioneering firm. Organizational regimes of high-technology firms are thus honed to accommodate the requirements of such settings.

Start-up "seed stage" high-technology firms often take on the guise of simple, entrepreneurial structures. Their primary mission is the development of a prototype upon which a sustainable business concern can be built. While on average, only one in twenty succeed beyond this stage, those that discover a winning formula can grow at a tremendous pace. However, in the process, they also outgrow the "simple" structure early in their life cycle.

Once established, the fundamental imperative is to respond quickly to nascent points of vulnerability or leverage by marshalling all of the firm's resources to focus on successive decisive points. This accounts for the critical structural difference between high-technology firms and variants of organic regimes; namely, hierarchical configurations and organizational arrangements which align the apex and the core in an attempt to unify strategic and operational command. This alignment *speeds up* the process of strategizing and acting, and provides the *cohesion* to maneuver the collective forces of the firm in unison, rather than as segmented units of a dispersed concern.

Contrasting Examples—The critical dimensions of this structural feature are best illustrated through a pairwise comparison of the two firms which were observed in parallel over a period of two years. At the time of the study, Firm A was 15 years old and had grown steadily to become a $500 million company in the telecommunications business and had over 7000 employees. The company was founded by a team of electronic engineers as a niche minicomputer company. It had successfully diversified into the telephone switching business and had later diversified further in order to capitalize on emerging opportunities in the "office of the future."

Firm A had undergone several major re-organizations over the years. A modified version of the initial functional structure had been retained after its first diversification in order to enhance strategic co-ordination between the two businesses. A divisional structure was later adopted to accommodate the growing size and complexity of its telecommunications business. Following entry into office systems, an autonomous division was set up to focus on new product development. This organization was revised after the introduction of the first series of office products. The new "hybrid" structure created a divisional sub-structure within a functional super-structure.

Firm B was founded during the early 1970s as a technological pioneer in the computer peripherals business. It had grown rapidly and broadened its product line—becoming a $250 million company with a workforce of nearly 3000—and had been acquired by a large multinational firm. By the early 1980s, Firm B had become a major supplier of storage devices for the "low-end" segment of the computer peripherals market.

Firm B had retained its initial functional structure, although this had been fine-tuned over the years. This arrangement had worked well, especially since many members of its original founding team had served in various executive capacities for a considerable period of time. However, after the acquisition, some of the key executives had left, prompting the parent to appoint a new president and a number of executives at senior levels from within its own ranks. Firm B was subsequently re-organized into four separate product divisions, a single sales and marketing division, and three administrative groups. The parent had also imposed some of its own organizational procedures on the subsidiary.

Both companies operated in volatile industries and exhibited a number of similar structural characteristics. The similarities included extensive use of task forces and project teams, frequent rotation of executives through different assignments, and extensive reliance on communication for co-ordination purposes. However, they differed along the critical dimension of alignment. Firm A was intentionally structured to align the strategic apex with the operating core; whereas this alignment was not evident in Firm B. The following account compares the two organizational regimes to elaborate on this structural dimension.

Cohesion of the Apex—Unity at the apex is a prerequisite for aligning and unifying strategic and operational command. Firm A achieved this cohesion through effective leadership, shared objectives, and extensive consultation and communication amongst members of the team. Members of the "Top Management Team" (TMT)—as the apex was known—had worked together for some time. The president (one of the founders) was considered an effective leader and the visionary behind the company's success. Members of the apex respected his judgment and considered him as the ultimate source of authority. This was crucial when conflicts had to be resolved at critical junctures.

Moreover, the TMT had a shared commitment to achieving the corporate goals. This was partially attributable to their ownership stakes in the company. Coupling of ownership and managerial interests generated a set of higher order criteria, which united their resolve in putting aside their personal differences in order to focus on their superordinate goals.

Frequent and direct consultation and communication amongst those at the apex gave them ample opportunity to make decisions as a team. The TMT held a three-hour weekly meeting for status updates, collectively reviewed all operational activities on a monthly basis, and addressed strategic issues every quarter during a three-day retreat.

In contrast, there was little discernible unity among Firm B's "Executive Staff." They had not worked together as a team for long, did not share similar objectives, and had instituted few forums for systematic consultation and communication. During a five-year time frame, the parent had appointed two different presidents from within its own ranks. While they possessed demonstrable leadership capability, they were not perceived as the final source of authority. Indeed, the Executive Staff often bypassed their own president and appealed directly to the parent for additional resources or approval of favorite projects. This opportunity to escalate issues undermined the president's ability to resolve conflicts quickly and resulted in many political maneuvers.

The absence of overarching objectives caused dissension, jockeying for position, and frequent pursuit of subunit goals. The problem was, in part, related to the reward system. Firm B's Executive Staff had no ownership stake in the company. Although they were granted minor stock options in the parent firm, the subsidiary's revenues only represented a small fraction of the parent's, and its performance would have little discernible impact on the parent's stock value.

Finally, the Executive Staff had few opportunities to discuss mutual concerns collectively on a frequent and systematic basis. A weekly staff meeting provided the only regular forum for joint decision making. Systematic strategic and operational reviews of the entire firm were the exception rather than the norm. In short, organizational procedures did not facilitate systematic discussion amongst those at the apex.

Fusion of Roles—Firm A's Top Management Team fulfilled operational roles, in addition to their strategic responsibilities. Every member was responsible for the performance of a different part of the firm. As indicated in Figure 3, this fusion of roles was facilitated by a hybrid structure which provided strategic *cohesion* through a functional superstructure, and operation *focus* through a divisional substructure.

During the study, every member of the TMT controlled a distinct functional activity. These incorporated smaller divisions and operating units which were in turn run by general managers. The TMT was in a position to co-ordinate interdependent divisional strategies, while delegating considerable operational autonomy to divisional general managers. This ensured that members of the TMT would not become preoccupied with their operational sub-goals at the expense of the overall corporate strategic goals.

Figure 3. Contrasting Organizational Structures

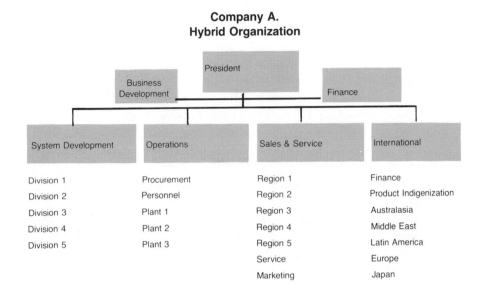

Company A.
Hybrid Organization

President

Business Development

Finance

System Development	Operations	Sales & Service	International
Division 1	Procurement	Region 1	Finance
Division 2	Personnel	Region 2	Product Indigenization
Division 3	Plant 1	Region 3	Australasia
Division 4	Plant 2	Region 4	Middle East
Division 5	Plant 3	Region 5	Latin America
		Service	Europe
		Marketing	Japan

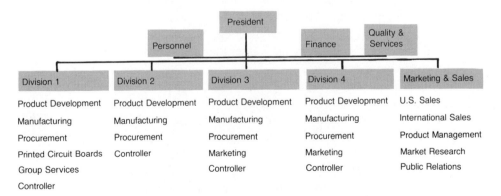

Company B.
Divisional Organization

President

Personnel

Finance

Quality & Services

Division 1	Division 2	Division 3	Division 4	Marketing & Sales
Product Development	Product Development	Product Development	Product Development	U.S. Sales
Manufacturing	Manufacturing	Manufacturing	Manufacturing	International Sales
Procurement	Procurement	Procurement	Procurement	Product Management
Printed Circuit Boards	Controller	Marketing	Marketing	Market Research
Group Services		Controller	Controller	Public Relations
Controller				

In contrast, Firm B's structure failed to fuse the strategic and operational roles of the apex. The Executive Staff considered their primary responsibility to be managing their own operating units and promoting their own divisional interests. This was exacerbated by the divisional structure which led to fragmentation of effort, lack of cohesion, and a minimal degree of strategic co-ordination at the apex.

Organizational Processes—Firm A had devised organizational forums to facilitate communication between the apex and the core on a frequent and systematic basis. For example, monthly operational review meetings were held over 3 consecutive days in which every divisional general manager and all members of the TMT participated. These gave the former an opportunity to get the TMT's input on pertinent issues and concerns. The TMT could review operations, find out about latest competitive and market developments, and address inter-divisional concerns.

In addition, the business planning process was devised to bring together divisional general managers and members of the TMT every quarter. These meetings provided a forum for addressing strategic concerns, prioritizing divisional action plans, allocating resources, and assessing interdependencies. They also provided the general managers with an opportunity to participate directly in the strategy-formation process.

Moreover, Firm A gave considerable operational autonomy to line managers and had a culture which was tolerant of failure and encouraged experimentation. Its senior executives openly admitted that they were prepared to tolerate failure as a price for giving autonomy to line managers, instead of relying on staff groups for monitoring line activities. However, the evaluation and reward system, which was devised to compensate tangible accomplishments, helped mitigate against the negative consequences of autonomy.

Firm B had no regular mechanisms to bring together the apex and the core, apart from crisis situations. Line managers operated with limited knowledge of strategic priorities and had few opportunities to give their collective input to the Executive Staff. Strategic planning had been subsumed under the parent's annual planning process and was designed to fulfill the parent's requirements, rather than to address the subsidiary's unique imperatives.

In addition, staff groups, including personnel and finance, were used to oversee line activities. For example, projects initiated by line managers were typically screened and evaluated by staff groups before being considered by the Executive Staff. This was largely attributed to the reporting requirements and the structural orientation of the parent, which used staff groups extensively.

In summary, the tight alignment between the apex and the core was a critical contributor to Firm A's success in its industry. This arrangement made it possible to identify opportunities early, devise and implement decisions quickly, and forge a spirit of community and commitment amongst its employees. In contrast, the organizational arrangements of Firm B impeded effective alignment between the apex and the core. The result was slow recognition and response to market developments, lack of focus in dealing with shifting opportunities, dispersion of resources, and poor morale. However, Firm B did possess the "genetic pool" and the capabilities to succeed, as exemplified by the number of very successful spinoffs which it spawned over a short period.

Implications and Conclusion

Implicit in the preceding discussion is the hypothesis that successful high-technology firms are organized to support the operating core. This is because the core is best positioned to simultaneously detect pertinent developments, devise appropriate responses, and undertake the necessary action. This line of reasoning leads us to conclude that the organization of high-technology firms is a "stratocracy," defined in an organizational context as "rule by the doers."

In the high-technology arena, the distinction between short-term operational activities and long-term strategic activities becomes blurred, and the time lag between decision and action is typically short. Therefore, the planning and formulation of strategy needs to be tightly coupled with its implementation in a dynamic feedback loop. The direct alignment of the apex and the core thus becomes the significant structural feature of stratocracies. It enables the organization to unify command and to quickly marshall all of its resources and focus on ephemeral opportunities and critical threats.

Structural characteristics of successful high-technology firms support the doers in various ways. Communication processes provide the means for co-ordinating line activities and for linking the apex and the core. Staff are used to support rather than to monitor and oversee line activities. Strategists fulfill operational roles and integrate thinking, planning, and acting. The use of hybrid structures facilitates the fusion of operational and strategic roles. Compensation systems are designed to reward tangible accomplishments, rather than seniority and spans of control.

Stratocracy is an organizational regime of the high-technology arena where strategic ends change constantly and organizational means have to be marshalled cohesively and be amenable to frequent adjustments. The doers are in charge because they are in a position to ascertain and undertake the actions necessary for accomplishing the firm's changing ends, and to rapidly re-focus its capabilities. This regime enables technology firms to maintain a sense of focus and cohesion, while retaining sufficient flexibility to cope with new imperatives.

References

1. For an economic perspective on the importance of organization, see A.H. Cole, "The Entrepreneur: Introductory Remarks," *American Economic Review,* 58 (May 1968):61-62; and K.J. Arrow, *Essays in the Theory of Risk Planning* (Chicago, IL: University of Chicago Press, 1971), p. 224. For a comprehensive account of the ecological perspective, see M. Hannan and J. Freeman, "The Population Ecology of Organizations," *American Journal of Sociology,* 82/5 (1977):929-964. On the historical evolution of the business enterprise, see A.D. Chandler and H. Daems, eds., *Managerial Hierarchies: Comparative Perspectives on the Rise of the Modern Industrial Enterprise* (Boston, MA: Harvard University Press, 1980).

2. A.D. Chandler, *Strategy and Structure: Chapters in the History of the American Industrial Enterprise* (Cambridge, MA: MIT Press, 1962).

3. R.A. Burgelman, "Applying the Methodology of Grounded Theorizing in Strategic Management: A Summary of Recent Findings and Their Implications," in R. Lamb and P. Shrivastava, *Advances in Strategic Management,* Vol. 3 (Greenwich, CT: JAI Press, 1985), pp. 83-99.

4. H. Mintzberg, "An Emerging Strategy of Direct Research," *Administrative Science Quarterly,* 24 (December 1979):582-589.

5. See M. Heidegger, *The Question Concerning Technology,* translated by William Lovitt (New York, NY: Harper and Row, 1977); and P.M. Sherman, *Strategic Planning for Technology Industries* (Reading, MA: Addison-Wesley, 1981).

6. See J. Kotkin and P. Grabowicz, *California, Inc.* (New York, NY: Rawson Wade Publishers, 1982).

7. These are consistent with the findings of other studies. See M.A. Maidique and R.H. Hayes, "The Art of High Technology Management," *Sloan Management Review* (Winter 1984), pp. 17-29.

8. H. Mintzberg, *Structure in Fives: Designing Effective Organizations* (Englewood Cliffs, NJ: Prentice-Hall, 1983), pp. 137-138.

9. R.A. Burgelman and L.R. Sayles, *Inside Corporate Innovation* (New York, NY: The Free Press, 1986).

10. On structural inertia, see M. Hannan and J. Freeman, "Structural Inertia and Organizational Change," *American Sociological Review,* 49 (1984):149-164.

11. For an assessment of the impact of new technologies on organizational structures, see J. Child, "New Technology and Developments in Management Organization," *Omega,* 12/3 (1984):211-223.

12. These terms are derived from Mintzberg's categorization scheme. See Mintzberg, op. cit., (1983).

13. For different forms of hybrid structure, see A.C. Hax and N.S. Majluf, "Organizational Design: A Survey and an Approach," *Operations Research,* 29/3 (May/June 1981):417-447.

14. See W.G. Ouchi, "Markets, Bureaucracies and Clans," *Administrative Science Quarterly,* 25/1 (March 1980):129-141; and T. Burns and G.M. Stalker, *The Management of Innovation* (London: Tavistock Publication, 1961).

15. D.M. Kreps, "Corporate Culture and Economic Theory," unpublished manuscript, Graduate School of Business, Stanford University, 1984.

16. These terms are derived from Leavitt's 3-part model of the managing process. See H.J. Leavitt, *Corporate Pathfinders* (Homewood, IL: Dow Jones-Irwin, 1986).

17. Burns and Stalker, op. cit.; Mintzberg, op. cit., (1983).

18. Burns and Stalker, op. cit., pp. vii, 119.

19. H. Mintzberg and A. McHugh, "Strategy Formation in an Adhocracy," *Administrative Science Quarterly,* 30/2 (June 1985):191.

Chapter 6

Hybrid Organizational Arrangements: New Form or Transitional Development?

Walter W. Powell

Markets and formal organizations, the twin pillars on which much of contemporary social science rests, are typically presented as alternative mechanisms for the allocation and control of resources. In markets, resources are allocated through bargaining over prices. Formal organization— whether represented by hierarchy, as in the language of economists, or by the state, in the vocabulary of political scientists—is a means of allocating resources through authority relations. Sophisticated analysts, of course, recognize that markets are often informally organized and that contractual agreements commonly contain hierarchical properties.[1] Similarly, formal organizations have become much more complex through the introduction of such market processes as profit centers and transfer pricing.[2] But even these more sensible amendments to orthodox theory may lag behind social and economic changes. Or to put it more boldly, analytical concepts such as markets and hierarchies may provide us with distorted lenses through which to analyze economic change. By looking at economic organization as a choice between markets and contractual relations on one side, and at conscious planning within a firm on the other, we fail to see the enormous variety that forms of cooperative arrangements can take.[3]

The business press is rife with reports of ostensibly dramatic transformations taking place in economic institutions. In one variant of these developments, firms have rediscovered the competitive marketplace, the hostile world of arm's-length relationships that characterizes the competitive model of microeconomic theory. Associated with this rediscovery are drastic efforts at cost cutting, fewer restrictions on managerial freedom in the deployment of labor, and intense efforts to reduce the restraints imposed by government regulation. These changes are intended to refashion firms in a

"lean and mean" manner in order to help them to survive intensified competition for jobs and contracts. In another variant of this trend, firms seek
to become more competitive and flexible by reorganizing the nature of production, in some cases by developing entirely new methods for organizing
competition. These firms are responding to high labor costs, not by
eliminating jobs, but by tying some portion of employees wages to company profits and by engaging employees much more actively in the operation of the company.[4]

In tandem with many of these internal reforms are a series of revamped
relationships with trading partners. The realignments may take the form of
new cooperative relationships with suppliers, or collaboration among small
firms to facilitate research and new product development. More generally,
internally generated and financed research is giving way to new forms of
external R&D collaboration among previously unaffiliated enterprises.
Indeed, in some industries, there appears to be a wholesale stampede into
various alliance-type combinations that link large generalist firms and specialized entrepreneurial start-ups. Nor are these simply new means to pursue
research and development; the new arrangements also extend to production,
marketing, and distribution. And, in some circumstances, large firms are
joining together to create "global strategic partnerships"[5] that shift the very
basis of competition to a new level—from firm vs. firm to rival transna-
tional groupings of collaborators.

These nonmarket, nonbureaucratic organizational arrangements are
highly significant features of the contemporary organizational landscape.
We see these hybrid forms in "traditional" craft-based industries, in a wave
of strategic partnerships and alliances in high-technology industries that
combine small firm flexibility with large firm muscle, and in the decomposition of large vertically integrated firms in supposedly mature mass-
production industries. This chapter describes the diversity of these hybrid
forms; offers some explanations for their proliferation; and speculates on
whether these changes will be short-lived or will represent more enduring
solutions to the problems of organizing production in an era of diverse consumer preferences, technological change, and sharp international competition.

Network Forms of Organization in Craft Industries

The distinction between craft-based work and formal organization is based
not only on the dissimilar way in which work is organized in the two settings, but also on differing sets of expectations about the location of authority. Craft work tends to be project-based, but in bureaucratic organizations
a product moves through a series of functional departments where different
activities are performed. In craft work (to borrow from the useful language
of Perrow)[6] each product is relatively unique, search procedures are non-
routine, and the work process depends to a considerable degree on intuition

and experimentation. The three examples presented below are surely not ideal-type illustrations of craft-based work, but they do represent well-researched cases that highlight the many network features associated with craft production.

- *Construction*—Robert Eccles, in his research on the construction industry, found that in many countries the relations between a general contractor and his subcontractors are stable and continuous over long time periods, and only rarely established through competitive bidding.[7] This type of quasi-integration results in what Eccles calls the "quasi-firm." Although most contracts are set under fixed price terms, no hierarchical organization arises, even though there are clear "incentives for shirking performance requirements." Instead, long-term and fairly exclusive association obviates the need for costly organizational monitoring. In an empirical study of residential construction in Massachusetts, Eccles found that it was unusual for a general contractor to employ more than two or three subcontractors in a given trade. This relationship obtained even when a large number of projects were done in the same year, and despite the fact that a number of alternative subcontractors were available.

- *Publishing*—An important development in the book publishing industry is the establishment of personal imprint lines within large trade publishing houses. Under these arrangements, successful editors enjoy freedom from corporate constraints, and authors enjoy the intimacy and closeness associated with smaller houses. These hybrid forms of organization allow an editor to rely on his or her own judgment and not have to appeal for higher level approval. The large firm is able to keep top-flight editors content and, at the same time, give them a greater financial stake in the books they bring in. Personal imprint editors are on their own as far as acquiring and nurturing authors, yet retain corporate clout for financing, sales, and distribution. Other publishers, in a related effort to hold on to key personnel, have "spun off" subsidiaries that operate autonomously within the boundaries of the larger company. These "boutique" operations permit, in the words of the head of one such company, "the intimacy of a small operation with no committee meetings and no bureaucracy."[8]

But these developments are merely reflections of a general phenomenon in certain sectors of the book trade. In trade and scholarly publishing, editors behave much of the time as if they are optimizing not their organization's welfare, but their own or the welfare of the social networks to which they belong. In scholarly publishing, editorial search and evaluation relies extensively on personal networks, which are based on loyalty and friendship, cemented over time. Bonds of allegiance shape the processes of access and discovery. These networks of personal relationships are also vital to economic success. Although competition among firms does, to some extent, influence the success or failure of particular publishing houses, these selection pressures are dampened by the dense associational ties and personal relations that support all publishing transactions. The fortunes of a scholarly publishing house often depend more on the rise and fall of various academic paradigms than on the efficiency of a firm's internal operations. In a sense, companies do not so much compete with one another as they hitch their fate to the success or failure of different academic networks and intellectual fashions.[9]

Both the spinoff arrangements and the quasi-organizations based on personal networks reflect the fact that editors occupy structurally ambivalent positions: Loyalty to their authors and their craft often outweighs allegiance to the firm that employs them. From the employer's perspective, the only means of responding to circumstances in which the most valued assets of the organization—the editor and his or her contacts— are highly mobile is either to allow the editors to set up shop on their own within the corporate boundaries or to try to influence editorial behavior unobtrusively.[10]

- *Textiles*—Charles Sabel and his colleagues describe the German textile industry, centered in the prosperous state of Baden-Württemberg in southwestern Germany, as an "association of specialists, each with unmatched expertise and flexibility in a particular phase or type of production."[11] This flourishing traditional craft industry employs a highly refined system of production that links small and medium-sized firms with a wide range of institutional arrangements that further the well-being of the industry as a whole. These support services include industry research institutes, vocational training centers, consulting firms, and marketing agencies. Most textile producers are highly specialized; and, as Sabel et al. argue, the more distinctive each firm is, the more it depends on the success of other firms' products that complement its own. This production system depends on an extensive subcontracting system in which key technologies are developed in collaboration. The subcontractors are also connected to overlapping inter-industry supplier networks. These linkages allow textile makers to benefit from the subcontractors' experiences with customers in other industries, and the suppliers are, in turn, buffered from downturns in any one industry. All of these arrangements strengthen the social structure in which textile firms are embedded and encourage cooperative relations that attenuate the destructive aspects of competition.

These three examples are not particularly unusual. Network forms of social organization are found in many cultural industries, in research and knowledge production, and in various industrial districts—such as the diamond trade, the garment and fashion business in Milan and New York, or the Lyonnaise silk industry. Many of the professions exhibit some network-like features. Architecture is a prime example; but so apparently is engineering: To judge from one recent study, the informal trading of proprietary know-how among professionals in competing firms is extensive.[12] What these different activities share is a particular kind of skilled labor force, one with hands-on experience with production and the strategic ability to generate new products to keep pace with changing market demands. The people who perform the work have fungible knowledge, that is, it is not limited to an individual task but applicable to a wide range of activities. The organizations that complement these human capital inputs are highly porous, with ill-defined boundaries, vague work roles, overlapping responsibilities, and strong work ties both across teams and to members of other organizations.

Strategic Partnering in High-Tech Industries

In many respects, partnerships and joint ventures are not new developments. They have been common among firms involved in oil extraction and petroleum refining as a means of spreading risks. Chemical and pharmaceutical firms have long conducted basic research jointly with university scientists. And some of the most complex partnerships have taken place in the commercial aircraft industry. The three major global players—Boeing, McDonnell Douglas, and Airbus Industrie—construct their planes via complex joint ventures among firms from many nations. Boeing and Rolls Royce teamed up to produce the Boeing 757, and much of the construction of the Boeing 767 is done, through joint ventures, in Japan and Italy. Airbus Industrie is a four nation European aircraft consortium, supported in part through loans (or subsidies, if you take the competition's view) from European governments.[13]

More generally, however, there is ample evidence that various kinds of interfirm agreements, collaborations, and partnerships have mushroomed—in some industries, in an unprecedented fashion.[14] Firms are seeking to combine their strengths and overcome weaknesses in a collaboration that is much broader and deeper than the marketing joint ventures and technology licensing that were used in the past.

These developments, not surprisingly, are particularly common in high-technology industries.[15] Both the motivations for collaboration and the organizational forms that result are quite varied. Firms pursue cooperative agreements in order to gain fast access to new technologies or new markets, to benefit from economies of scale in joint research and/or production, to tap into sources of know-how located outside the boundaries of the firm, to share the risks for activities that are beyond the scope or capability of a single organization, and to contract for complementary skills.

The ensuing organizational arrangements include joint ventures, strategic alliances, equity partnerships, collaborative research pacts or large-scale research consortia, licensing agreements, reciprocity deals, and satellite organizations. There is no clear-cut relationship between the legal form of the cooperative agreements and the purposes they are intended to achieve. The form of the agreement appears to be individually tailored to the needs of the respective parties, and to tax and regulatory considerations.

High-technology industries, such as microelectronics, telecommunications, and biotechnology, are graphic examples both of the range of different possible ways of organizing and allocating tasks and of their divergence from traditional patterns of industrial organization. Friar and Horwitch contend that there has been a marked shift in technology strategy: a general trend toward greater reliance on external sources for R&D, and more cooperation among competitors.[16] In interviews with members of a sample of 16 *Fortune 500* companies that spent at least $80 million on R&D in 1982, they found that external sources of technology had grown in relative importance at the expense of the central R&D lab. There was a significant increase in contract research, acquisitions, licensing, joint ventures, equity participation, the marketing of other companies' products, reciprocity agreements, and multiorganizational collaborations. In addition, Horwitch finds that large companies are moving away from centralized organization, using instead various internal ventures, such as extreme decentralization at 3M, managed autonomy at Hewlett-Packard, matrix forms at Texas Instruments, and new-venture groups at Exxon.

Similarly, Margaret Graham reports a sea change in corporate research and development.[17] She observes that most of the new approaches to innovation involve ways of obtaining technology from outside the firm, as an alternative to internal R&D. In the biotechnology field, various forms of collaborative relationships are particularly evident;[18] this trend is especially pronounced in Europe.[19] In the U.S., the great majority of biotechnology alliances have linked small, technology-driven, emerging companies with large, well-established companies with extensive manufacturing and marketing capabilities. In Europe, because significant venture capital for start-up companies is lacking, there is greater emphasis on, and government support for, industry-university collaborations and collective research efforts by teams of large companies.

In the past, the most common way in which large companies gained expertise or products that they were unable to develop on their own was to acquire another company with the needed capability. Mergers and acquisitions in high-technology fields have by no means disappeared, but the track record of acquisitions is generally poor. Recent efforts at various kinds of more limited involvement represent an important alternative to outright takeover. Equity arrangements—deals that combine direct project financing and varying degrees of ownership—are an example. A larger firm invests, rather than purchases, primarily for reasons of speed and creativity.

The movement in large companies away from in-house development to partial ownership reflects an awareness that small firms are much faster at, and more capable of, innovation and product development. General Motors explained its 11% investment in Teknowledge, a maker of diagnostic systems that use a type of artificial intelligence, by noting that "if we purchased the company outright, we would kill the goose that laid the golden egg." Equity arrangements can be quite complex. Some small companies have several equity partners, and large companies may find themselves in the novel position of negotiating product development contracts and licensing arrangements with companies that they partly own.

Collaborative agreements involve a wide variety of players. Although the joining together of small firms with entrepreneurial commitment and expertise in technology innovation and large-scale corporate organizations with experience in marketing and distribution represents the prototypical example, these arrangements are certainly not the only form of collaboration. Many large firms are linking up with other large companies, particularly in international ventures. Porter and Fuller suggest that coalitions seem well suited to the process of industry and firm globalization, as evidenced by AT&T's alliances with Olivetti and Philips.[20] Large telecommunications companies have been very active participants in collaborative research efforts. Siemens and ICL both have links with Fujitsu; ICL, Siemens, and Machines Bull have formed a joint research institute in Munich to pool their basic research. Machines Bull is also a partner in a joint venture with Honeywell and N.E.C.

In the U.S., collective industrial research is less common than on the continent or in Japan, but it is becoming more accepted. This new activity signals not only the changing nature of technological research, but also the declining ability of most companies to generate on their own the technical base required for continued growth. Another key motivation is the need to keep pace with the widespread network for collective research in Japan, a model in which government links private firms in a great number of R&D networks. In the U.S., research associations have assumed various forms. Industry associations have been established to conduct basic research at university facilities, as in the case of the Semiconductor Research Corporation or the Center for Biotechnology Research. Research corporations with their own facilities, such as the Microelectronics and Computer Technology Corporation (a for-profit corporation that receives funding and scientists from its 20 member companies), are another example. Because of the complexity and costs of R&D and rapid speed of technological development, cooperative arrangements appear to be an important new means of organizing work in high-technology industries.

Vertical Disaggregation

In an era when the pace of technological change was relatively slow, when production processes were well understood and standardized, and when production runs turned out large numbers of similar products, vertical inte-

gration was a successful strategy. But the disadvantages of large-scale vertical integration can become acute when the pace of technological change
quickens, product life cycles shorten, and markets become more specialized. Firms are responding to these new pressures in a variety of ways,
either by explicitly limiting the size of work units, or by contracting work
out, or through more collaborative ventures with suppliers and distributors.

The Minnesota Mining and Manufacturing Company (3M) is a good
example of a strategy of growing by becoming smaller. The top personnel
officer at 3M reports that "we are keenly aware of the disadvantages of
larger size." The company makes a conscious effort to keep its work units
as small as possible, because its officers think it helps keep them flexible.
The 52,000 U.S. employees of 3M are divided among 37 divisions and 9
subsidiaries. Among the company's 91 manufacturing plants, only 5 employ 1,000 persons or more, and the average company installation has 270.
Many of the recent successes of 3M are attributed to its strategy of "multi-
plication by division."

Another common way in which large firms are growing "smaller" is
through the use of subcontractors and temporary employees. To be sure,
neither the use of part-time workers nor contracting for various business
services as needed are new additions to the repertoire of organizations. But
these methods of accomplishing tasks have recently grown in importance.[21]
We do not yet know if these trends are merely a reaction to a difficult economic period or part of a fundamental change in the organization of work.
The answer is not clear, because practices such as subcontracting have a
double edge: They may represent a move toward relational contracting,
with greater emphasis on security and quality;[22] or they could be a return to
earlier practices, a part of a campaign to slash labor costs, reduce employment levels, and limit the power of unions even further. The auto industry
is a good place to start, both because it is undergoing profound changes
and because the ultimate direction of those changes is not yet determined.

Prior to the mid-1970s, the big three automakers operated in a comforta-
ble environment with little pressure from foreign carmakers and scant consumer demands for gas-efficient, high-quality cars. The auto companies
pursued a policy of vertical integration that led to a highly productive manufacturing system.[23] The automakers used this integration of production as
a means to guarantee their sources of supply during periods of peak demand, as well as to protect the secrecy of annual styling changes. Vertical
integration also helped to keep down the prices of the independent parts
suppliers with whom the companies traded. There was neither any give-
and-take nor trust between the automakers and the subcontractors. Contracts were lost because a supplier bid .01 cents per item higher than a
competitor.[24] The contracts were, in effect, hierarchical documents.[25] Automakers rigorously inspected supplier facilities, quality control procedures,
stability of raw material sources, cost data, and management quality and

depth.[26] Moreover, automakers were reluctant to permit a supplier to manufacture a complete system. Instead, they preferred a competitive situation in which several firms made the various components and the final assembly was done internally by the automakers.

Today this old system appears to be crumbling before the force of international competition and falling prey to the contradictions and short-term logic of the regime of competitive supplier relations. Heightened competition exposed a number of defects in the old methods of production and supplier relationships. Abernathy has argued that vertical integration in the auto industry led to inflexibility.[27] One consequence of tight technological interdependence is that change in any one part means the entire process must be altered. Pursuit of a cost-minimization strategy also reduced the automakers' ability to innovate. Susan Helper, in an excellent analysis of supplier relations, observes that under the old methods the auto companies prevented suppliers from developing expertise, thereby reducing the skill requirements of the suppliers' employees.[28] This make it hard for suppliers to develop non-automotive contracts and kept them dependent on the auto companies. It also had a chilling effect on innovation. There was neither any incentive nor capability for the suppliers to update equipment, suggest technological changes, or make long-range plans.

Because of the erosion of their profits and market share, the automakers have chosen to sacrifice some of their bargaining power vis-à-vis suppliers in order to get more innovative products. Helper reports the following changes in supplier relations: the length of contracts is increasing from one year to three or five years; the automakers and suppliers are doing more joint design work; sole sourcing arrangements, rather than cut-throat competition, are becoming more common; and, instead of inspecting every piece supplied to them, the automakers have almost eliminated receiving inspection, yet defect rates are much reduced.[29] These new, more collaborative arrangements involve less monitoring, particularly with regard to quantitative evaluations, but are reportedly more flexible and adaptive. The automakers have become more dependent on the technological expertise of the suppliers, whose long-run health is now a factor in the automakers' profits.

At the same time, however, the automakers are pursuing a second strategy: outsourcing to low-wage areas. They are simultaneously deciding which suppliers are worth investing in a long-term relationship with and which components can be obtained on the basis of price rather than quality. In these cases, there is little concern for coordination or supplier design work; instead, the effort is aimed at finding third-world suppliers that can provide parts at the lowest possible price. This two-pronged effort reflects the crossroads that many companies are at as they run up against the limits of vertical integration. The choice is between moving transactions back into the marketplace or establishing long-term, give-and-take relationships among more or less autonomous parties. When tasks involve relatively standardized activities that require little asset specificity, or when demand for a product is uncertain, firms are likely to turn to market relationships. But when tasks require knowledge and skill, and quality is important, firms are more likely to rely on relational contracting.

Evidence is accumulating that many firms are choosing to shrink their operations in response to the liabilities of large-scale organization. For example, Mariotti and Cainarca describe a "downsizing" pattern in the Italian textile industry, where there has been a decline in the number of vertically integrated firms and growth in "intermediate governance structures."[30] They attribute this development to three failures that plague vertically integrated firms: an inability to respond quickly to competitive changes in international markets; resistance to process innovations that alter the relationship between different stages of the production process; and systemic resistance to the introduction of new products. Wilkinson details related developments in Britain, where retailing, clothing, shoemaking, printing, and foodstuffs have under gone vertical disintegration, with the subsequent rise of small firms and numerous subcontracting relationships.[31]

Ronald Dore argues that networks of preferential, stable trading relationships are a viable alternative to vertical integration.[32] His work on the Japanese textile industry, particularly its weaving segment, aptly illustrates this point. The industry was dominated in the 1950s by large mills, most of which were vertically integrated enterprises with cotton-importing, spinning, and finishing operations. By 1980, the larger mills had closed and the integrated firms had divested and returned to their original base in spinning. This "devolution" has led to a series of stable relationships among firms of different sizes. The key to this system is mutual assistance. Dore gives the example of a finisher who re-equips with a more efficient process, which gives him a cost advantage. This finisher, however, does not win much new business by offering a lower price. The more common consequence is that merchants go to their own finishers and say: "Look how X got his price down. We hope you can do the same because we really would have to reconsider our position if the price difference goes on for months. If you need bank financing to get the new type of vat we can probably help by guaranteeing the loan." This type of relationship is, of course, not limited to the textile industry. A similar pattern of dense, reciprocal ties is repeated in the relationship between Toyota and its many subcontractors as well as in many other sectors of Japanese industry.[33]

Extended trading groups are by no means unique to Japan. In Britain, Marks and Spencer, the retail group known for its product reliability, does not manufacture anything and administers as little as possible. It even subcontracts its entire computer business. The company squeezes suppliers in times of trouble, but it does not ditch them as long as they maintain quality standards.[34] Robert Bosch, GmbH (the West German firm) is one of the world's most sophisticated automotive-parts manufacturers. It is well-known as an experienced supplier to many companies and as an organizer of its own complex subcontracting system.[35] The company has highly supportive relationships with a number of key subcontractors. The assistance that is provided ranges from technical advice to production collaboration. An unusual policy that requires subcontractors to do no more than 20% of their business with Bosch insures that the suppliers do not become overly reliant on Bosch, and Bosch learns from the work the suppliers perform for other companies. Some of the subcontractors, in turn, apply this model of organization to their own transactions.

What are the performance consequences of these kinds of trading relationships? Dore suggests that the security of the relationship encourages investment by suppliers, as the spread of robotics among Japan's engineering subcontractors amply attests. Trust and mutual dependency result in a more rapid flow of information. In textiles, changes in consumer markets are passed quickly upstream to weavers, and technical changes in production also flow downstream rapidly. There is, Dore asserts, a general emphasis on quality. The best indicator of consistent effort is product quality. One would not terminate a relationship when a party cannot deliver the lowest price, but it is perfectly proper to terminate a relationship when someone is not maintaining quality standards.

These examples highlight several general, and presumably related, trends: a movement toward the decentralization of enterprises, the downsizing of large corporate bureaucracies, the growth of smaller units of enterprise (a growth that comes at the expense of larger units and is not explained solely by the shift from manufacturing to services),[36] and the development of extended networks of trading groups.

What Factors Explain the Proliferation of Hybrid Organizational Forms?

No single factor accounts for the fact that hybrid organizational forms have become such an important feature of the economic landscape. In many individual cases the explanation is highly idiosyncratic. A broader interpretation would point to the effects of rapid structural change in the world economy, with the consequence that there is movement both away from an older set of industries (thus causing firms in these industries to shrink) and toward a new set of industries (in which most firms are still in a youthful stage). This transformation of the economic environment is a crucial part of the story. Hybrid organizational forms ostensibly represent a better fit with these new market and technological demands. The organizational factors that are most relevant in accounting for the proliferation of hybrids include: better adaptability to changing markets; the limits of large scale organization and the incentives associated with smaller firms; the fact that sources of know-how are located more diffusely and the attendant need for fast access to this knowledge; and the powerful role played by reputation and reciprocity.

Changing Environmental Conditions—Vertical integration and mass production represented a victory, achieved through advertising and merchandising, of price over quality. In recent years, however, there has been as apparent shift in consumer taste in favor of diversity, even customization. Piore and Sabel contend that the breakup and dissolution of mass markets for standardized products has led to a decline in productivity and to slower growth, thereby opening the door to alternative organizational forms.[37]

It is not clear what has led to the apparent growing diversity in consumer tastes. It may simply reflect a saturation of mass-produced consumer goods, or it may be a sign that mass markets and standardized production are associated with a lower standard of living, and in a more affluent period, consumer wants have expanded. The change may also reflect the narrowing of the gap in cost between mass and craft production, which has made it easier to draw customers away from mass-produced items. This narrowing of cost is a result, to some extent, of the diffusion of business skills (such as accounting and marketing) to a wider population of firms and business people, complemented by the spread of microcomputer technology and small-business software applications.

But whatever the causes, the shift toward more flexible forms of production, greater emphasis on innovation, and more specialized, higher-quality product lines is significant. Coping with this change requires greater technological sophistication and faster response time on the part of organizations. These new requirements have led to the decomposition of large integrated firms and the rise of smaller specialized organizations and new hybrid forms. We see these changes in supposedly mature mass-production industries (note the rise of profitable minimills in the steel industry and the spread of small specialty chemical producers), in traditional sectors where the techniques of craft production were never abandoned, and in the new high-technology industries. Even the auto industry—the symbol of mass production—is now moving toward more specialized production and emphasizing flexibility and innovation.

The Limits of Large-Scale Organization—In what kinds of settings are large, hierarchical organizations (defined by the number of levels of supervisors and managers) most likely to be found? They are typically located in environments that lack strong competitive pressures. In contrast, in highly competitive environments, such as semiconductors or biotechnology, where selection pressures are strong and result in a high rate of organizational mortality, the enduring organizational form is the firm that operates, in Ouchi's terminology, more like a clan than a hierarchy.[38] Even the largest firms in these competitive industries, such as an IBM or a Hewlett-Parkard, have as many clan-like properties as hierarchical ones. Environments with tight selection pressures require that firms be responsive to market demands. Such responsiveness to client and consumer needs is best provided by smaller firms—or flat, decentralized ones—not by large firms with multiple layers of hierarchy. The latter are more capable of realizing scale economies; hence it is not surprising that the most hierarchical organizations are found in concentrated industries (such as the U.S. auto and steel industries, particularly in the era before foreign competition) and in the public and nonprofit sectors (as in the case of the U.S. civil service, the Defense Department, or various religious institutions, where selection pressures are weak at best and entry barriers are high).

Large vertically integrated firms may perform quite well when mass production, strict routines, and well-specified procedures can be used to attack stable and predictable markets. But when organizations are confronted by sharp fluctuations in demand and unanticipated changes, the liabilities of large scale are exposed. Among the principal disadvantages of large-scale organization are a bias toward internal procurement and expansion, problems of structural inertia, risk aversion, and decreased employee satisfaction and commitment.

There is a pronounced tendency in large organizations for managers to cause their firms to grown beyond the optimal size. More subordinates apparently satisfies a manager's psychological needs, increases his or her social status within the firm, and provides tangible economic rewards—especially when compensation is linked to the number of employees reporting to a manager. The addition of extra staff, units, or departments may have only marginal effects on the overall organization, but it brings important benefits to the people in charge of these new positions. People—measured in number of staff or departments—are a form of wealth in organizations. For those in charge, new positions are resources for maintaining influence and enhancing status. As Weber alerted us decades ago, bureaucracies are remarkably efficient tools for accomplishing certain kinds of activities; but once in place, bureaucracy is highly resistant to change. Hence the natural tendency for large organizations to become ends in themselves, stripped of their intended purpose.

The strength of bureaucratic organization is its reliability (its capacity for producing collective products of a given quality repeatedly) and its accountability (its ability to document how resources have been used).[39] But these very features result in organizational routines that display substantial rigidity[40] or lead to structural inertia.[41] The larger the organization, the more behaviors will repeat themselves; as a result, the more predictable they become and thus the greater is the propensity to formalize them. For certain activities this is useful, but for others it can result in a serious mismatch between organizational outcomes and the demands of clients and customers in changing environments.

Peter Blau's extensive studies of the effects of size on organizations have demonstrated that size independently gives rise to increased structural differentiation and that differentiation independently generates the need for more managerial, administrative, and supervisory personnel.[42] Similarly, John Child found large organizations to have more rules and to require more documentation.[43] These findings suggest that large organizations will be characterized by two features: risk-aversion and lack of speed in processing information and in making decisions.

The information costs in large organizations are further compounded by motivational difficulties as well. One point that Alchian and Demsetz[44] and Williamson[45] implicitly demonstrate is that much of the internal structure of large organizations is designed to prevent collective action by employees. This basic attitude of suspicion may explain the finding by social psychologists that job satisfaction (as measured by turnover, absenteeism, and morale) declines with increases in organizational size and/or centralization.[46] The design of organizations can effect the behavior of their members in a number of powerful ways. In large hierarchical organizations, promotions up the career ladder are a key part of the reward structure. You have, then, little incentive to disagree with the operating decisions made by people above you in rank because they are the people who must decide on your promotion. The motivational consequences of hierarchical design run counter to the research findings that suggest that individuals will be more committed if they have participated in a decision and less committed if they have been ordered to undertake a particular task.[47]

The discussion of the limits of hierarchy suggests that the very factors that make a larger organization efficient at some tasks make it cumbersome and resistant to change when it comes to others. Yet, if this is the case, why don't smaller organizations, which are presumably "lighter on their feet," outperform larger organizations? The issue is a complex one to resolve. Two points seem particularly relevant. First, many large organizations do not find it necessary to change very frequently. They may be protected by regulation, entrenched in a position of strong market power, or located in a fairly stable economic environment. Second, although small organizations are able to adapt their internal structures more quickly to changing environmental conditions, an organization undergoing change is probably more vulnerable to environmental shocks.[48] Large size may very well increase the capacity for withstanding such shocks. In addition, large organizations can devote more resources to the task of change. Thus the joining together of small specialist firms with large generalist organizations or the decentralization of larger firms into smaller autonomous work units may be viewed as strategies to overcome both bureaucratic inertia and the lack of clout and legitimacy that plagues small companies.

The Importance of Speed and Information—A central feature in many technologically-driven industries is know-how. In these process-oriented fields, knowing how to make a product and how to make it work is absolutely critical to success. In recent years, as product life cycles shorten and competition intensifies, timing considerations and access to know-how have become paramount concerns. Teece and Pisano suggest that, increasingly, the most qualified centers of excellence in the relevant know-how are located outside the boundaries of the large corporation.[49] Whether it is the case that one firm's technological competence has outdistanced others, or that innovations would be hard to replicate internally even if R&D spending was high, there is a growing need for fast access to technological innovation. Porter and Fuller contend that partnerships or coalitions are a more rapid means of repositioning than internal development and are less costly, less irreversible, and more feasible than mergers.[50]

Know-how often involves a kind of tacit knowledge that is difficult to codify and that cannot be easily transmitted. Physical records do not capture the intricacies and nuances of the work process. It may even be difficult to communicate verbally to another person how the work is executed. In such cases, an employee knows more than he or she can tell another person. The tacit character of certain technological skills suggests high switching costs; it is difficult for both employees and the organization to shift to other lines of activity. Under these circumstances, a stock of idiosyncratic knowledge is built up over time. It may include empirical lore, stories about special cases, and general intuition. This kind of knowledge is not easily appropriated. The information is in the heads of people, not written down in manuals, blueprints, or handbooks. Acquiring the rights to a particular technological process, especially one still in the development stage, or buying the process outright through takeover does not guarantee that the necessary knowledge is acquired. Indeed, it may hinder the process because the most valuable assets—the minds of the innovators—may choose to walk away.

Hybrid organizational forms, then, represent a fast means of gaining access to sources of know-how located outside of the organization, without risking the chance that the know-how will dissipate. And, in contrast to merger, hybrid arrangements preserve some measure of independence for the smaller partner. With their network-like configuration, hybrid forms can process information in multiple directions. They create complex webs of communication and mutual obligation. By enhancing the spread of information, they create the conditions for further innovation by bringing together different logics and novel combinations of information.

Networks and Generalized Reciprocity—In several important respects, hybrid forms represent a modern version of a centuries-old means of allocating goods and services, a method that Polanyi termed "generalized reciprocity."[51] In this model of resource allocation, transactions occur neither through discrete exchanges nor by administrative fiat, but through

networks of individuals engaged in reciprocal, preferential, mutually supportive actions. Reputation, trust, tacit collusion, and a relative absence of
calculative quid pro quo behavior guide this system of exchange. In network forms of organization, individual units exist not by themselves, but
in relationship to other units.

A cornerstone of network forms is a long-term perspective, which af-
fords more give-and-take and a view that bridges will be crossed when
they are arrived at. Security and stability encourage the search for new
ways of accomplishing tasks. When repeat trading occurs, quality becomes
more important than quantity. The reputation of a participant is the most
visible signal of its reliability. Reputation bulks large in importance because
in many network-like work settings, there is little separation of formal business roles and personal social roles. One's standing in one arena determines
one's place in the other. As a result, there is limited need for hierarchical
oversight, because the desire for continued participation successfully dis-
courages opportunism. Monitoring is generally easier and more effective
when done by peers than when done by superiors. Performance evaluation
takes place through the kind of subtle reading of signals that is possible
only among intimate coworkers but that cannot be translated into explicit,
verifiable measures.[52] Consensual ideologies substitute for formal rules and
compliance procedures.

Networks are particularly apt for circumstances in which there is a need
for efficient, reliable information. The most useful information is rarely
that which flows down the formal chain of command in an organization, or
that which can be inferred from shifting price signals. Rather, it is that
which is obtained from someone whom you have dealt with in the past and
found to be reliable. You trust best information that comes from someone
you know well. Kaneko and Imai suggest that information passed through
networks is "thicker" than information obtained in the market, and "freer"
than that communicated in a hierarchy.[53] From this perspective, vertical
integration may represent a second-best solution, one in which the parties
lacked membership in a network of social relations and thus turned to
merger in order to mediate their exchange.[54]

Liabilities of Hybrid Forms

There are, of course, drawbacks associated with hybrid arrangements. As
these forms become more prevalent, we learn more about their peculiar
disabilities. Hybrids may, like most forms of social organization in which
there are enduring patterns of repeat trading, restrict access. By foreclosing
opportunities to newcomers, either intentionally or more subtly through
such organizational barriers as unwritten rules or informal codes of conduct, the nature of competition is shaped. In practice, subcontracting net-

works and partnerships can influence who competes with whom and/or can dictate the adoption of a particular technology, making it much harder for unaffiliated parties to join the fray.

A common concern about hybrid forms is that one partner will appropriate a disproportionate share of the value of the relationship. This fear, along with the worry that the partner will not perform according to expectations, explains why most potential partners approach an agreement with trepidation. These are typical and well-founded misgivings about any asymmetric exchange relationship. One party may make costly investments that render it more vulnerable. (One hears talk that this is occurring in the production joint venture, NUMMI, between General Motors and Toyota: GM is reportedly gaining little knowledge about Toyota's production expertise, but Toyota is acquiring experience in managing ethnically diverse male and female workers.) Finally, there is always the risk that the relationship will terminate, and one partner will then copy the other's more valuable assets.

Hybrid arrangements can also create a host of novel management problems, difficulties that are summarized nicely by Borys and Jemison.[55] They suggest that because hybrid partners have not previously worked together, they may misperceive one another's actions. Hybrid arrangements are not like start-up companies; they begin with considerable resources, obligations to the founding parties, and lofty expectations. Moreover, these expectations are externally imposed by stakeholders who usually have a financial need for fast results. Thus the pressures on hybrid forms to perform may be intense.

There are also inherent dangers in global partnerships, risks that are contested in the current "manufacturing matters" debate. There is an ever-present threat in all hybrid agreements that one party will capture the lion's share of the benefits; but when the issue is raised to the level of national capabilities, the perils are obviously greater. David Teece has noted that when technology becomes more public and less proprietary through easier imitation, it is critical for a nation to maintain strength in low-cost manufacturing in order to reap benefits from innovation.[56] Otherwise, low-cost imitator-manufacturers may capture all the profits. *Business Week*, in its well-known March 3, 1986 issue, cautioned against the growth of "hollow corporations," that is, firms that have disaggregated so radically that they are left without any core expertise. Others worry that U.S. partners to global ventures may provide only such services as assembly, distribution, and marketing, which add little value to the product. The key development work and the higher-paying, value-added jobs are taken overseas, and the U.S. firm merely completes the final stages. These issues are far from being resolved, but they point out the complex ways in which hybrid organizational arrangements may or may not contribute to a country's stock of organizational talents.

Future Prospects

How stable are hybrid forms of social organization? Are hybrids likely to endure as an institution? These are separate questions, because even if individual relationships prove to be short-lived, the parties engaged in short-term agreements could search for new partners. Hence, one scenario would entail a series of temporary associations that are continually recast and reshuffled; as a result, the organizational form persists. Another scenario suggests that hybrids are transitional phenomena. A profound shift in the methods of technological development robs incumbents of their clout and brings upstarts to the fore. Established firms must turn to partnerships and coalitions to remain competitive, but once their internal capability is built up, large firms will either absorb their trading partners or convert the relationship into a market transaction.

The question, then, is whether these developments represent a permanent jump to a new and different kind of interaction or are part of a cyclical upswing. Is the world that the large corporation has dominated changing in fundamental ways? Or is the change only temporary—will the dominant incumbents soon reemerge on top, albeit in a slightly altered fashion? These are fundamental questions; at present, we can only glimpse the answers. We can, however, speculate as to what kinds of hybrid forms are likely to have more stability. And we can predict, as I have above, when firms will turn to market relationships as opposed to more long-term collaborative arrangements.

Some hybrid arrangements require that the various participants work together in the performance of a common activity. When the partners are involved in ongoing, complementary contributions—such as the pooling of research staffs or joint production activities—the relationship is likely to be constant. The alternative to this form of organization is vertical integration. In contrast, agreements based on contracting for the performance or delivery of various services are likely to be discontinued when one party's internal skills "catch up" with those of the partner. The exchange of money for knowledge or access implies that there is a basic asymmetry to the relationship. This unequal status reduces the likelihood of a long-term, balanced agreement.

It is unusual to find a tight connection between an organizational form and specific environmental conditions. To be sure, some organizational arrangements are better suited to certain conditions than others; but a range of social, political, and historical factors may attenuate the linkage between form and environment. This is particularly true in a period such as the present, when there is a good deal of experimentation under way. Many organizations are currently torn by crosscutting pressures: circumstances that push them toward sharp-edged competitive practices which entail lower wages and a more intensive pace of work; and equally strong conditions that lead companies to search for policies that permit flexibility, promote quality and more collaborative relationships, and provide access to sources of know-how. To the extent that the latter conditions obtain, hybrid forms of organization are likely to proliferate.

References

1. Mark Granovetter, "Economic Action and Social Structure: A Theory of Embeddedness," *American Journal of Sociology*, 91/3 (November 1985); Arthur Stinchcombe, "Contracts as Hierarchical Documents," in A. Stinchcombe and C. Heimer, *Organization Theory and Project Management* (Oslo: Norwegian University Press, 1985), pp. 121–171.

2. Robert Eccles, *The Transfer Pricing Problem: A Theory for Practice* (Lexington, MA: Lexington Books, 1985).

3. For an elaboration of this point, see G.B. Richardson, "The Organization of Industry," *Economic Journal*, 82 (1972):883–896.

4. For a thoughtful discussion of these developments, see Martin Weitzman, *The Share Economy* (Cambridge, MA: Harvard University Press, 1984); Richard Walton, "From Control to Commitment in the Workplace," *Harvard Business Review*, 85/2 (1985):76–84.

5. Howard Perlmutter and David Heenan, "Cooperate to Compete Globally," *Harvard Business Review* (April/May 1986), p.136.

6. Charles Perrow, "A Framework for the Comparative Analysis of Organizations," *American Sociological Review*, 32 (1967):194–208.

7. Robert Eccles, "The Quasifirm in the Construction Industry," *Journal of Economic Behavior and Organization*, 2 (December 1981):335–357.

8. Lewis Coser, Charles Kadushin, and Walter W. Powell, *Books: The Culture and Commerce of Publishing* (New York, NY: Basic Books, 1982), p. 53.

9. For a discussion of the friendly competition and collaboration that typify scholarly publishing, see Walter W. Powell, *Getting Into Print: The Decision Making Process in Scholarly Publishing* (Chicago, IL: University of Chicago Press, 1985).

10. Ibid., pp. 144–157.

11. Charles Sabel, Gary Herrigel, Richard Kazis, and Richard Deeg, "How to Keep Mature Industries Innovative," *Technology Review*, 90/3 (1987):26–35.

12. Eric Von Hippel, "Cooperation Between Competing Firms: Informal Know-How Trading," Working Paper #1759–86, Sloan School of Management, M.I.T., 1986.

13. The commercial aircraft industry is unusual because of the very active role played by governments in insuring that their countries have a major presence in the industry (for a more detailed discussion of the political aspects of international coalitions, see Michael Porter, *Competition in Global Industries* [Boston, MA: Harvard Business School Press, 1987]). In this case, coalitions and joint ventures are driven more by political factors and pressures for economic nationalism than by organizational reasons.

14. For empirical evidence, see John Friar and Mel Horwitch, "The Emergence of Technology Strategy: A New Dimension of Strategic Management," *Technology in Society*, 7/2–3 (1985):143–178; David Teece, "Profiting form Technological Innovation: Implications for Integration, Collaboration, Licensing and Public Policy," *Research Policy*, 15/6 (1986):285–305; Patrizia Zagnoli, "Interfirm Agreements as Bilateral Transactions?" paper presented at conference on New Technology and New Intermediaries, Center for European Studies, Stanford, 1987.

15. P. Mariti and R.H. Smiley, "Co-operative Agreements and the Organization of Industry," *Journal of Industrial Economics*, 31/4 (1983):437–451; Zagnoli, op. cit.

16. Friar and Horwitch, op. cit.
17. Margaret Graham, "Corporate Research and Development: The Latest Transformation," *Technology in Society,* 7/2–3 (1985): 179–196.
18. William F. Hamilton, "Corporate Strategies for Managing Emerging Technologies," *Technology in Society,* 7/2–3 (1985):197–212; David Teece and Gary Pisano, "Collaborative Arrangements and Technology Strategy," paper presented at conference on New Technology and New Intermediaries, Center for European Studies, Stanford, 1987.
19. Mark D. Dibner, "Biotechnology in Europe," *Science,* 232 (June 13, 1986):1367–1372.
20. Michael Porter and M.B. Fuller, "Coalitions and Global Strategy," in M. Porter, ed., *Competition in Global Industries* (Boston, MA: Harvard Business School Press, 1987), pp. 315–344.
21. Jeffrey Pfeffer and James Baron, "Taking the Workers Back Out: Recent Trends in the Structuring of Employment," in B. Staw and L. Cummings, eds. *Research in Organizational Behavior,* Vol. 10 (Greenwich, CT: JAI Press, forthcoming); Katherine G. Abraham, "The Role of Flexible Staffing Arrangements in Short-Term Workforce Adjustment Strategies," in R.A. Hart, ed., *Employment, Unemployment, and Hours of Work* (London: Allen and Unwin, forthcoming); Katherine G. Abraham, "Restructuring the Employment Relationship: The Growth of Market-Mediated Work Arrangements," paper presented at conference on New Developments in Labor Markets and Human Resource Policies, Sloan School of Management, M.I.T., 1987; Garth Mangum, Donald Mayall, and Kristin Nelson, "The Temporary Help Industry," *Industrial and Labor Relations Review,* 38 (1985):599–611; Max Carey and Kim Hazelbacker, "Employment Growth in the Temporary Help Industry," *Monthly Labor Review* (April 1986), pp. 37–44.
22. Ian Macneil, "Contracts: Adjustment of Long-term Economic Relations Under Classical, Neoclassical, and Relational Contract Law," *Northwestern University Law Review,* 72/6 (1978):854–905.
23. William Abernathy, *The Productivity Dilemma* (Baltimore, MD: Johns Hopkins University Press, 1978).
24. Michael Porter, *Cases in Competitive Strategy* (New York, NY: Free Press, 1983).
25. Stinchcombe, op. cit.
26. Porter, op. cit. (1983), p. 278.
27. Abernathy, op. cit.
28. Susan Helper, "Vertical Relations in the U.S. Auto Industry," unpublished manuscript, Department of Economics, Harvard University, 1984.
29. Ibid.
30. Sergio Mariotti and Gian Carlo Cainarca, "The Evolution of Transaction Governance in the Textile-Clothing Industry," *Journal of Economic Behavior and Organization,* 7 (1986):351–374.
31. Frank Wilkinson, "Productive Systems," *Cambridge Journal of Economics,* 7 (1983):413–429.
32. Ronald Dore, "Goodwill and the Spirit of Market Capitalism," *British Journal of Sociology,* 34/4 (December 1983):459–482.
33. Michael Gerlach, "Business Alliances and the Strategy of the Japanese Firm," *California Management Review,* 30/1 (Fall 1987).
34. Richardson, op. cit.; Dore, op. cit.
35. Sabel et al., op. cit.
36. On this point, see Gary Loveman, Michael Piore, and Werner Sengenberger, "The Evolving Role of Small Business in Industrial Economies," paper presented at conference on New Developments in Labor Market and Human Resource Policies, Sloan School of Management, M.I.T., 1987.

37. Michael J. Piore and Charles F. Sabel, *The Second Industrial Divide* (New York, NY: Basic Books, 1984).
38. William Ouchi, "Markets, Bureaucracies, and Clans," *Administrative Science Quarterly*, 25 (March 1980):129–141.
39. Michael Hannan and John H. Freeman, "Structural Inertia and Organizational Change," *American Sociological Review*, 49/2 (April 1984):149–164.
40. Richard Nelson and Sidney Winter, *An Evolutionary Theory of Economic Change* (Cambridge, MA: Harvard University Press, 1982).
41. Hannan and Freeman, op. cit.
42. Peter M. Blau, *On the Nature of Organizations* (New York, NY: John Wiley & Sons, 1974).
43. John Child, "Organizational Structure and Strategies of Control: A Replication of the Aston Study," *Administrative Science Quarterly*, 17 (June 1972):163–177.
44. Armen Alchian and Harold Demsetz, "Production, Information Costs, and Economic Organization," *American Economic Review*, 62/5 (1972):777–795.
45. Oliver E. Williamson, *Markets and Hierarchies: Analysis and Antitrust Implications* (New York, NY: Free Press, 1975).
46. Lyman Porter and Edward Lawler, "Properties of Organization Structure in Relation to Job Attitudes and Job Behavior," *Psychological Bulletin*, 64/1 (1965):23–51; Chris Berger and L.L. Cummings, "Organizational Structure, Attitudes, and Behavior," in Barry Staw and L.L. Cummings, eds., *Research in Organizational Behavior*, Vol. 1, (Greenwich, CT: JAI Press, 1979).
47. Richard Hackman and Greg Oldham, *Work Redesign* (Reading, MA: Addison-Wesley, 1980).
48. Hannan and Freeman, op. cit.
49. Teece and Pisano, op. cit.
50. Porter and Fuller, op. cit.
51. Karl Polanyi, *The Great Transformation* (Boston, MA: Beacon, 1957).
52. Ouchi, op. cit.
53. Ikuyo Kaneko and Ken-ichi Imai, "A Network View of the Firm," paper presented at 1st Hitotsubashi-Stanford conference, 1987.
54. Granovetter, op. cit.
55. Bryan Borys and David B. Jemison, "Hybrid Organizations as Strategic Alliances: Theoretical and Practical Issues in Organizational Combinations," unpublished paper, Graduate School of Business, Stanford, 1987.
56. Teece, op. cit.

PART II

SPECIAL DIMENSIONS OF STRATEGY

Chapter 7

The Top Management Team: Key to Strategic Success

Donald C. Hambrick

*or the past fifteen years, strategy researchers and consul-
tants have been preoccupied by a quest for techniques and
tools that top managers can reliably use to improve their
firms' performance. Many such attempts have fallen flat when
tried in real competitive arenas. Others have emerged as useful*
rules of thumb or as rough guidelines, but carrying so many exceptions as
to be only narrowly useful. Also, once in the hands of all competitors in an
industry, many of these concepts simply result in a more sophisticated stale-
mate. Finally, some of the prescriptions—such as those dealing with
payoffs from market share, product quality, innovation, and employee productivity—are a bit like the advice to the investor: "Buy low and sell high."
They're unassailable but provide very little concrete guidance.

These disappointing results have caused some theorists to shift their
focus away from trying to find new strategic nostrums and toward trying to
better understand the process by which successful strategies emerge and
get implemented. At the heart of this concern for strategic processes is the
question, "What types of managers, in what combinations, have the best
chances of identifying, picking, and implementing successful strategies?"
Introduced as the "upper echelons model," this view contends that performance of an organization is ultimately a reflection of its top managers.[1] In
the face of the ambiguity and massive bombardment of information that
typifies the top management task, no two strategists will necessarily identify the same array of options; if they were to pick the same major options,

Bert Cannella, Jim Fredrickson, Mike Tushman, and Bob Yavitz made valuable suggestions
on earlier versions of this article. The article is based upon research conducted under the
sponsorship of Columbia University's Strategy Research Center.

87

they almost certainly would not implement them identically. Biases, blinders, skills, aptitudes, interpersonal dynamics and other human factors in the executive ranks greatly affect what happens to companies. The upshot is that general managers who want to improve their organizations' performance will work on improving their management teams.

Obviously, greatness within a team will not in itself assure strategic success. We have many examples of "high-caliber" management teams who have operated in ways that have nullified their raw talents.[2] However, team qualities are the essential foundation for a successful strategic process within the firm. The amounts of open-mindedness, perseverance, communication skills, vision, and other key characteristics that exist within the team clearly set the limits for how well the team—and, in turn, the firm—can operate.

This chapter proposes a framework for systematically assessing and reshaping top management teams. While the logic of the approach could be used at any managerial level, the major focus here is on how the general manager of a business unit should approach this critical task. Following the description of the framework in the next section, the case of a division president in a multibusiness firm who used the framework will be presented.

The analytic framework is diagrammed in Figure 1. It specifies the elements of this important process and identifies the range of issues the manager must consider. The starting point is a careful consideration of the context in which the management team will operate. This context includes external factors (societal, industry, and corporate) as well as internal factors (chosen strategy, competitive weapons, workforce profile, and so on). The profile of the ideal team for managing in this context can then be constructed. There are many dimensions on which managerial qualities can be assessed, but the focus here is on six broad arenas: values, aptitudes, skills, knowledge, cognitive style, and demeanor. The next step is to fairly and carefully assess the mix of qualities within the existing team. Finally, the manager must develop a concrete action plan for closing the gap between what is needed and what exists. There is a substantial array of levers for reshaping a top team—training and development, incentives, coaching and counsel, use of outside or contract talent, team replacements, and team additions.

The framework should not be taken primarily as a way for deciding who needs to be replaced. It may lead to such decisions, but at least in the firms where it has been applied so far, it has tended to lead to the enhancement and unleashing of individuals' talents while making the overall team far more fit for the competitive environment.

Three basic premises underlie this chapter and the framework presented in it. First, there is no such thing as a universally ideal management team. The appropriate mix of qualities depends on the context in which the managers must operate and how the individuals fit with each other. This means

Figure 1. Framework for Top Management Team Analysis

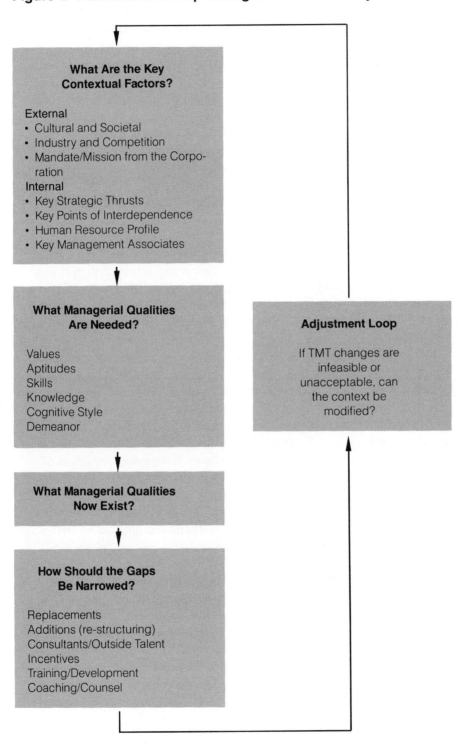

What Are the Key Contextual Factors?

External
- Cultural and Societal
- Industry and Competition
- Mandate/Mission from the Corporation

Internal
- Key Strategic Thrusts
- Key Points of Interdependence
- Human Resource Profile
- Key Management Associates

What Managerial Qualities Are Needed?

Values
Aptitudes
Skills
Knowledge
Cognitive Style
Demeanor

Adjustment Loop

If TMT changes are infeasible or unacceptable, can the context be modified?

What Managerial Qualities Now Exist?

How Should the Gaps Be Narrowed?

Replacements
Additions (re-structuring)
Consultants/Outside Talent
Incentives
Training/Development
Coaching/Counsel

that even the seemingly most desirable qualities can exist in counterproductive amounts. Second, the general manager can and must think proactively about his or her team. The view that the existing team's talents have to be taken completely as a given is an immense disservice to the business as well as to the members of the team. Third, managers must think about their teams in their own highly personalized ways. The ideal team is very much a function of how the general manager operates and what he or she values within the group. For this reason, canned inventories of managerial qualities are dangerous. For the same reason, it may eventually prove difficult for theorists to construct broadly applicable hypotheses about ideal team mixes, since the ideal is so dependent upon the general manager's own preferred mode of operating.

The view that so much hinges upon the general manager appears to imply that the upper echelon should be defined strictly as the top person. In support of such a position, recent research has found convincing evidence that the characteristics of general managers are related to the strategies they pursue[3] as well as to how well their organizations will perform.[4] Such findings are intuitively reassuring to most of us, since we—Americans in particular—tend to hold romantic views about strong leaders.[5] As a society, we seem to need and continually create singular managerial heroes and villains.

However, except in the most extreme cases, management is a shared effort. There are too many options and issues for one person to comprehend, so delegation and collaboration occur. The limited empirical evidence as to whether the top person or the entire top team is a better predictor of organizational outcomes clearly supports the conclusion that the full team has greater effect. Hage and Dewar found that the values of the entire top teams of health and social service agencies were better predictors of subsequent organizational innovation than were the values of the executive directors alone.[6] Similarly, Tushman, Virany, and Romanelli found in a sample of minicomputer firms that major organization changes, or "reorientations," were more likely to be successful when accompanied by changes in the entire top team than when accompanied by a change only in the CEO.[7]

One could also turn to anecdotal accounts of the importance of team dynamics. For example, Exxon's inability to achieve success outside the oil industry has been blamed on the extreme homogeneity and long tenures in the oil industry of Exxon's top management team.[8] Similarly, it was primarily due to the interplay among key partners, rather than due to any one person, that the venerable investment bank, Lehman Brothers, experienced a mutiny and was absorbed by Shearson/American Express[9] It seems clear that the composition of the top team is a crucial element in corporate behavior and performance.

Framework for Team Analysis

Context—The starting point for assessing a managerial team is in reaching a complete understanding of the context in which the team will be operating. Team designers often omit this stage or give it short shrift, preferring to move directly to more action-oriented questions, such as "Who should fill each slot?" However, unless the setting for managerial action is well comprehended, the mix of appropriate team qualities cannot be identified.

A good contextual analysis need not be laborious. Key factors are often readily apparent; moreover, in many firms, a major portion of the context is revealed as part of a good strategic planning process, with its emphasis on environmental opportunities and threats and internal strengths and weaknesses.

The context consists of factors both external and internal to the business. Following are descriptions of several of the key contextual elements that the team architect must grasp.

- *Cultural and Societal Factors*—What are the norms and needs within the broad society in which the business operates? What do *today's* (and tomorrow's) employees, customers, regulatory bodies, press, and other stakeholders require from the business and its managers? For instance, it is now widely observed that today's employees and customers are more highly educated and sophisticated than their predecessors 25, or even 15, years ago; yet, many firms still have not grasped the importance of having senior managers who can deal effectively in this new climate. Societal factors are also extremely important to understand in staffing foreign subsidiaries or even in staffing regional operations in the United States. For instance, many companies have found that very different styles and perspectives are needed for effectively managing West Coast, deep South, Midwest, and Midatlantic operations.
- *Business and Industry Environment*—What are the key success factors in this industry? Where are the big opportunities and threats? How turbulent is the industry? Answers to these questions change over the life cycle of an industry.[10] However, unpatterned pressures can arise as well. For example, the onslaught of low-price foreign competition has made cost controls an essential ingredient for success in the automotive industry. The recent insider-trading scandals that rocked Wall Street have profound implications for managerial selection in the large investment banks.
- *Mandate/Mission from the Corporation*—What is the role of this business in the firm's portfolio? Is it to generate cash flow? growth? technology? What constraints will be imposed? Obviously, a mandate for growth along with big infusions of cash requires very different managerial qualities and temperaments than a mandate for squeezing cash out of the business.[11]

- *Strategic Thrusts*—What product/markets segments have we chosen to emphasize? What will be our primary basis for competing? low unit costs? product innovation? customization and service? Each of these approaches to the marketplace, as well as others that could be envisioned, requires its own mix of managerial strengths. For instance, Miles and Snow found that firms which compete successfully by continual product innovation (prospectors) have relatively heavier representation of marketing and product development specialists within their top teams than do firms which compete successfully with a stable product line (defenders). [12]

    Obviously, if an enduring strategy has yet to be settled, the context then calls for team members who can contribute to development of a sound strategy. However, when a strategy has been decided, and the general manager has confidence in its correctness, it is then crucial that the team possess the special competences required for the plan's execution. [13]

- *Key Points of Interdependence*—Where do information flows, negotiations, and inter-unit decisions have to be particularly smooth and fast? between manufacturing and marketing? R&D and marketing? Derived both from the environment and the chosen strategy of the business, key collaborative nodes create the need for communication and negotiation skills, often even a certain "chemistry," between the parties involved. For example, a company attempting an aggressive product innovation strategy in the medical instrumentation industry found that the heads of marketing and R&D, while both very strong in their own areas, were not compatible or sufficiently compromising with each other. The strategy foundered severely and both individuals had to be replaced.

    External interdependencies must also be considered. The business may depend on a tight, symbiotic relationship with outside parties who need to be understood in considering an optimal team. For instance, a business engaged in defense contracting has to achieve a close familiarity with governmental procedures and personalities. The firm engaged in a high-technology strategy may need strong ties to, and an affinity for, university researchers.

- *Human Resource Profile*—What are the capabilities, values, and beliefs of the employees? Are they enthusiastic? cynical? frightened? out of date? The work of the business can only be done through its people, and the managers—particularly their communications and leadership abilities—must be suited to garnering the effective efforts from the workforce. This is a particularly important consideration in turnaround or depressed situations.

- *Key Management Associates*—What are the capabilities and repertoire, of the other key members of the management team? No executive position or person can be considered in isolation. There must be a thorough assessment of the people who are already part of the team, so that the desirable degrees of complementarity and depth can be achieved. Such considerations especially apply when a single position on the team needs to be filled.

Identifying the Ideal Team Profile—Having analyzed the context in which the management team must operate, the team architect turns next to establishing an ideal profile for the team. This can be done in broad overall terms or it can be attempted with substantial precision on a position-by-position basis. The latter approach is far better, since the presence of certain qualities in a specific position are usually far more important than their mere presence somewhere on the overall team. Put another way, there may be certain characteristics which everyone on the team should ideally possess and yet others which are desirable only in certain specific positions.

There are many potential dimensions for assessing managerial attributes. For instance, Levinson identifies 20 dimensions for evaluating leaders, including such factors as tolerance for ambiguity, sense of humor, and perseverance.[14] Similarly, Stringer describes an inventory of 36 managerial attributes which Pepsi-Cola International uses for evaluating managers.[15] The list includes such items as industry knowledge, writing skills, and drive.

These approaches are suggestive but far too limiting. They pretend to completeness and uniform appropriateness, although, in a given situation, neither may be the case.

The preferable approach is to propose very broad arenas of managerial wherewithal but then leave to the general manager the identification of specific dimensions for profiling the team. This choice of specific qualities should be based on the contextual analysis already conducted, as well as on the general manager's own highly personalized model of the key ingredients for managerial or team success. We turn now to a discussion of the broad areas in which the general manager will want to develop his or her own customized set of profiling dimensions.

- *Values*—The first broad area for considering executive makeup is values. Namely, what fundamental beliefs are important to have represented on the team? Values of humanism, aesthetics, hard work, wealth, novelty, and ethics are among those that might be considered in characterizing the ideal team. Values affect an executive's contributions to a team in three ways.[16] First, values cause executives to prefer certain behaviors and outcomes over others. Second, they affect the way in which the person searches and filters data used in decision making. Third, values affect the person's receptivity to any incentives and norms the general manager may try to establish.
- *Aptitudes*—Positions on the team also need to be mapped out according to the aptitudes, or personal capacities, needed among its members. Examples of aptitudes are creativity, intellect, tolerance for ambiguity, and

interpersonal awareness. Essentially, aptitudes are those qualities that are not amenable to short-term change. As such, they typically cannot be manipulated by training or incentives, at least in the short term.

- *Skills*—The team will also require a certain mix of skills. These are more concrete and usually more observable than aptitudes. Examples of skills that might be needed are communications, negotiation, economic analysis, planning, and delegating. Skills are somewhat dependent upon a person's aptitudes, but they are more prone to development and refinement.

- *Knowledge*—The context also imposes certain knowledge requirements on the ideal team. In-depth familiarity with certain industry, technical, or functional-area issues, legal or regulatory factors, and marketplace trends are illustrative of the knowledge bases that may be needed. Obviously, the more technically or legally complex the business, the greater the knowledge requirements. Compared to the other broad arenas, knowledge is perhaps most amenable to immediate and significant change within a person.

- *Cognitive Style*—It is widely accepted among psychologists that people differ appreciably in how they process information and make decisions. While the differences may not be as simple as ascribing "left-brain" and "right-brain" qualities, a major distinction is between orderly/analytic and nonlinear/intuitive thinkers.[17] The mix of the two modes within a team will greatly affect the team's strategic decisions—both their formulation and implementation. In turn, the appropriate mix of the two styles depends on the context in which the team must operate.

    For example, the CEO of a large firm consisting primarily of mature, medium-technology, industrial products concluded that his team of highly analytic, engineering-educated managers (including himself) were at a loss in comprehending and anticipating a new environment unfolding around them. Their industries were being rocked by radical technological breakthroughs, emergence of many new small competitors, and globalization. The team was well suited to digesting quantitative, tabular, incremental data, but it had little facility for grasping or acting upon the qualitative, incomplete, and rapid-fire explosion of information around them. The CEO complained, "We're typical engineers. We wait for data to become clear, firm, and graphable. By the time that happens, today's competition has passed us by."

- *Demeanor*—The intangible aura, style, or demeanor of members of a management team is a final area of consideration. Such qualities as enthusiasm, warmth, poise, or stateliness can be of central importance in constituting a management team. These characteristics would be especially relevant when constituencies are skeptical of the firm's prospects and motives, i.e., where the management team needs to provide some outward and immediate measure of legitimacy and strength.

These six arenas, comprising the range of qualities the general manager should consider for his or her team, serve as triggers for identifying specifically relevant dimensions for team success. The specific dimensions should be based on the earlier contextual analysis as well as on the general manager's highly personal view of the managerial ingredients needed for success of the business. As noted above, the general manager should attempt to specify the amounts of each quality that are needed for specific positions within the team, thus accounting for inherent differences in the tasks of individual positions.

Assessing the Existing Team—A manager of an on-going business rarely has a blank slate for a team. People are already in most, if not all, of the positions. The next step in the team analysis, then, is to carefully and fairly assess the qualities of the incumbents on the dimensions specified in the process discussed above.

Managers typically pride themselves in being good judges of people and in having an accurate and complete sense of the talents of their team members. Yet, many managers—even very good ones—carry only partial, fragmented views of their subordinates' repertoires. Appraising members of the team is something that must be vigorously worked at. It will not occur without pointed effort.

The manager must engage in continual observation, testing and probing, not in a threatening or adversarial manner, but in a way that somehow allows the boundaries of each person's repertoire to become apparent. Talking to each person's peers and subordinates is an important way of gathering insights. Also, getting out from behind the desk—or what Peters and Waterman would call "managing by wandering around"[18]—to watch each person carry out his or her job is an important part of the data-gathering process. Depending on the general manager's style and beliefs, he or she may wish to use standard psychological or assessment techniques with the assistance of trained consultants.[19] However, the reliability of such techniques is mixed, and their administration to senior colleagues is usually not well received. There is simply no substitute for careful, persistent observation of people engaged in a range of real managerial challenges.

Narrowing the Gaps—After the ideal team profile has been constructed and the incumbents have been gauged against the ideal, a plan for closing, or at least narrowing, the gaps between ideal and actuality must be designed. Required is a blend of ingenuity, open-mindedness, tough-mindedness, and humaneness on the part of the general manager. If the gaps are large, changes must be made or the business has a dim future. Fortunately, the array of possible changes is often immense, some involving less turmoil and discomfort than others.

Several broad categories of options can be considered. Since usually several types of gaps exist, these approaches will typically be used in combination rather than in isolation.

The first three options involve bringing new people on to the team:

- hiring or promoting replacements,
- hiring or promoting additions to the team, which essentially amounts to a re-structuring (either creating a new post or elevating an existing post to the top team level), and
- using consultants or outside talent as adjuncts to the team.

This last option, rarely considered, is particularly useful when a major knowledge deficiency exists within the current team. The use of limited-term adjuncts to managerial teams is a trend of growing importance, and one which provides the general manager maximum flexibility and quickness in securing needed skills.[20] However, "contract players" usually can only be used in staff support areas, since any supervisory or line powers can create serious morale problems among other members of the team.

The remaining three options involve efforts to secure more or different types of contributions from existing members of the team:

- incentives,
- training and development, and
- coaching and counsel.

Basically, these methods should be used if the general manager believes that the targeted team members have the inherent values and aptitudes that are needed in their posts, but that on other key dimensions—particularly skills, knowledge, or demeanor—they are delivering less than is needed. These methods hold great promise for stimulating or re-directing even the most senior executives.[21]

The choice of whether and how to use the six gap-closing alternatives depends on the general manager's assessment of the benefits and costs of each. The general manager should apply his or her own criteria, but at least four tests of each option should be considered.

- What is the *dollar cost*? Namely, can we financially afford to try to re-shape the team in this way?
- What is the *organizational cost*? That is, how would this action affect morale, intensity of effort, and team interactions?
- *How quickly* would this action have its desired effect? Often certain avenues are closed because they would simply take too long to achieve their end.
- Finally, what is the likelihood or *assurance* that the action would have its desired effect? Some actions, including the hiring of new people, simply have low or unknown probabilities of solving the problem.

The general manager needs to face up to these sometime remote possibilities and be sure not to undertake costly actions just on the "off-chance" they will work.

Looping-Back to the Context—After applying these tests to the most promising options for closing gaps on the team, the general manager may conclude that the needed changes are flatly infeasible. This could be because of strong norms or personal preferences about removing people, the costs involved, or the amount of time involved. In short, it is possible that the gaps simply cannot be closed, at least not in the timeframe needed for competitive success.

If this impasse occurs, the manager must loop back in his or her analysis and re-think the context in which the team will operate. In short, if the team can't be changed, then the context must be changed. It may be that the manager will have to readjust the intended strategy—the markets emphasized or the competitive weapons used—in order to accommodate the talents now on the team. The manager may also need to modify his or her way of operating with the team—perhaps delegating less than was hoped, requesting more frequent reports from subordinates, serving as mediator, and so on.

In sum, the effective manager understands the critical role of the management team in achieving strategic success. He or she is creative and far-reaching in identifying options, but tough-minded about bringing the team into alignment with the competitive context in which the business must operate. At the same time, however, the successful team architect understands the constraints on the task and possesses the flexibility and fluidity to be able to creatively re-think his or her original game plan. In this way, the exceptional strategist conceives of the top team as a key element of both strategy formulation and implementation.

Case of the Scribe Division

Following is a disguised case about a general manager who applied the framework for team analysis as part of his overall effort to turn around the performance of an ailing business. As will be seen, he followed the general logic stream of the framework while tailoring it to his own circumstances and style. Therefore, his approach should not be taken as the only or best way to systematically assess a team, but simply as an illustration of the perspective set forth in this chapter and as an indication of the array of issues and options it helps identify.

A New Strategy—Walter Newberry was brought in from a competing firm to be general manager of the Scribe writing instrument division of a large multibusiness firm. The division, with sales of $300 million, had languished for the previous five years, losing market share and making only modest profits. Its strategy during this period had mirrored some major trends in the industry: offshore (Far East) production, minimal promotion expenditures, price-based competition, and heavy emphasis on the price-sensitive government and commercial markets. Unfortunately, Scribe's moderate market share simply did not allow it the low unit costs to compete well in its chosen segments.

After three months of intense analysis and deliberations with his managers and consultants, Mr. Newberry developed a strategy which he thought would yield a solid future for Scribe. The summary of his strategy, as presented to and approved by corporate top management, was as follows:

> Scribe must do things differently if it is going to compete with the giants. Above all, Scribe must avoid head-on price competition at the low end of the product spectrum. Instead, the emphasis should be on aggressive development of new products and product variations (new product features, new styling, new packaging, etc.) that will sell at a mid-level price (between BIC and Gillette on the one hand and Cross and Parker on the other hand). An integral part of this strategy depends on being able to segment the market and develop innovations to match. Scribe must become a marketing company, adept at market research, translation of market research into product development, and media advertising. This strategy of innovation requires change in the distribution of our product. We will decrease our emphasis on small stationery and drugstores, as well as the commercial and government markets. A major push will be through national drug, department store, and gift/bookstore chains.

The Team Context—Newberry knew that the success of his new strategy depended on his management team. He had had a chance to work with these people—particularly the five functional heads who reported directly to him—during the process of formulating the new strategy. He had watched these people closely during this time, trying to observe their range of capabilities and potential. He had formed a number of impressions, but as so often happens, he felt he was lacking a coherent, overarching sense of the team. He felt the same way about his sense of what would constitute an ideal team. He had some scattered, piecemeal thoughts, but he did not feel he had a complete or well-developed picture of the talents he would need. He decided to approach this critical task systematically, using a tailored version of the process discussed in this chapter.

His starting point was to carefully assess the context in which the team would have to operate. His assessment of the external context led him to several conclusions. First, he knew that all external parties—customers, press, distributors, and so on—had higher standards for business communication and openness than had ever existed before. Second, when he looked at the writing instrument industry, he saw increasing price competition from imports and the consequent likelihood that other major firms would try, like Scribe, to escape by moving into higher styled, more differentiated segments. The industry was going to be more competitive than ever. Third, his mandate from the parent firm was very clear: "We want Scribe to be a balanced generator of profits and growth. We will make modest infusions of cash for up to three years in order to allow the business to achieve this balanced strength."

The key features of the internal context stemmed primarily from the new strategy. The key strategic drivers were going to be product innovation, styling, and creative marketing. In manufacturing, cost control would be important, but quality would be essential. Key points of interdependence— where negotiations and cooperation would need to be fluid—were between marketing and R&D, as well as between manufacturing and R&D. In assessing the human resource profile, Newberry concluded that the limited remaining U.S. production workforce was technically capable but probably lacking in concern for quality. It was among the marketing and sales employees that Newberry was most concerned. Few marketing people, *per se*, even existed, and the unpolished sales force consisted largely of "order-takers" whose primary selling angle had always been price and delivery. Overall, Newberry also saw a general malaise and cynicism among employees.

The Ideal Team Profile—It was against this backdrop that Newberry set out to identify the attributes he would need on his team. He began only with the six broad categories—values, knowledge, etc.—and then identified specific dimensions of importance under each. The resulting list of 18 dimensions is shown in Table 1.

It is important to emphasize that Newberry's list of profiling areas is uniquely his. As noted earlier, there can be no standard, universal approach to this important task. The choice of areas of concern is derived from the contextual analysis as well as from the general manager's own values and style. In Newberry's list, for instance, knowledge about Gift and Premium Buyer Behavior and aptitude for Social and Cultural Awareness follow directly from the imperatives of the new strategy. Newberry's inclusion of the value, High Standards for Business Performance, was largely due to his strong feeling that his colleagues in his former company had been content to be survivors and lacked the will to excel. He thus had a "hang-up" about high standards, seeing this dimension as crucial to team success.

After generating his array of relevant team qualities, Newberry turned to an assessment of how important each quality would be for each position on the team. He decided to approach this step quantitatively, although a numerical approach is neither necessary nor, perhaps in some eyes, even desirable. Newberry's quantitative ratings are presented here not because they are a preferred way, but because they allow a relatively concise portrayal of a complex process. (To Newberry's credit, he had many pages of personal notes which accompanied his numerical tallies.)

Table 1. What Managerial Qualities are Needed?

	General Manager	Director of Marketing	Director of R&D	Director of Manu-facturing	Controller	Director of Human Resources
Values						
High Standards for Business Performance	5	4	4	4	4	4
Commitment to Aesthetics	5	5	5	5	3	3
Work is Fun; Good Humor	5	4	4	4	4	4
High Ethical Standards	5	5	5	5	5	5
Aptitudes						
Creativity	4	5	5	4	3	3
Intellect	4	4	4	4	4	4
Social/Cultural Awareness	5	5	4	3	2	4
Skills						
Interpersonal and Communications	5	5	4	4	3	4
Business/Economic Analysis	4	5	3	5	5	3
Negotiation/Compromise	5	5	4	5	2	3
Knowledge						
Writing Instrument Technology and Markets	4	5	5	5	3	2
Gift and Premium Buyer Behavior	5	5	4	3	3	3
State-of-art Management Concepts	4	5	3	4	4	3
Cognitive Style						
Orderly/Analytic	3	3	4	4	5	3
Nonlinear/Intuitive	5	5	5	3	3	4
Demeanor/Style						
"Stylish/Classy"	5	5	3	4	3	4
Open/Flexible	5	5	5	4	4	4
Sense of Enthusiasm/ Dynamism	5	5	5	4	4	4

Newberry rated each of the six positions on his team, including the general management position, by asking this question of himself: "On a scale of one (very low) to five (very high), what is the minimum amount of each quality that should be held by the ideal incumbent?" Obviously, realism must be borne in mind—all fives are not possible. While it is desirable that the points on such a scale have absolute meaning, in actuality a concrete meaning for, say, a 5, is not essential; what is important is that the same relative frame of reference be used for this step (rating ideals) as for the next step (rating what now exists).

As can be seen, Newberry wanted homogeneity on some dimensions (such as most of the values) and heterogeneity, or complementarity, on other dimensions (such as cognitive style). Not surprisingly, he set very high standards for the marketing and R&D positions, since he considered them of paramount importance for execution of the new strategy.

Evaluating the Current Team—Drawing upon his several months of observation of his team, he then rated each member of the current team on all 18 dimensions (see Table 2). The director of manufacturing had retired just before Newberry arrived and had not yet been replaced, therefore no incumbent ratings were conducted for that position. Otherwise, all ratings were attempted. Asterisks in Table 2 denote gaps between the ideal and what actually existed.

A number of patterns emerged, but several in particular warrant noting. First, the director of marketing seemed to have serious, pervasive shortcomings for his position. Newberry had found him very bright and hardworking, but gruff, stubborn, and interpersonally and socially ill at ease; he also didn't have the creativity or intuition Newberry thought were needed in the job. The director of human resources was rated below the ideal on 14 of the dimensions, with serious shortfalls in attitudinal areas— good humor and enthusiasm/dynamism. The controller had several shortfalls, perhaps most notably in business/economic analysis and state-of-the-art management concepts.

Taking a different view, by looking across the columns, it can be seen that team-wide deficiencies existed in two major areas: knowledge of gift and premium buyer behavior and openness/flexibility.

It is worth noting that Newberry rated himself below the ideal on several dimensions. Whether he was sufficiently self-critical we cannot assess, however he appeared willing to admit that he himself had room for improvement.

Closing the Gaps—With his assessment done, Newberry began to consider actions. First, he concluded that he would have to modify his new strategy. He had planned to make the complete switch to the higher-priced, higher-styled strategy over a two-year period. Now fully appreciating the

Table 2. What Managerial Qualities Now Exist?

	General Manager	Director of Marketing	Director of R&D	Director of Manu-facturing	Controller	Director of Human Resources
Values						
High Standards for Business Performance	5	4	3*		4	3*
Commitment to Aesthetics	5	3**	4*		3	2*
Work is Fun; Good Humor	5	4	5		3*	2**
High Ethical Standards	5	5	5		5	5
Aptitudes						
Creativity	4	3**	5		3	2*
Intellect	4	5	4		5	3*
Social/Cultural Awareness	4	3**	4		3	3*
Skills						
Interpersonal and Communications	4*	3**	4		3	3*
Business/Economic Analysis	4	5	3		3**	2*
Negotiation/Compromise	4*	4*	4		2	2*
Knowledge						
Writing Instrument Technology and Markets	2**	5	5		3	3
Gift and Premium Buyer Behavior	4*	3**	2**		1**	1**
State-of-art Management Concepts	3*	4*	3		2**	3
Cognitive Style						
Orderly/Analytic	3	4	4		5	3
Nonlinear/Intuitive	5	2**	4*		3	3*
Demeanor/Style						
"Stylish/Classy"	5	3**	4		3	3*
Open/Flexible	3**	3**	5		3*	3*
Sense of Enthusiasm/ Dynamism	5	5	5		3*	2**

* is 1-point shortfall
** is 2-point (or more) shortfall

limitations of his team—particularly its lack of knowledge of the gift and premium market, but other notable shortfalls as well—he decided to carry out the transition over a four-year period. Thus, his team analysis led to a strategy modification. If he had done a careful team analysis earlier, he might have factored the results into the initial strategy formulation as part of a customary strengths and weaknesses analysis. The important point, however, is that Newberry recognized how crucial the team's abilities would be to successful execution of the new strategy and had the good sense to know that those abilities simply did not exist and probably could not be acquired or developed on the tight timetable he had envisioned.

This change of strategy then led to a change in structure. It was clear to Newberry that he would essentially have to run the old and the new businesses in parallel for the foreseeable future. He decided to create a structural subunit for the old business—which he called Government and Commercial—and appoint a director for it. He did not have to look far for the ideal candidate. The current Director of Marketing, although ill-suited for the new high-styled business, was ideally suited for broadened responsibilities in Scribe's traditional domain. His intellect, analytic and business skills, and in-depth knowledge of the writing instrument industry all fit well with the strategic challenges facing the Government and Commercial Market: intense negotiations with off-shore producers, marketing with an emphasis on volume and price, and establishment of efficient logistical systems. Whether Newberry came up with the idea of this new position before or after he had the Director of Marketing in mind for it is not clear. What is very apparent is that the systematic team analysis led to a clarity of options and issues.

In turn, there was the need for a director of marketing for the new line. Newberry turned outside and hired a person whose profile matched very closely with what was needed, including having significant experience in the gift and premium market. One of the first things Newberry asked this new person to do was to design a series of one-day workshops for the entire top management team dealing with the gift and premium market. The new person was to identify the top outside experts in the field to conduct these sessions. He was also charged with setting up a series of visits for Newberry, himself, and the R&D director to major gift and premium buyers. Thus, Newberry used his team analysis to identify the qualities needed in a new hire, but just as important was his use of the analysis to develop a plan for leveraging the new person's repertoire in a way to enhance the whole team.

Newberry decided to have a heart-to-heart, after-hours talk with the human resources director. Fully expecting that he would have to replace this person, Newberry encountered new insights about him. He had known already that the man was going through a divorce, but he had not known how traumatic it had been or that it had caused serious problems for the man's teenage children. Newberry essentially concluded that his assessment of the person had been, or may have been, off the mark. The man's apparent lethargy, distraction, and uninspired behavior were not inherent; they were temporary. The two questions in Newberry's mind were: "Can all this be overcome in time for this guy to be a productive team member? Can I play a role in the process?" The personal meetings continued; Newberry worked hard at listening and encouraging; he worked to make the man feel an integral part of the team, whereas he had been a secondary figure under Newberry's predecessor. Circumstances and good managing allowed this person to become an effective, fully contributing member of the team over the ensuing months. Here, an interesting lesson emerges. Namely, our assessments of people can sometimes be wrong; however, an explicit process of assessment can help guide us to where the problems may lie and where we may want to especially reaffirm our data.

The situation with the controller was somewhat similar. In a one-on-one, after-hours meeting, it became apparent to Newberry that the controller's lack of enthusiasm and good humor came from the fact that he was certain he would be fired. He was out-of-date with his profession, and he knew it. He was sure Newberry would replace him with a younger person, better versed in modern control and information systems. Newberry did come close to firing him, but he kept coming back to the man's strengths, including a great deal of evidence that he was fundamentally a smart, analytic person. Newberry then laid a developmental plan. He asked the controller to head a special project to analyze the economics of the new product strategy. Other insiders would serve on the task force and it would also be supported by outside consultants from the parent firm's auditors. Newberry's implicit agenda was twofold (beyond getting the study done): he wanted the controller to learn a great deal at the hands of the outside consultants, and he wanted the controller to develop confidence in his ability to learn. Newberry made these somewhat uncustomary goals clear to the senior outside consultant when he approached the firm. The result was that the controller made substantial progress—learning a great deal, developing an enthusiasm for learning more, and becoming an integral, effective part of the team.

Newberry's experiences with the controller and the human resources director warrant attention. In both cases, Newberry set out to establish a more intimate and accurate information exchange than he thought could be accomplished in everyday business activity. This did not come naturally for Newberry. In fact, he was struggling to overcome the aloofness and autocratic style that superiors and peers had criticized him for throughout his managerial career. He had taken these criticisms to heart in rating himself (Table 2). In his dealings with these two members of his team, we observe a purposeful, albeit strained, experiment with tremendously positive results for the business and for the people involved. In sum, if the team analysis is well done, it can lead to self-insight and self-development for the general manager himself or herself.

All of these actions, as well as establishment of new aggressive incentives based on overall performance of the business, were carried out within Newberry's first six months in the Scribe division. Two years after Newberry took over, Scribe was recognized within the parent firm as a dramatic turnaround success. Sales were up 35 percent, with about half the gains coming from the traditional line and half from the new line (which achieved an impressive ten percent of its served market within a year of introduction). Profits had doubled, and the division's return on assets was above (well above) the parent firm's average for the first time in many years.

Summary

The strategic success of a business depends not on just one person but on the entire top management team. If the aptitudes, values, skills, and knowledge base of the top few people do not fit with what is required by the competitive environment, or if they do not mesh with each other, the business will encounter serious trouble. Conversely, the business with a top team whose qualities are well suited to emerging trends in the environment, as well as forming a complementary whole, will have the best chance of competitive success.

This chapter has presented a comprehensive framework for conducting this important managerial task. While leaving room for ample tailoring to the general manager's own style and preferences, the framework provides a generalized procedure:

- understand the context in which the team will operate,
- develop a profile of the ideal team for that context,
- fairly and carefully assess the current team, and
- develop a plan for closing the gaps between what is needed and what exists.

Ideally, a well developed, on-going executive development system will reliably address many of these issues. However, at times, an in-depth, *ad hoc* analysis may be important.

The case of Walt Newberry at Scribe illustrates how the framework can help greatly sharpen the issues and options confronting a team architect. His successes were no doubt aided by good fortune and other factors, but his integrated approach to team design was instrumental in the advances he was able to make. Managers who, like Newberry, face increasingly competitive environments must understand the real key to strategic success is the group of people who formulate and implement the strategy. The task of selecting, developing, and molding that group into a fit team is at the heart of the general manager's job.

References

1. D.C. Hambrick and P.A. Mason, "Upper Echelons: The Organization as a Reflection of Its Top Managers," *Academy of Management Review,* 9 (1984):193-206.
2. G.T. Allison, *The Essence of Decision: Explaining the Cuban Missile Crisis* (Boston, MA: Little Brown, 1971); I.L. Janis and L. Mann, *Decision Making: A Psychological Analysis of Conflict, Choice, and Commitment* (New York, NY: Free Press, 1977); B.W. Tuchman, *The March of Folly: From Troy to Vietnam* (New York, NY: Ballantine, 1984).
3. D. Miller, M.F. Kets DeVries, and J.M. Toulouse, "Top Executive Locus of Control and Its Relationship to Strategy-Making, Structure, and Environment," *Academy of Management Journal,* 25 (1982):237-253; D. Miller and J.M. Toulouse, "Chief Executive Personality and Corporate Strategy and Structure in Small Firms," *Management Science,* 32 (1986):1389-1409.
4. A.K. Gupta and V. Govindarajan, "Business Unit Strategy, Managerial Characteristics, and Business Unit Effectiveness at Strategy Implementation," *Academy of Management Journal,* 27 (1984):25-41.
5. J.R. Meindl, S.B. Ehrlich, and J.M. Dukerich, "The Romance of Leadership," *Administrative Science Quarterly,* 30 (March 1985):78-102.
6. J. Hage and R. Dewer, "Elite Values Versus Organizational Structure in Predicting Innovation," *Administrative Science Quarterly,* 18/3 (September 1973):279-290.
7. M.L. Tushman, B. Virany, and E. Romanelli, "Executive Succession, Strategic Reorientations, and Organizational Evolution," *Technology and Society,* 7 (1985):297-313.
8. M. Shao, "Exxon's Mining Unit Finds It Tough Going," *Wall Street Journal,* August 31, 1982, p. 1.
9. K. Auletta, "The Fall of Lehman Brothers: The Men, The Money, The Merger," *New York Times Magazine,* February 24, 1985, p. 36.
10. W.L. Moore and M.L. Tushman, "Managing Innovation Over the Life Cycle," in M.L. Tushman and W.L. Moore, eds., *Readings in the Management of Innovation* (Boston, MA: Pitman, 1982), pp. 131-150; M.W. Porter, *Competitive Strategy* (New York, NY: Free Press, 1980).
11. M. Gerstein and H. Reisman, "Strategic Selection: Matching Executives to Business Conditions," *Sloan Management Review,* 24/2 (Winter 1983):33-49; Gupta and Govindarajan, op. cit.
12. R. E. Miles and C.C. Snow, *Organization Strategy, Structure, and Process* (New York, NY: McGraw-Hill, 1978).
13. A.K. Gupta, "Matching Managers to Strategies: Point and Counterpoint," *Human Resources Management,* 25 (1986):215-234.
14. H. Levinson, "Criteria for Choosing Chief Executives," *Harvard Business Review,* 58/4 (1980):113-120.
15. R.A. Stringer, Jr., *Strategy Traps* (Lexington, MA: Lexington Books, 1986).
16. G.W. England, "Personal Value Systems of American Managers," *Academy of Management Journal,* 10 (1967):53-68; D.C. Hambrick and G.L. Brandon, "Executive Values," in D.C. Hambrick, ed., *The Executive Effect: Concepts and Methods for Studying Top Managers* (Greenwich, CT: JAI Press, 1987).
17. H. Mintzberg, "Planning on the Left Side and Managing on the Right," *Harvard Business Review,* 54/4 (1976):49-58; W. Taggart and D. Robey, "Minds and Managers: On the Dual Nature of Human Information Processing and Management," *Academy of Management Review,* 6 (1981):187-195.
18. T.E. Peters and R.H. Waterman, Jr., *In Search of Excellence* (New York, NY: Harper and Row, 1982).

19. Gerstein and Reisman, op. cit.
20. S. Lee and S. Flack, "HiHo, Silver," *Forbes,* March 9, 1987, pp. 90-98.
21. J.F. Bolt, "Tailor Executive Development to Strategy," *Harvard Business Review,* 63/6 (1985):168-176; D.C. Hambrick and C.C. Snow, "Strategic Reward Systems," in C.C. Snow, ed., *Strategy, Organization Design and Human Resource Management* (Greenwich, CT: JAI Press, 1987).

Chapter 8

The Strategic Use of Corporate Board Committees

J. Richard Harrison

Much recent attention has been focused on committees of corporate boards of directors—particularly the audit, compensation, and nominating committees—as mechanisms for monitoring management and protecting shareholder interests.[1] Board committees can also serve strategic purposes for the firm. This chapter discusses some of the strategic uses of board committees, focusing on maintaining corporate legitimacy, protecting directors from excessive exposure to liability, and contributing to the formulation of corporate strategy.

Types of Board Committees

Over the last 25 years, boards have displayed an increasing tendency to establish committees. This trend can be seen clearly in Figure 1, which is based on samples of several hundred large manufacturing firms.[2]

There are two generic types of board committees. One type is the *management support* or *operating* committee, which advises management and the board on major business decisions. The executive committee and the finance committee are examples of management support committees. The other type of committee is the *monitoring* or *oversight* committee, intended to protect shareholder interests by providing an objective, independent review of corporate affairs, particularly with respect to the legality, integrity, and ethical quality of corporate activities. Monitoring committees are composed primarily of outside directors, and include the audit, compensation, and nominating committees. The use of these committees has increased dramatically in the last few years. Another type of committee, which rapidly emerged in the 1970s but which cannot be clearly classified as either

Figure 1. Existence of Board Committees

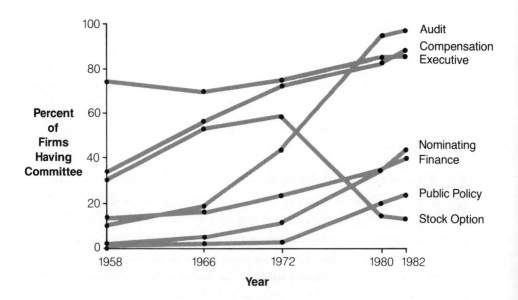

management support or monitoring, is the public policy or social responsibility committee.[3] The strategy or planning committee, the newest type of
board committee, also does not fall clearly into either the management support or monitoring category; it will be discussed in detail in a later section.

Corporate Legitimacy

Increasing emphasis has been placed on boards of directors as being responsible and accountable for the actions of their corporations. As Kenneth
R. Andrews observed:

> Under pressure from the public, from the Securities and Exchange Commission, and
> indirectly from the U.S. Senate's Subcommittee on Shareholders' Rights, the board
> of directors is undergoing revitalization as the only available source of legitimacy for
> corporate power and assurance of corporate responsibility, given the archaism of
> corporate law and the dispersed ownership of the large public corporation.[4]

Particular attention has been directed toward the committee structure of the
board. In 1980, the U.S. Securities and Exchange Commission noted that

"the attention focused on the board of directors as a key to enhanced corporate accountability has been directed . . . to the importance of a committee system enabling the board to devote attention to pecific areas of responsibility."[5]

For purposes of accountability and legitimacy, the most important committees are the monitoring or oversight committees. In 1978, the SEC adopted requirements (effective in 1979) that proxy statements disclose the existence, membership, and function of audit, compensation, and nominating committees of the board.[6] The American Bar Association has advocated audit, compensation, and nominating committees, composed of non-management directors, for corporate boards.[7] Since 1978, the New York Stock Exchange has required all U.S.-based firms listed on the Exchange to have audit committees of their boards, composed of directors independent of management, and audit committees have been strongly recommended by both the American Stock Exchange and the National Association of Securities Dealers.[8] Connecticut recently became the first state to mandate a board committee, adopting a statute requiring audit committees for domestic corporations with at least 100 record holders.[9] The courts have also recognized the accountability value of monitoring committees by requiring that audit and nominating committees composed of independent outside directors be established in the settlements of shareholder lawsuits against Phillips Petroleum and Northrop Corporation.[10]

Monitoring committees enhance corporate accountability by providing a mechanism for independent oversight of corporate activities; they serve a further purpose of promoting corporate legitimacy. Legitimation has been defined as "the process whereby an organization justifies to a peer or superordinate system its right to exist, that is, to continue to import, transform, and export energy, material, or information."[11] Similarly, legitimacy has been viewed as necessary for an organization's continued access to society's resources and hence for its survival.[12] A corporation's success and even its survival depends, then, among other things, on maintaining its legitimacy; this has long been seen as a primary function of its board of directors.[13]

Organizations can pursue legitimacy by adapting their methods of operation to conform to socially acceptable standards,[14] or to what Meyer and Rowan call "institutional norms."[15] For a board of directors, its committee structure symbolizes its method of operation, which itself is not readily observable. With the increasing attention focused on board committees by the SEC disclosure requirements, the New York Stock Exchange regulations, the AMEX, NASD, and ABA recommendations, and the courts, the board's committee structure is becoming increasingly visible and important for legitimacy maintenance. These organizations have, in effect, established acceptable standards for the board's committee structure—namely, boards should have audit, compensation, and nominating committees composed primarily of outside directors. These standards, or institutional norms, have been reinforced by the fact that most firms have adopted audit and compensation committees, and are rapidly adopting nominating committees.

Meyer and Rowan argue that organizations gain legitimacy, resources, stability, and enhanced survival prospects by conforming to institutional norms concerning their formal structures.[16] DiMaggio and Powell contend that once the adoption of particular structural elements reaches some threshold—as is the case for the three major monitoring committees of the board—there are high rewards in terms of legitimacy for adopting these structural elements.[17] The adoption of monitoring committees of the board may be viewed, then, as a strategy for maintaining corporate legitimacy. One immediate advantage of establishing an audit committee is in terms of director recruitment; many potential directors refuse to serve on a board which does not have an audit committee.[18]

The adoption of a structural element, such as a particular type of board committee, does not have legitimacy value through conforming to institutional norms until a norm has been established, or, as DiMaggio and Powell argue, until its use in a population of organizations has reached some threshold level. This raises the question of why a new structural element is initially adopted by the first few firms, if it has no legitimacy value, and focuses attention on the process whereby a structural innovation diffuses through a population of firms. Although it is very difficult to determine why structural innovations are initially adopted, a pattern for their diffusion can be clearly observed. My research on the adoption of board committees showed that large firms are likely to be the first to adopt a new type of board committee.[19] That is, the large firms are the first movers or trend setters, followed by medium-sized and small firms. This pattern is illustrated by Figure 2, which shows the diffusion of audit committees by firm size.[20] Once a normative threshold is reached, the rate of adoption of board committees by the remaining firms was found to be unrelated to firm size.[21] It appears that once a norm has been established for a particular type of committee, all remaining firms can realize the same legitimacy benefits by adopting the committee.

Corporations have recognized the advantages of conforming to the institutional norms concerning the board's committee structure. This can be seen by the rapid rise in the use of monitoring committees, but is most dramatically illustrated by the demise of the stock option committee (see Figure 1). In 1972, most firms had both a compensation committee (often called the salary and bonus committee) and a stock option committee. As the compensation committee became institutionalized as the legitimate board unit for considering executive compensation in the 1970s, most firms changed the name of the salary and bonus committee to the compensation committee and also assigned responsibility for awarding stock options to this committee, eliminating the stock option committee. In other words,

Figure 2. Audit Committee Existence by Firm Size

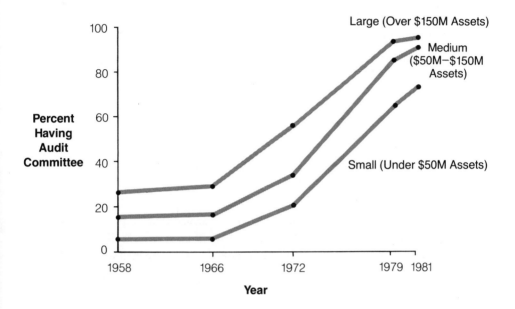

conformity pressures displaced the stock option committee as a legitimate structural unit, and its use rapidly declined.

The conformity strategy is, in a sense, a symbolic one. That is, it is effective because of the appearance it creates. Irving S. Shapiro referred to the existence of board committees as "a signal to the outside world."[22] Since it is very difficult to observe what work these committees actually do, however, there is the possibility that monitoring committees will be established to create a favorable appearance, but that they will do very little in terms of active oversight of the corporation's activities. The SEC has shown its awareness that the existence of a board committee projects an image of responsible activity to the external environment, regardless of what, if anything, the committee actually does. They noted that recent pressures for disclosure have produced the necessity of maintaining this image, but observed that data from their Proxy Disclosure Monitoring Project showed that 16% of the firms studies were not able to affirm that their audit committees had reviewed the results of the corporate audit, and that 26% were not able to affirm that their audit committees had reviewed the audit plan—two essential functions for audit committees.[23] They stated that a poorly functioning audit committee "may be worse than having no audit committee at all by creating the appearance of an effective body while lacking the substance."[24]

The courts have also demonstrated an awareness of this possibility. A classic example is Falstaff in 1977, which publicized an audit committee which never met. The D.C. District Court in 1978, ruling on *SEC v. Falstaff*, held that:

> Falstaff's statement in its 1977 Proxy Statement that it had an audit committee was false and misleading in that the committee existed in name only. . . . The proxy statement thus falsely conveyed to Falstaff's shareholders the impression that effective oversight was being exercised by the Board of Directors.[25]

In affirming the District Court decision on appeal, the U.S. Court of Appeals for the District of Columbia in 1980 stated:

> The existence of a committee implies a structured investigation and analysis of a company's fiscal welfare . . . formal entities such as committees create at least the impression of great care and precision through detailed review and oversight.[26]

Former SEC Chairman Harold Williams observed that "at present, many audit committees are, undoubtedly, not yet working fully effectively, and some may serve more to provide window-dressing rather than to add substance to the accountability process."[27] Creating such committees to project a favorable image may serve a strategic purpose of legitimacy maintenance, but if the committees are not active, it runs the risk of legal repercussions as well as shortchanging shareholders and being unethical.

The strategy of conforming to standard practices with respect to the board's committee structure may extend to other board committees, depending on the firm's industry. For example, technology, safety, or trust committees of the board may be common in some industries. Firms need to be aware of the types of board committees that are prevalent in their industries, since these constitute the standards against which conformity is assessed.

Director Liability

In recent years, director liability has become a major problem for American corporations, brought on by an increasing number of shareholder lawsuits and larger awards by the courts. Liability insurance for officers and directors (D&O insurance) has become either unavailable or unaffordable due to skyrocketing costs, and the deductible amounts and the coverage exclusions have increased dramatically. As a consequence, some companies have experienced wholesale director resignations, and many are finding it difficult to attract qualified directors.[28]

One strategy for reducing directors' exposure to liability is the use of board committees. The use of a board committee tends to limit the liability of directors who are not members of the committee for actions taken by the committee, and for actions taken by the board on the basis of information provided by the committee, if the non-committee directors have no reason to believe that the committee was not acting reasonably and in good faith. Nonmember directors can further protect themselves by ensuring that the committee is composed of competent directors and, in the case of the oversight committees, of directors who are independent of management influence; by ensuring that the committee is meeting regularly and following reasonable procedures; and by seeing that the committee makes regular reports and provides minutes of meetings to the full board.[29]

Committee members are normally protected from liability if they are attentive to the maintenance of reasonable procedures, follow a standard of care typically used by other directors in similar circumstances, maintain records to document their activities, and act in good faith and in a manner reasonably believed to be in the best interests of the corporation.[30] Additional steps are advisable for members of the audit and compensation committees. Audit committee members should ensure that the committee's duties are spelled out either in the corporation's By-Laws or in a board resolution, that the committee's role and limitations are disclosed to shareholders, and that procedures for the committee's operations have been formulated. Compensation committee members should ensure that specific actions are taken to assure the fairness of executive compensation. The necessary steps for these committee members have been specified by the ABA.[31]

The American Bar Association has emphasized the liability advantages of using the three major monitoring committees. According the ABA, "Given its increasingly widespread use, the absence of an Audit Committee may become a consideration in weighing whether or not the directors of a publicly-held corporation have met the standard of care set forth in many state corporation laws."[32] The Audit Committee's role has grown in importance following the passage of the Foreign Corrupt Practices Act of 1977. Based on their assessment of the laws of most states, the ABA also concluded that having management compensation set by a compensation committee composed of directors independent of management would shift the burden of proof for the fairness of the compensation to the attacking party.[33] The existence of a nominating committee composed of non-management directors, in the view of the ABA, "should be an important factor in securing judicial acceptance of the overall fairness of the decision-making process" for decisions involving the interests of individual directors, primarily because it provides a vehicle for impartial decisions concerning the selection and retention of directors.[34]

The liability issue is not independent of the issue of conformity to institutional norms discussed in the previous section. The ABA emphasized the concern of the board committee structure's "compliance with legal norms or contemporary practices."[35] Similarly McSweeney, while observing that committees are used to protect the board by obtaining more information on the corporation than management may be willing to supply, also noted that too many committees, or committees that are quite active, may expose directors to increased liability risks, implying that the best committee structure from a director liability standpoint is one that is common or widely shared—that is, one that conforms to the norms for board committee structures.[36] It appears, then, in terms of a strategy for maximum liability protection, that a board should use the three major monitoring committees and other committees commonly used in the firm's industry, but no others, and that committees should match their levels of activity and standards of care to those used by other committees in similar circumstances.

Strategy Formulation

Establishing the objectives and strategies for the corporation is widely believed to be a primary function of boards of directors, but researchers have consistently found that the boards of large corporations are typically not involved in this function. Myles L. Mace terms the board's involvement in corporate strategy a "myth."[37] While some movement in the direction of more board involvement in the strategy formulation process has been observed in the last few years, most boards still leave strategic planning to the CEO and the corporate staff.[38]

A common reason cited for the lack of board involvement is that CEOs oppose it.[39] Kenneth R. Andrews attributes CEO opposition to the fact that corporate strategies are often not articulated, to the belief that outside directors are not capable of useful input because of time and knowledge constraints, and to a concern that CEO power will be diminished by board involvement.[40]

Most authorities on corporate governance, however, argue for greater board involvement in the strategic planning process as a means to improve the quality of strategic decision making and to better discharge the board's responsibility to represent shareholder interests.[41] If boards are to become more involved, two important issues need to be addressed. One is whether the board should be actively involved in developing strategy, or should play an oversight role both to ensure that management is engaging in a sound process of formulating strategy and to review and approve the strategic plans developed by management. The second issue is whether the board should have a committee responsible for considering strategy.[42]

There are differing views on the appropriate role for boards involved in strategic planning. Andrews advocates an oversight role: "It is not the board's function to formulate strategy but to review it and to monitor the process that produces it."[43] Others argue for an active board role in strategy formulation.[44] In surveys of large American corporations, both Henke and Waldo found that boards were more likely to be involved in an oversight role than in a formulation role.[45]

The issue of the structure of board involvement is of primary concern here. In particular, the use of a board strategy committee will be examined. Andrews has been a leading advocate for the creation of strategy committees. In his view, a strategy committee would oversee the corporation's strategic management process, permit the board to evaluate individual decisions in the context of the company's purpose, and enable the board to respond to major problems constructively at an early stage, rather than responding with the traditional removal of the CEO after the problems have become critical.[46]

Given the increasing emphasis on board involvement in corporate strategy, it is surprising that very few corporations have established strategy committees. My examination of 1982 proxy statements for 753 large American manufacturing firms revealed that only 15 firms reported having strategy committees. This number could be underrepresentative, since the SEC does not require the disclosure of strategy committees on proxy statements. However, Brown's comprehensive study of annual reports and Conference Board surveys found only 16 strategy committees for manufacturing firms and 13 strategy committees for other types of firms as of 1980.[47] Henke's early 1980s study found a number consistent with these findings, and Ballout's analysis of 1984 proxy statements found the number unchanged from my 1982 results.[48] Several other companies have board committees such as finance, executive, and nominating to which the strategy function has been added. Brown found that with the exception of two strategy committees created by utilities in the 1960s, all of the strategy committees were created between 1972 and 1980. Figure 3, based on Brown's data, shows the growth in the number of strategy committees during the 1970s.[49] It appears that the number remained essentially constant between 1980 and 1984, although sampling procedures, response rates, and disclosure uncertainties associated with the various recent studies admit the possibility that some new committees have been overlooked. My study revealed only one firm, Bendix, which eliminated its strategy committee (by merging it into its finance committee, removing several outside directors in the process); it is interesting to note that Bendix eliminated itself shortly thereafter as a result of its abortive attempt to take over Martin Marietta. (Another Bendix board committee, its pension committee, ensured the success of Martin Marietta's "pac-man" defense when it fulfilled its fiduciary responsibilities by tendering all of the Bendix shares held by the pension fund to Martin Marietta.)[50]

A major reason that so few boards have strategy committees is the uninvolvement of most boards in the strategy function (as discussed earlier). For those boards which *are* involved, Andrews suggests an explanation for the scarcity of strategy committees. He observes that CEOs may want to keep strategy out of the hands of a qualified, informed committee, preferring instead to have strategy addressed by the full board, which is more likely to give routine approval to management recommendations than to

Figure 3. Strategy Committee Existence

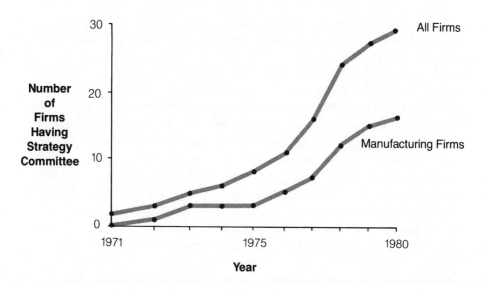

delve deeply into strategic questions.[51] Henke found that boards with strategy committees are likely to be more involved in the strategic planning process and are likely to be involved in a broader range of strategic issues; his findings lend support to Andrews's reasoning and also show the value of a strategy committee for increasing board involvement. He found the highest level of board involvement for boards with committees which had strategy as their *only* function.[52]

Brown's study included questionnaire responses from CEOs and interviews with executives and directors. His respondents indicated that strategy committees were more suitable for firms under certain conditions. The circumstances under which strategy committees were thought to be most appropriate included firms with a new CEO, firms facing rapid change, and firms in which management had not been actively involved in planning. Circumstances under which strategy committees were deemed inappropriate included firms whose full boards were actively involved in strategy, firms with other board committees performing the strategy function, and firms whose businesses were stable or narrow in scope.[53] It is interesting that Henke's findings described in the preceding paragraph indicate that firms in the first two "inappropriate" conditions could improve the board's strategic involvement by forming strategy committees. This discrepancy also illustrates a more general point—whether the issue is a strategy committee or protecting shareholder interests in general, the preferences and prescriptions of CEOs and directors concerning the nature of board involvement may not be consistent with the most effective utilization of board resources.

It is tempting to speculate on the conditions under which a strategy committee would be most useful, based on theoretical considerations rather than CEO and director opinions. It is my view, however, given the importance of strategic considerations, that all firms could benefit from a strategy committee. The advantages may be obvious for firms that are large or diversified; for firms facing high risks, rapidly changing environments, or global competition; for firms in emerging or declining industries; and for firms with a new CEO. On the other hand, a small firm could benefit because, lacking an extensive corporate staff and the funds to hire consultants, the board may be the only source of strategic assistance available to the CEO. (Since small firms typically have small boards, the full board could serve on the strategy committee in this case. The advantage of forming the committee would be that the meetings would focus exclusively on strategy.) Firms with narrow, stable businesses, facing low risks, with restricted competition, or in stable industries may be lulled into assuming that their present, and relatively stable, operating conditions will continue indefinitely without significant changes, ignoring or underestimating the inherent uncertainties of the business world. Kahneman and Tversky use the term "conditionality" to characterize decision making under these circumstances; conditionality can lead to overconfidence and inadequate contingency planning.[54] Firms with long-tenured CEOs or with well-developed corporate planning systems are also subject to conditionality, since after a period of time, strategic planning is likely to become routinized. A strategy committee, particularly with directors independent of management, could help to reduce conditionality by questioning the assumptions embodied in the internal planning process.

The question of whether the board should be involved in an oversight role or actively involved in strategy formulation (discussed earlier) is also relevant for the strategy committee. Should the committee be an oversight committee or a management support/operating committee? As in the case of the full board role, opinions differ on the appropriate function for the strategy committee. Andrews advocates an oversight role, while Waldo believes the committee should be actively involved in strategic planning.[55] The results of empirical studies are inconsistent on this issue. Both Brown and Henke found that strategy committees are more likely to play an oversight role, with some committees involved in strategy formulations.[56] My study of proxy statements showed that 7 of the 10 strategy committees whose functions were described in detail included a strategy formulation role for the committee. All strategy committees appear to have an oversight role, whether or not they are involved in strategy formulations. The findings of Brown and Henke may in part reflect the relative emphasis placed on these two committee roles. If and when strategy committees become more common, conformity pressures may lead to a standardization of their roles. While the oversight role is very important, firms can fully utilize the wisdom and experience of strategy committee members only by involving them in strategy formulation. Perhaps the best approach would be to assign the strategy formulation role to the strategy committee and the oversight role to the full board.

A variety of committee names are used by those boards that have strategy committees. No name is dominant, but Strategic Planning is the most common. Other names include Strategy, Planning, Long-Range Planning, Corporate Development, and Corporate Objectives. Some acquisitions committees also consider broader issues of corporate strategy.[57]

My proxy statement study showed that strategy committees range in size from three to nine members, with an average size of six members; they averaged about four outside directors and two inside directors (including retired executives of the firm). Brown's findings on the size and composition of the strategy committee were essentially identical to mine, with the exception of one utility and one highly diversified firm which had constituted their full boards as strategy committees.[58] These composition findings are consistent with Waldo's recommendation for strategy committees staffed primarily by outsiders.[59] Andrews, however, believes the committee should be composed completely of outsiders; Henke argues for an equal number of insiders and outsiders on the committee to balance the committee's strategic orientation, based on his finding that outsider-dominated committees tended to focus on the firm's environment while insider-dominated committees tended to focus internally.[60] Henke also found that committees chaired by outsiders were likely to be more involved in strategy.[61]

The most common types of directors serving on strategy committees are show in Figure 4. These composition data indicate that the committees are staffed primarily by directors with experience and knowledge relevant for strategic planning, particularly CEOs and retired CEOs. University professors may be the most controversial committee members. Andrews noted one CEO who was skeptical of "noncombatants" lacking operating management experience, while another liked professors because he didn't have to listen to "how we do it in my company."[62] The composition of the strategy committee is constrained by the types of directors serving on the board; considerations of directors needed to effectively staff the strategy committee may have implications for the types of director recruited for the board.

Figure 4. Composition of Strategy Committees

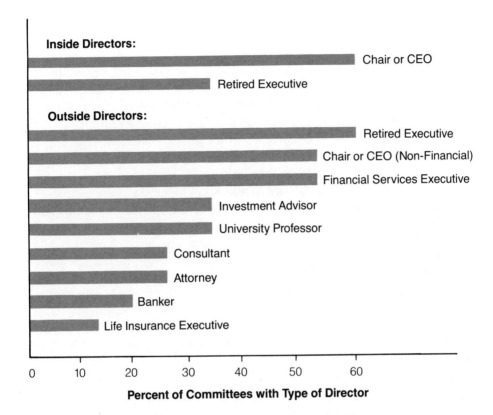

Percent of Committees with Type of Director

Since other board committees, particularly the finance and executive committees, may be involved in issues with strategic implications, it is important to coordinate their activities with those of the strategy committee. One way to accomplish this is through committee interlocks—that is, some members of the strategy committee can also serve on these other committees. Most of the boards with strategy committees that I examined appeared to be using this approach.

In summary, most authorities see the firm's board of directors as a strategic resource and advocate greater board involvement in strategic planning. The use of a strategy committee of the board can effectively increase the board's strategic involvement. Important decisions concerning the use of this committee include what function the committee will have (strategy formation or simply oversight of the strategic planning process), who will serve on the committee, who will chair it, and how the committee's activities will be coordinated with those of other board committees. The reluctance of CEOs to involve the board in strategic planning has been noted;

any effort to increase the board's strategic involvement, whether by committee or otherwise, seems unlikely to succeed without the active support of the CEO.

Conclusion

While corporate board committees are receiving an increasing amount of attention, little of this attention has been directed to strategic considerations of the board's committee structure. This chapter is intended to focus attention on strategic aspects of board committees and to consider how these committees can be used to promote the firm's strategic interests. Board committees—particularly the audit, compensation, and nominating committees—can be used to help the firm maintain its legitimacy and to protect directors from exposure to liability. With respect to these concerns, structure is, in a sense, a strategy. Most firms don't use the strategy committee, but should seriously consider establishing this board committee as a way to promote the board's involvement in strategic planning.

Since few firms have a strategy committee, creating this committee may be seen as deviating from standard practice and as introducing the potential for exposing directors to additional liability risks. This reasoning is probably not applicable to the strategy committee, however. Whether they are involved or not, directors are legally responsible for the firm's strategy and for the outcomes of strategic decisions—the firm's performance. Given the increasing emphasis on director accountability, especially in a climate where mergers, takeover attempts, responses to foreign competition, and other events of major consequence for the corporation are prevalent, it would seem that boards have much to gain by being better informed and more involved in corporate strategy—and the strategy committee can provide valuable assistance in this respect.

The more effective use of board committees can lead to more responsible behavior by corporate boards and to stronger protection of shareholder interests. It is my belief that those interested in corporate strategy, whether managers, advisors, public policy makers, or academics, should be more concerned with the board's committee structure. It is also believed that board committees provide an interesting focus for those interested in the structure and behavior of organizations.

References

1. See, for example, U.S. Securities and Exchange Commission, Division of Corporate Finance, *Staff Report on Corporate Accountability* (Washington, D.C.: U.S. Government Printing Office, 1980); American Bar Association, Committee on Corporate Laws, "The Overview Committees of the Board of Directors," *Business Lawyer*, 35 (1980):1335-1364.
2. Solomon Ethe and Roger M. Pegram, *Corporate Directorship Practices* (New York, NY: National Industrial Conference Board, Studies in Business Policy, No. 90, 1959);

Jeremy Bacon, *Corporate Directorship Practices* (New York, NY: National Industrial Conference Board, Studies in Business Policy, No. 125, 1967); Jeremy Bacon, *Corporate Directorship Practices: Membership and Committees of the Board* (New York, NY: The Conference Board, Conference Board Report No. 588, 1973); J. Richard Harrison, *The Committee Structure of Corporate Boards of Directors* (Unpublished doctoral dissertation, Graduate School of Business, Stanford University, 1986). One committee not shown in Figure 1, for lack of historical data, is the pension committee, which has become more common following passage of the Employee Retirement and Income Security Act of 1976 (ERISA). This committee, sometimes granted an independent or quasi-independent status by the board with fiduciary responsibility for the pension fund, was found in 32% of the manufacturing firms I examined in 1982.

3. Phyllis S. McGrath, *Corporate Directorship Practices: The Public Policy Committee* (New York, NY: The Conference Board, Conference Board Report No. 775, 1980); Duane Windsor, "Public Policy and Corporate Ethics Committees," in George C. Greanias and Duane Windsor, eds., *The Changing Boardroom: Making Policy and Profits in an Age of Corporate Citizenship* (Houston, TX: Gulf, 1982).

4. Kenneth R. Andrews, *The Concept of Corporate Strategy,* revised edition (Homewood, IL: Richard D. Irwin, 1980).

5. SEC, op. cit., p. F156.

6. U.S. Securities and Exchange Commission, "Securities Exchange Act Release No. 15384," *Federal Register,* 43 (1978):58522-58532.

7. American Bar Association, Committee on Corporate Laws, "Corporate Director's Guidebook," *Business Lawyer,* 33 (1978):1620-1644;American Bar Association, op. cit., (1980). Throughout this chapter, I refer to the American Bar Association for convenience; the articles referred to were actually prepared by its Committee on Corporate Laws, which provided the arguments and recommendations discussed.

8. SEC, op. cit., (1980).

9. ABA, op. cit., (1980).

10. Thomas M. Jones, "Shareholder Suits: Good News and Bad News for Corporate Executives," *California Management Review,* 23/4 (1981):77-86.

11. J.G. Maurer, *Readings in Organization Theory: Open-System Approaches* (New York, NY: Random House, 1971), p. 361.

12. Talcott Parsons, "Suggestions for a Sociological Approach to the Theory of Organizations," *Administrative Science Quarterly,* 1 (1956):63-85.

13. Talcott Parsons, *Structure and Process in Modern Societies* (New York, NY: Free Press, 1960); Andrews, op. cit.

14. Charles Perrow, *Organizational Analysis: A Sociological View* (Monterey, CA: Brooks/ Cole, 1970); John Dowling and Jeffrey Pfeffer, "Organizational Legitimacy: Social Values and Organizational Behavior," *Pacific Sociological Review,* 18 (1975):122-136.

15. John W. Meyer and Brian Rowan, "Institutional Organizations: Formal Structure as Myth and Ceremony," *American Journal of Sociology,* 83 (1977):340-363.

16. Meyer and Rowan, op. cit.

17. Paul J. DiMaggio and Walter W. Powell, "The Iron Cage Revisited: Institutional Isomorphism and Collective Rationality in Organizational Fields," *American Sociological Review,* 48 (1983):147-160.

18. This position was frequently taken by directors I interviewed anonymously in the early 1980s.

19. Harrison, op. cit.

20. Ethe and Pegram, op. cit.; Bacon, op. cit., (1967); Bacon, op cit., (1973); SEC, op. cit., (1980); U.S. Securities and Exchange Commission, "Analysis of Results of 1981 Proxy Statement Disclosure Monitoring Program," *Federal Register,* 47 (1982):10792-10804.

21. Harrison, op. cit.
22. Irving S. Shapiro, "Corporate Governance," in Harold M. Williams and Irving S. Shapiro, eds., *Power and Accountability: The Changing Role of the Corporate Board of Directors* (Pittsburgh, PA: Carnegie-Mellon University Press, 1979), p. 52.
23. SEC, op. cit., (1980).
24. SEC, op. cit., (1980), p. F65, quoting a 1978 SEC report.
25. Quoted in SEC, op. cit., (1980), p. F66.
26. Ibid.
27. Harold M. Williams, "Corporate Accountability and Corporate Power," in Williams and Shapiro, eds., op. cit., p. 19.
28. See, for example, Roswell B. Perkins, "Avoiding Director Liability," *Harvard Business Review,* 64 (May/June 1986):8-14.
29. ABA, op. cit., (1980).
30. SEC, op. cit., (1980); ABA, op. cit., (1978); ABA, op. cit., (1980).
31. ABA, op. cit., (1980).
32. Ibid., pp. 1352-1353.
33. Ibid.
34. Ibid., p. 1342.
35. Ibid., p. 1338.
36. Edward McSweeney, *Managing the Managers* (New York, NY: Harper and Row, 1978).
37. Myles L. Mace, *Directors: Myth and Reality* (Boston, MA: Division of Research, Graduate School of Business Administration, Harvard Business School, 1971). The terms "strategy formulation," "strategic planning," and "developing strategy" are used interchangeably throughout this section.
38. James K. Brown, *Corporate Directorship Practices: The Planning Committee* (New York, NY: The Conference Board, Conference Board Report No. 810, 1981); John W. Henke, Jr., "Making the Board of Directors' Involvement in Corporate Strategy Work," paper presented at the Strategic Management Society Conference, Paris, October ,1983; Charles N. Waldo, *Boards of Directors: Their Changing Roles, Structure, and Information Needs* (Westport, CT: Quorum, 1985). Henke noted that although a majority of board chairs responding to his survey reported that their boards were not involved in strategic planning, the responses indicated that nearly all boards were involved in making decisions in areas related to strategy, such as resource allocation. The methodologies of each of the three studies referenced here will be described later.
39. See, for example, Kenneth R. Andrews, "Directors' Responsibility for Corporate Strategy," *Harvard Business Review,* 58 (November/December 1980):30-42.
40. Ibid.
41. See, for example, Statement of the Business Roundtable, "The Role and Composition of the Board of Directors of the Large Publicly Owned Corporation," *Business Lawyer,* 33 (1978):2083-2113; Andrews, *The Concept of Corporate Strategy,* op. cit.; Andrews, "Directors' Responsibility for Corporate Strategy," op. cit.; Kenneth R. Andrews, "Replaying the Board's Role in Formulating Strategy," *Harvard Business Review,* 59 (May/June 1981):18-26; Kenneth R. Andrews, "Corporate Strategy as a Vital Function of the Board," *Harvard Business Review,* 59 (November/December 1981):174-184; Henke, op. cit.; J. Kreiken, "Board Role in Strategic Planning and Resource Allocation," in Edward P. Mattar and Michael Ball, eds., *Handbook for Corporate Directors* (New York, NY: McGraw-Hill, 1983); Waldo, op. cit.
42. A third, highly controversial issue related to the extent of board involvement in strategy, which will not be discussed here, is whether the board chair and CEO positions should be held by the same person.
43. Andrews, "Corporate Strategy as a Vital Function of the Board," op. cit., p. 174.

Waldo, op. cit., agrees with Andrews on the full board's role, but has a different view of the role of the strategy committee, to be discussed later.

44. See, for example, Statement of the Business Roundtable, op. cit.; Kreiken, op. cit.

45. Henke, op. cit.; Waldo, op. cit. Henke's study was based on a survey of the board chairs of 234 large American firms, and Waldo's study was based on a survey of 163 directors from 50 large American manufacturing firms; both surveys were apparently conducted in the early 1980s, although neither author provides this information. Waldo found that *no* director he surveyed reported that his board was involved in strategy formulation.

46. Andrews, *The Concept of Corporate Strategy,* op. cit.; Andrews, "Directors' Responsibility for Corporate Strategy," op. cit.

47. Brown, op. cit.

48. Henke, op. cit.; Hassan Ballout, "Strategy Committees in Large Manufacturing Firms: Empirical Research and Recommendation for Further Investigation," unpublished paper, School of Management, University of Texas at Dallas.

49. Brown, op. cit.

50. Harrison, op. cit.

51. Andrews, "Corporate Strategy as a Vital Function of the Board," op. cit.

52. Henke, op. cit.

53. Brown, op. cit.

54. Daniel Kahneman and Amos Tversky, "Intuitive Prediction: Biases and Corrective Procedures," *Management Science,* 12 (1979):313-327.

55. Andrews (see Note 39); Waldo, op. cit.

56. Brown, op. cit.; Henke, op. cit.

57. Brown, op, cit.; Ballout, op. cit.; and my proxy study.

58. Brown, op. cit.

59. Waldo, op. cit.

60. Andrews, "Directors' Responsibility for Corporate Strategy," op. cit.; Henke, op. cit.

61. Henke, op. cit.

62. Andrews, "Corporate Strategy as a Vital Function of the Board," op. cit., pp. 175, 181, respectively.

Chapter 9

Business Alliances and the Strategy of the Japanese Firm

Michael Gerlach

T*he American business landscape in the 1980s is being trans-*
formed by a range of forces, including those of foreign com-
petition, stock-market-induced industrial restructuring,
and the proliferation of new forms of business alliances. The
rapid increase in foreign competition, particularly from East
Asian economies, across a wide range of product lines in which U.S. firms
were formerly dominant is leading to calls for enhancing the "competitiveness" of American industry. At the same time, because of the remarkable
increase in activity in the U.S. stock market, investors are placing new
pressures on managers to improve corporate financial performance. This is
resulting not only in an increase in the volume of transactions taking place
and the volatility of share prices on the stock exchanges, but even more
importantly in a transformation of the market for corporate control. A wave
of mergers, takeovers, and divestitures is significantly reshaping American
industrial structure, a structure which is also being altered by the proliferation of strategic alliances among firms as they seek new ways of promoting
technological innovation and market development. Joint ventures, research
consortia, cross-licensing, and other arrangements are now a common pattern in many industries.

These seemingly disparate forces are brought together in an important
institutional innovation of the U.S.'s leading trading partner and competitor, Japan. This innovation is the Japanese bank-centered business alliance, also known as *kinyu keiretsu* (financial lineage) or *kigyo shudan*
(enterprise group). These alliances have transformed the Japanese economy
and the operations of its businesses in fundamental ways, with significant
implications for the Japanese corporate system vis-à-vis its American counterpart. In order to understand this, we need to think strategically about the

relationships between firms and their investors (i.e., banks and shareholders). U.S. firms have increasingly had to consider capital market arrangements in their overall corporate plans. Among the *Fortune 500* in 1986 alone, twelve companies took themselves private though leveraged buyouts. Thirteen others disappeared from the list as they were acquired by other *Fortune 500* corporations.[1] Proportions of debt and equity are now being shifted in response to real and potential takeover threats from outside shareholders, while an increasingly large share of capital comes from overseas sources, particularly from Japanese investors.

Japanese firms are themselves facing a transformed capital market environment with the dramatic rise in the value of the yen during the mid-1980s and the internationalization of capital flows. What has remained, however, are the strategic relationships Japanese firms have forged with their capital suppliers and trading partners. These relationships were studied as part of a three-year project on Japanese business alliances carried out by the author while living in Japan. To summarize, companies in Japan rely particularly heavily on their banks for outside capital, while equity capital is held primarily by closely affiliated trading partners. Mergers and acquisitions are infrequent, and hostile takeovers are all but nonexistent. Firm-investor relationships have in turn shaped the strategy and organization of the Japanese firm, including the stability of internal employment patterns, the quality of interfirm information flows, and the ability of firms to make long-term expansion decisions. The Japanese economy has done a remarkable job of funneling capital and other resources into new, higher-value-added sectors; yet this very success raises important concerns regarding the ideal way to structure the relationship between providers of capital (investors) and users of capital (corporate managers).

The Importance of Business Alliances in Japan

Among the most significant but poorly understood features of the Japanese economic landscape is the organization of firms into coherent groupings which link them together in significant, complex, long-term ownership and trading relationship. These I refer to as "business alliances." Being neither formal organizations with clearly defined, hierarchical structures nor impersonal, decentralized markets, business alliances operate instead through extended networks of relationships between companies. They are organized around identifiable groupings and are bound together in durable relationships based on long-term reciprocity.

The bank-centered enterprise group is representative of the larger pattern of investor-manager relationships in the Japanese economy. This form of alliance is composed of a central commercial bank, other financial institutions, a trading company, and a highly diversified set of large manufacturing firms. Of the six main enterprise groups in Japan, Mitsubishi, Mitsui, and Sumitomo are direct descendants of the prewar holding companies (the *zaibatsu*) while the other three were formed during the postwar period around the large commercial banks of Fuji, Sanwa, and Dai-Ichi Kangyo. Although these groups are not legally defined organizations, they have nevertheless been able to express themselves as significant social forms through the ways in which they have structured interaction among their members and created an ongoing symbolic framework within which this interaction takes place. This has been achieved through three integrating mechanisms:

- the creation of high-level executive councils which symbolically identify group members and the boundaries of the social unit, as well as provide a forum for interaction among group firms;
- the structuring of exchange networks—specifically, debt, equity, directorship, and trade networks—that define the position of individual firms in the group and establish group-wide constraints on behavior; and
- group-wide industrial and public relations projects which affirm the existence of the kigyo shudan as a coherent social unit.

The focus here is on the second of these mechanisms, and particularly on the role of affiliated companies as creditors and shareholders.

Alliances and the Reliance on Bank Capital—The role of business alliances in structuring the market for capital must be put in perspective of the overall patterns of corporate finance in Japan as distinguished from its American counterpart. Most significant is the particularly heavy use of borrowed capital in Japan, with the resulting development of close relationships between firms and their sponsoring banks. Japanese firms have long had among the highest ratios of debt to equity of any developed country. Typical estimates have debt covering about 80% of total external capital, as compared with only 50% in the U.S.[2] Banks are particularly important. During the period from 1966–1978, banks provided over half of firms' external capital, double the proportion of that provided by U.S. banks.[3] Close relationships between firms and banks are furthermore promoted by the fact that Japan has never had an equivalent of the Glass-Steagall Act, which in the U.S. forbids bank ownership of companies' equity shares. Furthermore, Japanese banks are typically among their client companies' main stockholders.

The Japanese bank's status as number-one lending institution (the company's "main bank") carries with it the expectation that the bank will not only provide a significant portion of the firm's capital, but will also look after its interests in a wide variety of ways. The main bank acts as a signal to other banks of the financial health of the company, ensuring that the company is able to gain loans from other banks as well—a process known as "pump priming," or *yobi-mizu* (lit., "calling water"). In 1971, for example, the Sumitomo Bank applied to the Ministry of Finance and the Bank of Japan for approval of a plan under which it would guarantee loans by local and mutual banks to its clients, including, prominently, other Sumitomo firms.[4]

Bank assistance also extends to helping its clients find business customers. As a Sumitomo Bank executive explained:

> "Sumitomo Metal Industries does a lucrative business now selling sheet steel to the Matsushita companies, the Nissan companies, and Toyo Kogyo, among others. They enjoy this business because the bank provided a large part of the financing for these companies and acted as go-between to get this business for them. There are many, many arrangements such as this in the group."

When the company gets involved in financial problems, the main bank is expected to come to its client's rescue. For example, Akai Electric, a major tape-deck manufacturer, had run into financial difficulties during the early 1980s and was under financial reconstruction. Significantly, it was Akai's main bank, the Mitsubishi Bank, that took charge of this reconstruction. (Mitsubishi was Akai's leading shareholder and creditor, owning 8% of Akai's shares and lending 16% of its borrowed capital.) As part of the assistance, Mitsubishi sent three people to Akai—the chief secretary to the president, the department manager in charge of International Business Operations, and the department manager for International Finance—and extended additional loans to the company.

In the enterprise group, the main bank relationship is expanded from that of a bilateral relationship to that of a larger alliance of firms, each of which employs the group bank as its main bank. These firms, moreover, are connected directly to other group companies through ownership, personnel, and trading networks. The maintenance of the central position of the group banks was ensured by the postwar economic reforms pushed by the U.S. occupation, which broke up the zaibatsu holding companies but not the zaibatsu banks. As a result, and in conjunction with the Japanese government's policy of allocating scarce capital to the city banks through its own financial organs, these city banks became the leading sources of capital for group companies and were in a position to give preference to their own long-standing clients. Firms themselves were growing rapidly and had extremely high external capital requirements that could not be met by the relatively undeveloped equity market. Thus, they turned increasingly to the banks.[5] Groupings formed around these banks as companies were willing to forego a degree of independence in order to gain access to scarce but needed capital, particularly during the economic resurgence of the mid-1950s. Figure 1 depicts schematically how these relationships among the leading companies now appear in one group, Sumitomo.

Alliances and the Structure of Equity Networks—Business alliances are critical in structuring shareholder relationships. In Japan, as in the U.S., equity ownership legally defines control over the firm. However, in practical terms, corporate ownership in Japan is not a neutral commodity, traded

Figure 1. Intra-Group Borrowing Dependency of the Leading Companies in the Sumitomo Group

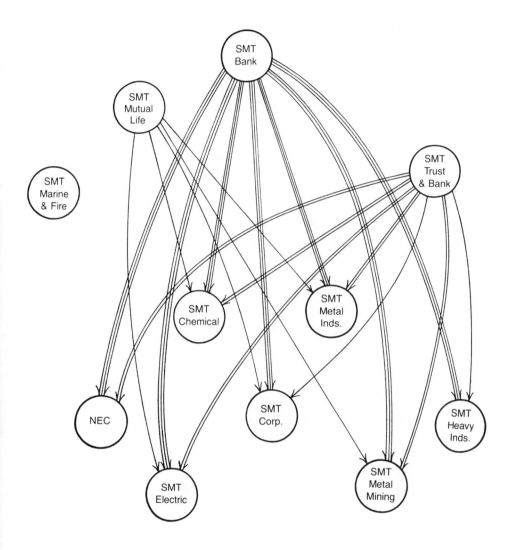

≡≡≡≡≡ **Main lender**

≡≡≡≡ **Loans in excess of 10% of company's borrowed capital (but not main lender)**

—————— **Loans of 1-10% of company's borrowed capital**

Note: SMT = Sumitomo
Source: Date from *Industrial Groupings in Japan* (1982).

anonymously among actors who have little vested interest in the firms in which they have shares. Ownership of the firm sets the framework within which the firm's internal operations take place, and the issue of *who* owns companies—the structure of corporate control—is a critical one.

Among publicly traded Japanese companies, institutions have replaced individuals as the primary controller of shareholdings. About 43% of shares of U.S. firms were held by institutional investors in the early 1980s, while in Japan the figure was even higher at 62%.[6] More important, however, is the nature of this relationship. In the U.S., nearly two-thirds of institutional shareholders are representatives for pension funds and personal trust funds, investors for whom the primary incentives come in the form of portfolio returns rather than in trading relationships with the firms they hold. Institutional ownership retains an identity separate from that of management.

The interests of institutional shareholders in Japan differ dramatically. Equity shareholdings take on symbolic meaning in signifying relationships with other firms, rather than as straightforward investments for capital gains. The role of shareholder becomes merged with that of business partner. In the words of one executive, "There is no sense in holding shares in a company with which business ties are slim." Equity positions become embedded in other ongoing relationships between the firms and remain highly stable over time. The symbolic role of intercorporate shareholdings to the Japanese has been pointed out by Rodney Clark:

> Unlike Western institutional shareholders, which invest largely for dividends and capital appreciation, Japanese institutional shareholders tend to be the company's business partners and associates; shareholding is the mere expression of their relationship, not the relationship itself.[7]

This is particularly clear in the relationship between firms and their client banks, where the embedding of equity and loan positions transforms their roles. Credit, in the form of bank loans, resembles equity in allowing creditors flexibility in repayment by deferring interest and principal payments and by reducing compensating balances during times of financial adversity. Loans are rolled over as a matter of practice. Furthermore, banks become active participants in the management of their client firms, particularly when the company is in trouble. Common stock, in contrast, takes on many of the characteristics Westerners associate with debt. Shareholders demand relatively fixed returns on their investment (in the form of stable dividend payments) but do not ask for active influence over management.

The relationship between equity shareholders and firms remains a durable one, as shareholders are a stable constituency of well-known trading partners. As an executive in Sumitomo Life Insurance, the largest holder of shares in the Sumitomo group, described it: "If group shares go up, we don't quickly sell them off, though naturally we're happy. If the value of a company's shares goes up, that improves the financial conditions of all group companies." Estimates of holdings by "stable shareholders" (*antei kabunushi*) run somewhere between 60-80% of total shares on the Tokyo Stock Exchange. Aoki estimates that banks account for only 2.9% of transactions on the Tokyo Stock Exchange, life insurance companies only 0.8%, and non-financial corporations 6.9%.[8] In other words, while institutional investors hold two-thirds of total shares issued, they account for only 10% percent of total transactions on Japanese stock exchanges.

In comparison, U.S. institutional shareholders are extremely active traders in corporate securities—and are by implication, unstable shareholders. Mintz and Schwartz report U.S. institutional investors account for 60% of all transactions, while holding only 40% of issued shares.[9] U.S. institutional shareholders, therefore, hold only two-thirds the proportion of shares held by their Japanese institutional counterparts, yet they engage in six times the share of transactions. When controlling for the smaller proportion of shares held by U.S. institutional investors, this means that they engage in almost *ten times* the number of stock transactions (as a proportion of shares held) as do Japanese institutional investors.

Institutional shareholding in Japan has furthermore developed into a pattern of interlocking ownership, or *kabushiki mochiai* ("stock joint-holdings"). The term *mochiai*, construed narrowly, means "to hold mutually." But it also carries additional connotations of "helping one another," of "shared interdependence," and of "stability." Crossholdings, as Japanese businessmen point out, "keep each other warm"—*hada o atatame-au*.

Corporate ownership of business alliances is structured into internalized networks of crossholdings with other group firms. Overall, according to the Japanese Federal Trade Commission, an average of 15-30% of a group company's shares are held by other companies in the group.[10] This figure, however, considerably understates the significance of intra-group shareholding, since it includes in this total a large number of scattered smaller shareholders. If, on the other hand, we consider only firms' *leading* shareholders, the percentages of internalization of ownership more than doubles. Table 1 shows the extent of crossholdings among the leading shareholders (defined as those in the top 20 for a company) of Japan's largest firms, broken down by group membership.

The table indicates that share crossholdings are over 30% for all six groups, and in the range of 55-74% for the three zaibatsu groups. Percentages of shareholdings *across* groups, on the other hand, are small. Mitsui group companies, for example, hold only 1.7% of the shares of companies in the Mitsubishi group and in the Sumitomo group, in contrast to 55.2% of the shares of other Mitsui companies. Conversely, among their own shares, only 5.4% are held by Mitsubishi group companies and only 7.3% by Sumitomo companies.

In the process of holding each other's shares, *mochiai* becomes self-cancelling—a *kami no yaritori*, or "paper exchange"—thereby removing

Table 1. Share Crossholdings Within and Across Groups
(Top 100 Manufacturers and Top 23 Financial Institutions, 1973)

Company Issuing Shares (and No. of Top Companies)	Companies Holding Shares						
	Mitsui	Mitsu-bishi	Sumi-tomo	Fuji	Dai-Ichi	Sanwa	Inde-pendent
Mitsui (12)	55.2%	5.4	7.3	4.9	2.1	—	25.2
Mitsubishi (13)	1.7	74.2	0.8	3.8	3.8	1.0	14.8
Sumitomo (10)	1.7	0.3	68.8	3.6	1.6	0.2	23.9
Fuji (14)	3.5	6.4	6.8	49.2	5.5	4.9	23.6
Dai-Ichi (10)	4.2	9.1	4.7	6.2	42.3	2.4	31.1
Sanwa (12)	3.2	5.6	2.6	12.7	11.3	32.8	31.8
Independent (52)	11.2	13.0	9.8	9.2	9.5	7.2	40.0

Notes: Figures indicate percentage of shares held by group firms (underlined) versus other-group and independent firms. Limited to the top twenty shareholders in each company.
Source: Translated and adapted from Yuusaku Futatsugi, *Gendai Nihon no Kigyo Shudan—Dai-Kigyo Bunseki o Mezashite* [Enterprise Groups in Contemporary Japan: Focusing on an Analysis of Large Frms] (Tokyo: Toyo Shinposha, 1976), p. 33, Table 1.9.

shares from open public trading. Offsetting shares constitute better than half of all holdings among group firms. Futatsugi has calculated these for companies in the three zaibatsu groups (excluding life insurance companies, whose shares cannot be held) and found them to account for 56% of Mitsubishi group companies' holdings, 57% of Mitsui's, and 68% of Sumitomo's.[11] In other words, in these groups between 56% and 68% of shares have corresponding shares held by the other firm. Figure 2 shows the specific patterns of crossholding for the leading companies in the Sumitomo group.

The issue of why a self-cancelling shareholding system developed in Japan was well phrased by an executive in the Mitsui group over twenty years ago: "What's the use of owning two or three hundred shares in related companies? If we had the money, we would put it to better use in equipment or something else."[12] No answer was provided by this executive, but the question is a good one. By normal economic logic, borrowing heavily from financial institutions in order to use a significant portion of this to make equity investments in other firms does not make sense, for companies are paying interest on that borrowed capital. The reasons for share crossholdings seem to lie instead in their importance in shaping the *qualitative* relationships between firms. With the symbolic function that ownership implies, and its importance in linking firms in other ongoing transactions, share crossholdings among group companies create a structure of stable, mutual relationships among trading partners.

Figure 2. Stock Crossholdings of the Leading Companies in the Sumitomo Group (Top 10 Shareholdings only)

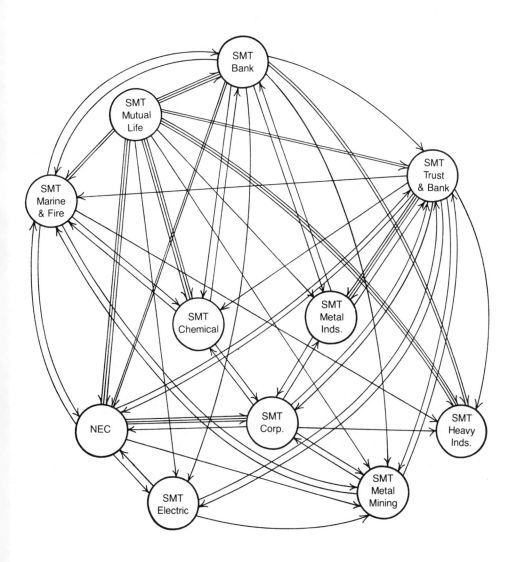

≡≡≡≡≡ **5% or more and leading shareholder**

═════ **5% or more (not leading shareholder) or less than 5% and leading shareholder**

────── **One of top ten shareholders but less than 5%**

Note: SMT = Sumitomo
Source: Data from *Industrial Groupings in Japan* (1982)

Reconceptualizing the Corporation: The Impact of Business Alliances on the Japanese Firm

The alliance represents an important institutional alternative that has linked Japanese corporation with their environments in ways fundamentally different from that in the U.S. Through it, the market for corporate assets and control has been transformed, as has the nature of the corporation itself. Consider the relationship between investor and manager in the U.S. What is striking is the extent to which shareholders of the firm have become differentiated from the activities of the firm itself, and from its employees, lenders, and trading partners. Today in the U.S., a large constituency of institutional investors share common interests with each other, but little ongoing interest in the firms in which they hold shares. These investors are likely to vote similarly and based solely on the criteria of financial performance—share price, dividend policy, etc. Indeed, laws of fiduciary responsibility in the U.S. demand this of them.

In Japan, in contrast, the business alliance becomes the key link between firms and their environments, and it does so in ways that alter their nature. In the market for corporate control, arm's-length shareholders—e.g., large institutional investment trusts seeking portfolio returns—are replaced by a closely connected community of mutually positioned, long-term trading partners. The firm is not a commodity to be exchanged on an open market, but a social collective to be preserved and protected within the framework of the joint business alliance. As a result, mergers and acquisitions take place only among parties closely familiar with each other, and hostile takeovers are virtually nonexistent.

The process of acquisition in Japan is a long, time-consuming one, not unlike an extended courtship. A Japanese consultant specializing in mergers (there are only a few such individuals) described the process as follows: "Price is only the last item of discussion, in contrast with the U.S. approach. Instead, we emphasize the advantages to the company itself. In particular, we show them how the acquiring firm can help the company expand into international markets and gain new access to new technologies." Another consultant said, "At first the Japanese owner can't accept the fact that he is selling his company, and so we talk about the foreign company taking a percentage of equity . . . . Most importantly, the sellers want guarantees that they and their people are not going to be dismissed."

The firm's key constituencies must be properly courted, or the marriage is likely to fall through. For example, in the ill-fated merger attempt between Sumitomo Bank and Kansai Sogo Bank in the mid-1970s, both employees and affiliated firms joined forces in opposition. Together the employees, branch offices, and customers of the much smaller Kansai Sogo Bank formed the Kansai Bank Preservation Association ("Kansai Sogo Ginko o Mamoru-Kai") with the intention of frustrating merger plans due to concerns that they would be relegated to second-class status. This group carried out a campaign widely picked up by the Japanese media, which played on themes of Sumitomo's social responsibility, on the importance of the preservation of smaller companies, and even on the necessity of maintaining the employee's *ikigai* (their purpose or meaning in life). Sumitomo eventually abandoned its merger efforts.

If mergers and acquisitions among large firms are relatively infrequent in Japan, then hostile takeovers of the kind now prevalent in the U.S. are all but nonexistent; and this fact reveals clearly the degree to which the "market" for corporate control takes place not among arm's-length traders in impersonal stock markets, but among firms which maintain longstanding relationships with each other.

The factors affecting the merger and acquisition market in Japan apply *a fortiori* to hostile takeovers. This is particularly true when foreign firms are involved. Foreign ownership of Japanese stock has increased substantially over the last two decades, and accounted for 5.1% total shareholdings in 1983, up from only 1.4% in 1961. Moreover, because of the tendency of Japanese institutional investors to hold onto their shares, foreigners now account for about 20% of all trading on the Tokyo Stock Exchange.[13] In 1971, the Finance Ministry revised the securities exchange to allow foreign takeovers of Japanese companies. However, despite this liberalization, there have been virtually no interfirm transactions in corporate assets involving foreign firms in Japan. In 1985, for example, a British-U.S. group attempted a hostile takeover of the Japanese company, Minebea. This attempt was defeated, however, when the investors found Japanese shareholders unwilling to sell their shares. The market is open in principal, but in reality it is internally regulated by the parties involved.

Protection from external takeover threats is implicit in the alliance structure of corporate ownership. A good example of the ways in which such groups rally round to protect other firms occurred in 1984 and involved the Mitsubishi group. At the time, Texaco held a 50% position in Mitsubishi Oil. However, it had just finished a purchase of Gulf Oil and wanted to unload this position in order to raise needed capital. The Mitsubishi group agreed to buy back Texaco's share in Mitsubishi Oil rather than risk letting it fall into unfriendly hands.

The Resulting Transformation of Japanese Corporate Strategy and Organization

In order to put into perspective the ways in which the organization of business alliances has transformed the linkage between capital and productive activities in the Japanese economy, consider first another important institutional innovation, the modern joint-stock corporation. By establishing division of labor between holders of capital and management, and limiting the liability of the former, the corporate form simultaneously opened up new sources of capital for faster growth, allowed for the specialization of the management function, and diffused risk across a broader set of investors. Development of the corporation also established arrangements whereby ownership interests could still be represented—including most importantly, the board of directors and the general shareholders' meeting. While within the corporation, the invisible hand of anonymous traders was replaced by the quite-visible hand of corporate managers,[14] the firm itself was to be disciplined externally through these shareholder institutions.

The business alliance retains the advantages of the corporate form of organization, as each of its firms operates as a legally independent entity. Outside capital is therefore made broadly available, the division of labor is maintained, and risk is diffused. But the sources of external discipline are changed dramatically, for capital comes primarily from affiliated companies, particularly group financial institutions, while stockholdings are reciprocal and based in long-term positions among companies' trading partners.

There are three important consequences of these alliance relationships for Japanese business strategy and organization. Alliances have simultaneously

- allowed for development of stable, reliable business relationships, including internal labor markets and "lifetime employment,"
- improved information flows between companies, and
- promoted aggressive, long-term growth policies.

Stabilized Business Relationships—Among the most interesting features of Japanese business, as we have seen, are the ways in which Japanese firms have constructed strategic alliances with capital suppliers to *remove* firms from stock-market influence and to maintain a high degree of internal control over their operations. The system of mutual shareholding establishes a kind of implicit hands-off policy in managing the internal affairs in other group companies quite different from the highly rationalized capital found in the U.S. that drives firms towards continually focusing on those features of the organization most easily measured (particularly the firm's current profitability). In addition, the normal fluctuations of the business cycle are buffered by the heavy reliance on stable, outside trading partners. Banks, in particular, provide a steady source of capital to their close affiliates, while external subcontractors provide a reliable source of production to buffer firms from economic swings. Furthermore, the group provides external assistance in times of duress. Under the "Japanese-style layoff system," employees in firms in depressed industries (e.g., aluminum) may be transferred to their alliance affiliates in growth industries (e.g., consumer electronics). Similarly, during the mid-1970s oil shortage in Japan, most oil companies continued to provide oil to their longstanding partners at below-market prices. In the U.S., in contrast, this kind of reliability has declined significantly with the unpredictability of new industrial arrangements resulting from continual restructuring. The president of a large Japanese tool manufacturer, for example, complained that his American partner had gone through three ownership changes over the past decade. "We never know who we are dealing with," was one comment.

The forging of stable external relationships has gone hand-in-hand with the development of stable internal relationships as well, allowing Japanese firms to focus on product market competition, technological innovation, and the development of employee skills. Among the many interesting features of Japanese organization, perhaps the most widely commented on is the so-called "lifetime employment system" (*shushin koyo seido*)—the personnel policy of hiring (male) employees directly after graduation from high school or college and keeping them employed until retirement at age 55–60. This system is the most tangible expression of the more general redefinition of the modern, large-scale Japanese firm, in which managers and employees have become the dominant constituency and the firm's *raison d'etre*.[15]

The high degree of external stability developed through alliance relationships has permitted the lifetime employment system to persist even during economic downturns. The first major test of the system came in the mid-1970s oil shocks. Despite dire predictions at the time, firms were to a large extent able to maintain their commitment to their workers. When, for example, Toyo Kogyo, builder of Mazda automobiles, was facing collapse in the mid-1970s, its main bank, Sumitomo, took the lead in extending new credits, arranging for special terms on sales and purchase agreements from other Sumitomo group companies, and arranging for group companies to buy additional shares of Toyo Kogyo's stock.[16] Similar arrangements are now being forged in response to new challenges imposed by the dramatic rise in the value of the yen since 1985. Overall unemployment in Japan has so far risen by less than half of a percentage point.

Improved Interfirm Information Flows—The basic dilemma in governing the investor-manager relationship is that managers have more information about how investors' funds are being utilized, but less incentive to utilize those funds in the investors' best interests.[17] While these problems are not entirely resolved in the business alliance, the close relationship between investors and managers has brought these two constituencies considerably closer together.

In gaining access to information, business alliance partners are able to utilize sources not available to outside shareholders. They have learned about each other through ongoing trading relationships and through various collaborative projects and other forms of interaction that provide information not available in financial statements. If, for example, product quality is beginning to decline, the group trading firm and other affiliated trading partners are likely to be among the first to know this through their purchasing connections, while the kind of in-depth information that the firm's "main bank" acquires in order to extend loans is utilized in its decisions as shareholder.

Alliance partners are also linked through various forms of personnel connections. Group projects and other cooperative projects are prevalent in Japan and serve as an important forum for interaction among management and technical personnel. Employee transfers, both temporary (usually two years) and permanent, are common among business partners, particularly between banks and their client firms and between large manufacturers and their subcontractors. Another forum for interaction is the interfirm executive council, which brings together managers from various levels in firms within the bank-centered and vertical subcontracting groupings. The Sumitomo group, for example, has ten different monthly councils, including those for the presidents of group companies, the chairman, and vice presidents of corporate planning and of research and development.

Aggressive, Long-Term Growth Policies—Perhaps even more important than the transformation of the information properties of the investor-manager relationship is that of its *incentives*. With the emergence of coherent "mini-economies," in the form of the *kigyo shudan*, has come a shift in the level of competition from a purely firm-against-firm level to one in which groups themselves are involved. The alliance becomes one of the strategic tools at the disposal of firms in their quest to improve their positions in the larger business community, and competition increasingly takes place at the inter-*group* level.

The aggressiveness of Japanese firms in pursuing market share, in expanding capacity even in economic downturns, in improving product quality and diversity, and in moving into high-value-added fields is evident in a wide range of industries—from steel to semiconductors. To a significant degree, this is due to the alliance organization of business, which has brought together investment and managerial decisions in an ongoing relationship between firms. Capital has been moved closer to the action, resulting in a general pattern of rapid, aggressive entry into new industries by existing firms, with the early and continued support of affiliated companies. Group firms, as equity shareholders, receive first-order returns on their investment when other group firms are profitable. More important, however, are second-order returns to trading partner. Product improvement and volume expansion rebound to the benefit of group financial institutions that extend loans for new investments, trading concerns that will manage the goods that result, and those manufacturers that use the products.

As a result of these features, new market entry in Japan has been dominated by the entrance of larger and older firms, with substantial backing from their supporting financial institutions. There is really nothing equivalent in Japan to California's Silicon Valley, though pockets of regional high-tech entrepreneurialism exist (notably, in Kyoto and parts of Kyushu island). Rather, the "future industries" (e.g., biotechnology, semiconductors, new materials) have been entered by well-established firms seeking expansion into new, but related, growth areas, and achieved with the backing of their larger group. While this may discourage some entrepreneurs, it means that new entrants have a ready market to tap in the form of other group firms. In addition, when industries reach a point at which plant and equipment with greater capacity become necessary, these firms have a larger pool of capital to access, through their banking relationships, that is not available to smaller firms.

Moreover, these relationships have allowed Japanese firms to persist in markets even during economic downturns and despite the inevitable mistakes that will occur in the early stages of market entry. As Abegglen and Stalk point out, "Rather than cutting back when demand is weak, [the Japanese company] with a growth bias typically steps up its levels of investment. Product variety is increased, prices are cut, and distribution is expanded."[18] Despite the conspicuous recent successes of Japanese firms, Japanese market penetration in the U.S. is the result of efforts over long years of developing distribution networks, and it includes major strategic mistakes as well as victories.[19] Alliance structures have buffered firms during lean years—e.g., the Japanese semiconductor industry in the mid-1980s— while pushing firms to maintain a market presence for its eventual benefits to the wider group. U.S. firms in the same industries, therefore, compete not merely against single companies, but against an extended set of firms.

With the merging of shareholding positions into ongoing trading relationships, returns on equity positions become considerably less important to investing firms, while the long-term viability of the firm as a reliable supplier and customer becomes much more important. The continual improvement in the quality and features of the firm's product line takes on a significance in-and-of-itself, even where these improvements are not captured in improved equity returns, because investors receive benefits in other forms. Financial institutions, for example, are generally among the top shareholders in large Japanese firms, yet their equity positions are typically only a fraction of the loans and other business they carry on with the same firms. To take one case, the top shareholder of NEC in 1982 was its affiliated life insurance company, Sumitomo Mutual Life. While Sumitomo Mutual Life held 8.1% of NEC's shares, valued at $15.8 million, its outstanding loans to NEC were over eight times higher, $126.0 million. NEC's second-leading shareholder was also a Sumitomo affiliate, Sumitomo Bank, which held 5.8% of NEC's shares. This accounted for $11.3 million in external capital, but was only a small fraction of the bank's total commitment, since during the same year Sumitomo Bank extended $184.0 million in loans to NEC.[20]

These leading "shareholders" are concerned, quite rationally, with the firm's long-term viability rather than the relatively minor equity returns it brings. Continued expansion of the firm, even where returns are low, leads to new business not only for the group banks and insurance companies (in the form of loans, deposits from employees of group companies, and other business), but for the group trading firm (as commercial representative of the firm's products) as well as for other affiliated manufacturing concerns that will use the product.

Conclusion

For all the attention that various dimensions of Japanese business have received, the significance of interfirm relationships and the role of business alliances in the organization of the Japanese economy has been largely ignored. The alliance structure of capital and control in Japan is demonstrably different than its American counterpart. This institutional environment has set the context for the development of the distinctive ways in which Japanese firms have pursued their external strategies and managed their internal operations; and it is here, as much as in Japanese managerial insight or culture, that the sources of Japanese business behavior are found.

Perhaps the strongest argument for the Japanese business system has been its remarkable ability and willingness to experiment, to try new things, and to look outside and learn. This has been carried out enthusiastically on all fronts in the development of Japanese technical, organizational, managerial, and production skills. Japanese industry has been marked by rapid entry into new fields by firms that have the early and continuing support of affiliated companies. Understanding this approach requires thinking about not only competitive strategy, but *cooperative* strategy.

Within the U.S., significant legal barriers to interfirm cooperation exist which are largely absent in Japan. These include antitrust policies (which prohibit forms of business reciprocity common in Japan) and financial regulations (particularly the Glass-Steagall Act, which forbids commercial bank ownership of corporate shares). However, some of these restrictions are now in the process of breaking down, presenting opportunities for American firms to forge new kinds of cooperative alliances with other firms, both U.S. and foreign. While the forms these will take remains an open question, Japan shows that among the most critical of all alliances are those between firms and their investors.

References

1. *Fortune*, April 27, 1987, p. 359.
2. Cross-national comparisons are complicated by institutional differences in accounting practices (some of which underrepresent equity and overrepresent debt values in Japan), but estimates even after adjustment suggest that these rates are somewhere around 65%.
3. Daniel I. Okimoto, Takuo Sugano, and Franklin B. Weinstein, *Competitive Edge: The Semiconductor Industry in the U.S. and Japan* (Stanford, CA: Stanford University

Press, 1984), p. 141. The reliance on borrowed capital in Japan is high even in comparison with that for European countries. Futatsugi, using a different data base, finds that for the period 1967–1972, Japanese firms borrowed on average 15.9% more of their total capital than did French firms, 20.3% more than did West German firms, and 23.2% more than did British firms. Yuusaku Futatsugi, *Gendai Nihon no Kigyo Shudan - Dai-Kigyo Bunseki o Mezashite* [Enterprise Groups in Contemporary Japan: Focusing on an Analysis of Large Firms](Tokyo: Toyo Shinposha, 1976), p. 33, Table 1.9.

4. T.F.M. Adams and Iwao Hoshii, *A Financial History of the New Japan* (Tokyo: Kodansha International, Ltd., 1972).

5. Where firms' debt capital had accounted for only 10% of total capital in the 1930s, it rose to over 50% in the 1950s. Meanwhile, equity as a portion of external capital declined during the postwar period, from 39% to only 8% in the 1950s. Raymond A. Goldsmith, *The Financial Development of Japan, 1868–1977* (New Haven, CT: Yale University Press, 1983), pp. 143 ff.

6. For statistics, see Masahiko Aoki, "Aspects of the Japanese Firm," in Masahiko Aoki, ed., *The Economic Analysis of the Japanese Firm* (Amsterdam: North-Holland, 1984), pp. 9–11.

7. Rodney Clark, *The Japanese Company* (New Haven, CT: Yale University Press, 1979), p. 8.

8. Aoki, op. cit.

9. Beth Mintz and Michael Schwartz, *The Power Structure of American Business* (Chicago, IL: University of Chicago Press, 1985), p. 97.

10. Kosei Torihiki Iinkai [Japanese Federal Trade Commission], "Shuyo Dai-Kigyo no Kabushiki Shoyu no Jokyo ni Tsuite" [On the State of Stock Ownership of Important Large Companies], 1983.

11. Futatsugi, op. cit.

12. Quoted in *Oriental Economist* (March 1961), p. 143.

13. *Business Week*, October 15, 1984, pp. 44–47.

14. Ronald H. Coase, "The Nature of the Firm," *Economica* (1937), pp. 386–405; Oliver E. Williamson, *Markets and Hierarchies: Analysis and Antitrust Implications* (New York, NY: Free Press, 1975); Alfred D. Chandler, *The Visible Hand: The Managerial Revolution in American Business* (Cambridge, MA: Harvard University Press, 1977).

15. Recent empirical evidence suggests that employment relationships in even medium and smaller Japanese firms are considerably more stable than their U.S. counterparts. Hashimoto and Raisian find that average eventual employee tenure in medium and larger Japanese firms is about 50% higher than in the U.S., while that in the smallest Japanese firms is about *double* that in the smallest U.S. firms.

16. See Richard Pascale and Thomas Rohlen, "The Mazda Turnaround," *Journal of Japanese Studies* (1983).

17. See Michael C. Jensen and William H. Meckling, "Theory of the Firm: Managerial Behavior, Agency Costs and Ownership Structure," *Journal of Financial Economics* (1976), pp. 305–360, and Eugene F. Fama and Michael Jensen, "Separation of Ownership and Control," *Journal of Law and Economics* (1983), pp. 301–326, for theoretical discussions of the "agency costs" of bringing the divergent interests of management and investors in line.

18. James C. Abegglen and George Stalk, Jr., *Kaisha: The Japanese Corporation* (New York, NY: Basic Books, 1985).

19. Pascale's study of Honda's early failures in the U.S. market quite convincingly punctures the myth of the omniscient Japanese strategist, while pointing out the importance of perseverance in markets. Pascale and Rohlen, op. cit.

20. Calculated form data provided in *Industrial Groupings in Japan* (Tokyo: Dodwell Marketing, 1982).

Chapter 10

Strategic Decision Processes in Silicon Valley: The Anatomy of a "Living Dead"

L. J. Bourgeois, III   **Kathleen M. Eisenhardt**

I*n the fast-paced world of Silicon Valley, the entrepreneur's dream is to found a high-technology company which will grow with sufficient speed and prosperity to present a "winning" image and go public. The dream is propelled by intense desire to build a unique product, and, in the process, a successful organization. The fuel for the dream is often venture capital.*

From the venture capitalist's perspective, the objective is to fund a sufficient number of promising ventures such that the enormous gains from a few winners far outweigh the cost of the failures. For a typical venture portfolio, two or three ventures out of ten might be big winners. An equal number will fail early, not surviving the first or second round of financing. The remaining four or five might live on, past the third, fourth, or even fifth rounds of financing, and they may raise $10 or $20 or even $30 million. For this last group, success appears always to be "just around the corner," as the companies continually fall short of their targets and consume money and time. The financial backers cannot extricate themselves because there is no clear market for the company. The ventures themselves are insufficiently successful to be taken public, but neither are they clear enough failures to die. The venture capital community refers to these firms as the "living dead" of their portfolios.[1]

Although much has been written about successful firms like Apple Computer and unsuccessful ones like Osborne, little has been written about the majority of firms who are, in fact, in neither category, but rather

We wish to thank our graduate assistant, Theresa Lant, for her invaluable help. An earlier version of this article was presented at the TIMS National Meetings, May 1987, New Orleans, in the session, "Innovation in American Corporations: Best Practices and Competitive Advantage."

occupy the limbo of the "living dead." By contrast, this chapter examines the strategic process within one of the "living dead" among our sample of microcomputer companies.

The company was studied as part of an ongoing investigation into the competitive strategies and strategic decision processes of firms in the computer industry. The motivation for the project was to study firms in unusually fast change, high-technology environments. Prior research on strategic decision making emphasizes large corporations such as Xerox, Chrysler, and DuPont,[2] nonprofit organizations,[3] and laboratory simulations.[4] Our study extends this work by examining executives making actual decisions in firms operating in high-speed, high-technology environments.

Background

Our earlier research reported some of the decision processes that appeared to differentiate the successful microcomputer firms from the unsuccessful firms.[5] A key conclusion was that successful firms combine paradoxical decision practices. For example, the top managers of successful firms made their strategic decisions in a deliberately analytic manner, but also very quickly. That is, major decisions were arrived at in virtual "textbook" fashion (conducting industry and competitor analyses, identifying distinctive competences, etc.), but they were usually made within a short three-month period. By contrast, the poor performers were usually reactive in their decision processes and tended to take as long as 18 months to two years from initiation to conclusion.

A second characteristic of successful firms was that their CEOs appeared to act decisively and retain the power to set strategic direction, but would leave the power to articulate strategy implementation with the functional VPs. Power maps drawn for these firms indicated that while the chief executive exercised occasional power over functional decisions, he was frequently second to the functional vice-presidents in influence in any given area. Only among the low-performing firms did the CEO exercise the most power over every decision area.

A third success characteristic was the taking of major decisions that were often bold and risky, and yet making them "safer" through "execution triggers" which permitted last-minute adaptation. That is, bold commitments to action were tempered by carefully planned execution cycles in which specific actions were triggered by events, and multiple implementation options were retained as long as possible.

In sum, our previous research indicated that successful firms appeared to resolve a series of competing or paradoxical tensions in their strategic decision processes. These included:

- simultaneously rapid and deliberate strategic decision processes;

- simultaneously powerful, decisive CEOs and powerful top management team members; and
- simultaneously bold, innovative decisions and safe, incremental execution.

By contrast, we found that unsuccessful firms were reactive and slow, had all power centralized with the CEO, and tended to make major strategic decisions incrementally. That is, the unsuccessful firms lacked most, or even all, of the above characteristics. What happens when only some of the characteristics are missing? As we will describe in the case that follows, the "living dead" have several characteristics which are associated with success, but their executives are ultimately unable to deal with the competing tensions of analysis and speed, autocratic and collegial power, and innovation and incrementalism. These firms tend to then slip into the category of the "living dead"—somewhere between success and failure.

The Omicron Story

Omicron Computers was founded in 1981 by a pair of successful computer executives, Bill Smith and Ron Adams.[6] Omicron was created to take advantage of the increasing interest by businesses in smaller computers. By combining multi-tasking functionality with the small size and high power of supermicros, Smith was able to design a unique multiprocessor architecture around 16- and 32-bit chips. The result was a unique and successful blend of hardware and software.

Taking early advantage of new software and computer architecture concepts and VLSI technology, Omicron was able to establish itself quickly as the price/performance leader in its market segment. The visible entry of a well-known competitor into this segment enhanced credibility and added impetus to Omicron's early success. The first few years of growth were strong:

1981—founding, first-round financing
1982—$5 million in sales
1983—$21 million
1984—$37 million

Until 1985, the company was meeting its original business plan targets and was considered to be well on its way towards becoming a success story. If it were to have reached its $75 million target for 1985, the investors could probably have taken the firm public and counted Omicron among the winners in their respective portfolios.

However, this was not to be. In 1981, Omicron had been one of the first entrants into its market, but by 1986 the number of competitors had grown from 5 to 43. Newcomers had computers which were now outperforming those of Omicron in industry benchmark tests of CPU speed and price. Total sales for 1985 dropped to $34 million, and the firm continued to lose money even as other start-ups became profitable in the same market.

Perhaps the pace of early growth had exhausted the Omicron executives. Perhaps they were blinded by early success. What is clear is that by 1985 Engineering was no longer developing new products, and Sales was not exploring new markets. As Andy Wong, Vice President of Engineering, put it:

> "We didn't renew our product strategy early enough. We lost the performance gap that permitted us to charge premium prices. Because we're not good at marketing, we [Engineering] were driving the Marketing group. We pushed Marketing to think about new products. No one outside Engineering was pushing us to develop new products."

The status of "living dead" was difficult to accept after the early taste of success. The fall into what John Wilson describes as "dragging out a miserable existence as a 'living dead' "[7] was recognized retrospectively by several of Omicron's top managers:

> "A year and a half ago, we were a winner. Now we must do a strategy in order to move. People [in Omicron] want a strategy, but there is lots of controversy about what it should be. Everybody wants the dream (of getting rich, the successful startup) to happen. But . . . time is passing by."—*Nancy Remington, VP Sales*

The following is the story of Omicron Computers: how they fell behind, how the top management recognized their deteriorating position, and how the executive team addressed strategy issues now that they were rapidly becoming members of the "living dead." The story is based on a series of interviews with the seven top executives, as well as on their responses to a questionnaire and our observations of these executives in an all-day strategy session.[8]

Tracing A Strategic Decision: "Do We Need To Change Our Strategy?"

When we first investigated Omicron in the spring of 1986, the company was in the midst of rethinking its overall business strategy. We studied two major decisions at Omicron: the decision to reformulate its business strategy, and the determination of that new strategy itself. The first (whether to change strategy) was traced through multiple interviews with all those involved. The second (the new strategy) was studied through observation of executive meetings, and follow-up interviews.

The decision to revamp strategy evolved over about 18 months through a series of meetings and interactions. Although the executive team did not recognize it at the time, the actual process began a few months before the firm experienced a series of sales declines. After their explosive growth in 1984, Omicron had a soft January (1985), which was shrugged off as a fluke. But the downturn continued, and by May production schedules were being cut back, inventory was growing, cash flow was negative—all the traditional signs that there may be strategic problems.

Three members of the top management team had actually anticipated these problems *prior* to the downturn in sales. These three, whose stories follow, were Bill Smith (President), Ron Adams (VP Marketing), and Andy Wong (VP Engineering). They each read different signals and interpreted them from different perspectives, yet the three came to the same conclusion—the firm's strategy needed to be examined.

Bill Smith, President—The president sensed problems through his dealings with the firm's venture capitalists. These investors were becoming skeptical about the company and were translating their skepticism into a lower stock price. As the president told us:

> "With every financing after the first round [early 1981], it became increasingly clear that we needed a long-term, articulated strategy—in word, if not in fact. The financial community wondered what we would do when the big companies entered our niche. Venture capitalists don't put much emphasis on execution ability; they look for sizzle—for proprietary products that push back technological frontiers. But we were not pushing back on those frontiers. We had second and third financing rounds in the fall of 1983 and the winter of 1985. It became a bigger and clearer issue with each round. That is, challenges from the VCs made it evident that we needed to rethink our strategy."—*Bill Smith, President*

Ron Adams, VP Marketing—While the president sensed upcoming problems from investor signals, the VP of Marketing saw problems on the horizon because of increasing entries into Omicron's market segment.

> "The idea of needing a new strategy first came up about 18 months ago, around the beginning of 1985. Kind of a conversation Bill [the president] and I were having about how our market was taking off—it looked great, but I realized that a lot of competition would come, maybe 40 to 50 players. I started seeing more people licensing similar technology. Perhaps I was reading a magazine and saw that the fourth company or so was on board. The technology bandwagon was starting to get publicity then. I suspect Bill was thinking the same thing."—*Ron Adams, VP Marketing*

Andy Wong, VP Engineering—Andy Wong anticipated problems through a third information source. Engineering's pipeline of new products was running dry, and the rank and file engineers (who were also stockholders) were agitating for direction. Wong described the situation as follows:

> "Engineering was in the process of defining the next generation of product. We had defined the short term—the immediate next product —but we had to look beyond that. We knew which microprocessor to use, but didn't know anything else. The staff was pressuring me directly: 'What do you want to design here? Give us some parameters to work with. What should the machine do?' It all revolved around a lack of a clear concept of what Omicron was and where it was going. This was particularly important in Engineering. 'If we don't know what we're going to be when we get big, then we can't work on a product design for you.'"—*Andy Wong, VP Engineering*

Since these three executives usually met on a regular basis as the company's product planning group, they began to shift that group's agenda from tactics to a broader mission. They began to track competition and lay out assumptions about the future of the industry, before the financials turned downward. At first, they were a bit haphazard in their approach. They had had a few off-site meetings with the full executive team to discuss corporate values and culture. Somewhat later, the smaller product planning group began to focus on competitor analysis, technology trends, and the firm's distinctive competences. The president described these meetings as not necessarily rethinking strategy, but rather laying the groundwork for it by developing a sense of the possible.

> "We developed a list of assumptions about the marketplace. We started with what we thought to be true, and used a five-year planning horizon. What crystallized our thinking was realizing that every major company should have a supermicro and our advantage of being a small company would go away. We also made technical assumptions. For example, we assumed that the 32-bit microprocessor would be a plateau and that parallelism would be the computer architecture of the future."—*Bill Smith, President*

The Signals Get Stronger—With the exception of Smith, Adams, and Wong, the top management of Omicron was optimistic in the face of the sales downturn of early 1985. However, by the summer of 1985, the other executives began to recognize the seriousness of the problems as well, and they began groping for causes. The management team became introspective. At staff meetings people would ask, "What's going on?" There was a lot of focus on quality issues. There were manufacturing problems with one of the machines. There were turnover problems within sales. In addition, new firms with superior machines had entered the market and made it more competitive.

When asked to describe his first sensing of problems, Steve Jones, VP Finance, reported:

"When we missed plan regarding June revenue, and the board asked us why, we put together a litany of reasons: we said 'One, they were old products; two, the market is tough (slow) in the summer; and three, quality problems.' Then we missed the plan in July—by 50%—and again in August, and we said, 'Holy S——! This looks like a trend, we have a problem.'"

From Nancy Remington, VP Sales:

"June was a revenue disaster and July wasn't much better. From January to June we staffed up from 120 to 180 employees, and moved into this fantastic building, 'Versailles,' costing us over $2 million a year. The problem was that we were losing our competitive edge. It was becoming harder to differentiate Omicron. A lot of companies started to look like us."

Throughout the fall months, the top management team carefully analyzed the problems and considered whether they should change their strategy. Several of the executives thought that Omicron needed a strategic redirection to cope with their changing marketplace. The other executives held to the view that the firm simply needed to execute better, particularly in sales and manufacturing. Several of the executives developed a good grasp of their competitors and the assumptions, especially regarding technology, that formed the basis of their industry. The top management team was able to agree on the basic goals and values for the firm (they all wanted profitable growth in order to go public), and on the existence of several clear alternatives to meet current financial problems. In other words, the team exhibited the kind of careful and complete analytical approach to decisions which we noted in very successful firms.

We also observed a highly collegial team at Omicron, which was also a characteristic of successful firms. The entire team was involved in the decision process. There was open disagreement, but that disagreement did not impair the top executives' feelings of mutual respect and shared values.

However, there were hints of problems. During the fall, the president had decided to look for a consultant to help the firm with its overall operations. He wanted to gain an external viewpoint, and he had made that search one of his top priorities. He was reluctant to decide whether to reformulate strategy without settling this matter. Partially because of this, the decision process at Omicron was taking a long time. The decision to rethink strategy stretched from late 1984 through the fall of 1985, and on into early 1986. By contrast, our successful firms had made the same type of decision regarding strategy reformulation in 3 months or less, without sacrificing thorough analysis.

What happened at Omicron? Most of the executives blame the president. His indecisiveness was perceived to lengthen the decision process, which in turn meant missed opportunities and initiatives. The following quotations from three members of the executive team summarize the sense of frustration with the delays and indecision.

> "Around June it was clear to everyone at our level that either a new strategy was required, or a reaffirmation of the current strategy. In July and August, Bill was dealing with too many issues. It was clear he wasn't committing time to the strategy issue. In September, Bill made it clear that he wasn't ready to deal with the strategy until he had the consultant's report. A lot of us said we couldn't run the company without a strategy, but Bill held firm.
>
> "The problem is, the consultant took much longer than we thought he would. Three times the 60 or 90 days it should have taken. Frustration built up because of this. It caused a morale problem—a sense of decision delays in the company. I think the problem was that the consultant was threatened by the freedom Bill wanted to give him in the strategy area."—*Andy Wong, VP Engineering*

> "I probably had the most radical ideas about doing something different. But most of my input was to Bill, 'Do something now, do something now, do something. . . .' The worst thing we could do was nothing. Any change would be positive. Bill responded by acknowledging the need—an intellectual response. He said OK, but continued to be preoccupied."—*Steve Jones, VP Finance*

> "In retrospect, Bill's procrastination may have produced the problem. Should we have been more aggressive? Yes, you don't know any more even though you wait. Maybe we saw too much mystery and maybe we needed more gut."—*Nancy Remington, VP Sales*

Very simply, the Omicron executives were very good at half of the task—being analytical and collegial—but they did not figure out the other half—being quick and decisive. In retrospect, the executives realized these problems and lamented the lost opportunities.

From the foregoing, we arrived at a picture of a fast-track start-up unable to adapt to a changing environment. Omicron had a strong executive group, the backing of premier venture capitalists, and an excellent product, but they slipped into the limbo of the "living dead." Imitators with better price/performance figures came in just as the computer market was encountering its first real slowdown. The president was indecisive and the strategic decision process stalled.

Tracing A Strategic Decision: "What Is Our New Business Strategy?"

Early in 1986, the entire team agreed that it was essential to change the strategic direction at Omicron. In the fall of 1985, they had had the alternative option of focusing on better execution of the existing strategy. Five months later, all agreed that the pace of marketplace change had eliminated that option. It was time to decide: What is our new strategy? What market are we in? What product shall we sell? What sales channels should we use?

The process began in a way which was reminiscent of the past. The entire team agreed to meet in a full-day strategizing session. Once again, the team was united in its perception of the core business values of the firm— values of integrity and customer service. Also once again, there were disagreements about direction, but these conflicts were rarely personalized.

However, the executives at Omicron did make some changes in their approach to making major decisions. The president had appointed Andy Wong to oversee strategic planning. Wong, in turn, organized the strategizing session into a brainstorming event. To stimulate thinking, he developed an unusual proposal by which to reorganize the firm. The following is an abbreviated transcript of that strategy session, which illustrates the strategic decision-making process at Omicron.

A Strategy Meeting—The strategy meeting occurred in the spring of 1986 and lasted approximately five hours. All seven of the top executives were present, seated around a doughnut-shaped table. All were in business suits, except for Steve Jones (VP Finance) in baggy jeans and a plaid shirt. Steve stood apart from the group, occasionally leaning against the wall, for about the first hour.

(12:00 noon)

Andy Wong *opens the meeting with a presentation of franchising as a potential model for the computer business. He discusses McDonald's and Radio Shack as typical approaches to franchising and considers the implications for* Omicron. *There is much group discussion of the proposal, and the discussion is flowing smoothly until the following comment.*

(12:45)

Steve Jones:	*[pushing himself off the wall]* Are you serious? Are you waiting for me to ask "Is this a joke?"
Nancy Remington:	We've gone 15 minutes with no one saying "bullsh-t."
Ron Adams:	We're addressing the wrong issue, and it's not franchising, but whether to sell direct or not.
Steve Jones:	This is a non-incremental transition (for us) we're talking about.
Bill Smith:	This is a big decision. How will the new strategy work? We're talking about changing our damn company, not something that's already set up! Let's focus on what type of decision this is, how much change it will entail.

This is followed by a flurry of comments regarding level of risk and incrementalism versus radical change. Twenty minutes pass.

(1:15)

Steve Jones:	*[after having listened in silence for several minutes]* I was really connected to this up till I realized—BLAM, this is a way of doing business that is so different it's WEIRD. Why? Why not use channels we already have?

Volume and strain of voices rises.

(1:30)

Jim Faire:	Will we be in the systems business or hardware business that bundles software? Value Added Resellers [VARs] are requesting more software tools. What business DO we want to be in? What are the key issues?

(1:50)

Steve Jones:	Last meeting we said we don't want to manufacture. *[NB: Omicron is an assembler.]*

This is followed by 20 seconds of silence.

Bill Smith:	Does everybody have their own sense of the distribution channel we're discussing?
Ron Adams:	No. I don't even have a sense of the product. We're trying to make a decision without understanding the product we're selling to the channels.
Bill Smith:	We're not getting anywhere. We've got to eliminate variables. Competition. Health care market versus banking market. Distribution channels. Costs. Let's eliminate some alternatives.

(1:59)

Jim Faire:	The bottom line is, are we a systems house or a box *[hardware only]* house? I don't think we can win the box game.
Ron Adams:	I think we have consensus there. The disagreement is strategic, regarding distribution channels and market. We don't have a clear fundamental understanding of any distribution channel except VARs. It's the only one I'm comfortable talking about unless we bring in someone who's an expert at some other channel and include him in these meetings.

(2:10 to 2:30)

The group takes a break for sandwiches and soft drinks and to check in-baskets. Discussion during the break continues between Bill, Andy, *and* Ron *regarding distribution versus product and which decision to make first*. Jim Faire *[VP Manufacturing] comments to us in an aside that* "this is how decisions get made around here—between these guys during the break."

(2:30)

The group reconvenes.

Bill Smith:	It's hard to make a decision in a big group environment. We have to decide how to make a decision; how to agree on a strategy. We can exchange ideas in this setting. Maybe I feel frustrated.
Ron Adams:	We've set up a mechanism here to choose strategy: You come up with a strategy and we shoot holes in it. That's why you feel defensive.
Jim Faire:	We feel comfortable with what we do because we know it. A change is bound to make us feel uncomfortable.
Bill Smith:	How do you approach this as a process? How do we decide on a market segment?
Jim Faire:	Where are the majority of VARs? What market? Let's do a sanity check. Should we be in this business? What are our alternatives?

Various alternatives are then discussed for distribution channels and products.

(2:43)

Steve Jones:	Maybe we're whipping the wrong horse. If we were executing the way we should be, we wouldn't need this meeting. We're trying to borrow an idea and in our financial position we're going to miss the window. We need something *everyone* can believe in, and I don't think we have that.
Bill Smith:	What's your suggestion for finding this burning source? Essentially this is what the franchise idea is all about.
Steve Jones:	I keep leaping ahead to the bottom line, and I can't see myself or anyone else investing in it. It gets lots of points for novelty, but not for fundability.

Bill Smith: What is fundable? If you can't tell me, then I disregard the statement.

Disagreement between Bill and Steve—would they fund someone like us?

Ron Adams: We're being too hard on ourselves.

Bill Smith: Sure, characteristic of this company.

Jim Faire: Characteristic of venture capitalists. They're pulling the cork sooner these days.

(3:20)

Steve Jones: This group should come up with a set of rules for making the decision, set up criteria. Do we have the expertise for this?

Ron Adams: Yes.

Bill Smith: No.

Andy Wong: No.

Steve Jones: We just like to play company.

(3:25 to 4:00)

Several attempts to structure the decision process are made by the various speakers. Various alternatives for eliminating variables and conducting studies are mentioned.

Jim Faire: We're floundering here.

The group continues to discuss whether more search for alternatives is needed, how to conduct it, how much search has already been done, and who should do it.

(4:10)

Bill Smith: We should try not to bound this search to narrowly.

Steve Jones: That's exactly how strategy should be made—i.e., bounded.

Bill Smith: *[agitated]* I'm so used to jumping on things and making decisions quickly. Now that I'm trying to take my time, you're suggesting that I not. We're not betting the company.

Nancy Remington: We came in here to talk about a big change, and now you say we're not betting the company.

Steve Jones: We've been analyzing for two years.

Andy Wong: Have we made a strategic shift?

Steve Jones: Yes.

Bill Smith: Yes.

Andy Wong: No. This process takes too long.

The Aftermath—Subsequent to the strategy meeting, several of the executives expressed frustration about the whole process—the floundering, the lack of clear direction from the top, the expenditure of seven people's energy for a seemingly fruitless exercise. The discussion was wide-ranging and free, but as Nancy Remington, VP Sales, expressed it,

> "Most successful computer companies have someone with a personality driving the company such as DeCastro at Data General, Watson at IBM, Olsen at DEC. No successful companies are run with committees. I wanted Bill to dictate and not to waste time in meetings to bring consensus. I had more pressing problems to worry about."

The resounding theme seemed to be a strong desire for the president to decide strategy. There seemed to be a "get on with it" sense of urgency among most of senior management. However, as in the past, the decision process bogged down. The president continued to strive for a consensual approach to strategy making. The team concentrated more on the "right way" to make the decision than on the decision itself. They had difficulty coping with the lack of hard data in such a fast-paced environment. They became paralyzed—unable to act quickly, boldly, and decisively in the face of ambiguity.

Eventually, the president seized the initiative and ended the group process. He, Ron Adams, and Andy Wong began to work on the strategy themselves—often on weekends. Soon Smith ended that process as well and set the strategy himself. He described his thinking in the following way.

> "I saw two viable ideas: Andy's strategy, and mine. A week or two later, I stopped our meetings. Then one night I went home after Andy had been really high on his idea. I slept on it and canned it. I pursued my idea and its related technologies. It is a great fit—same customers and same sell as our existing approach."—*Bill Smith, President*

The president's strategy relied on the same sales approach to some of the existing customers, but it was a very innovative move in terms of exploiting a new vertical market with an industry-first product. The strategy required significant engineering development to create a systems, rather than hardware, customer solution. The strategy looked like a good way to create competitive advantage, but it was also risky because it could prove to be an expensive waste of engineering talent. Nonetheless, it was, at long last, a decision.

With this decision, Omicron was finally beginning to exhibit some of the speed and decisiveness of our successful firms. Now that the president had finally been decisive, perhaps the firm was ready to regain success. If they had followed the pattern of our successful firms, they would have then combined their innovative, but admittedly risky, strategy with a carefully planned, incremental execution. The Omicron executives could then have maneuvered and adjusted their decisions as events unfolded.

However, this did not happen. The bold strategy initiative was not followed by careful implementation by strong functional heads. In fact, when we examined power maps[9] for the Omicron team, we found a power pattern at Omicron midway between the autocratic power structure of poor performers (i.e., CEO as the key decision maker in every functional area), and the collegial structure of successful performers (i.e., functional VPs as the key decision maker in their functional area) that we had found in our earlier research.[10]

As we left the firm, it was not clear that much was really changing at Omicron, despite the rapid change occurring in the marketplace. The strategy appeared not to be implemented at all, other than a few project reassignments in Engineering. Omicron Computers was still stuck in the limbo of the "living dead."

Implications for Managing in High-Velocity Environments

Other scholars of strategic decision making have focused their efforts on large, often nonprofit organizations in stable environments.[11] But the constraints faced by firms in fast-paced environments are much different from those of large bureaucracies in stable situations. As we have observed, most managers cannot sit back and wait to see what will happen in the marketplace, as IBM did in personal computers. They cannot do what everybody else does, as some new ventures in the overcrowded disk drive industry tried. They cannot afford to make mistakes either, as Osborne Computer did in announcing its follow-on product too soon. The velocity of the microcomputer industry and industries like it forces managers to confront the critical constraints of speed, decisiveness, innovation, analysis, and caution in a way in which managers in more stable environments perhaps need not do. Although some small-group researchers such as Vroom and Yetton[12] and Janis[13] have thought in terms of trade-offs such as decision quality vs. speed vs. implementation, the luxury of such trade-offs is unavailable to the executives of firms such as Omicron.

We have drawn several conclusions from the Omicron story. First, the two decisions—the decision to reformulate strategy and the strategic decision itself—were carried out very carefully and deliberately, but very slowly. In both instances, the president was very careful not to rush into a decision, and a large range of alternatives was considered. The president wanted as much information as possible in order to proceed with decision making, and he wanted full involvement by the top management team. The result was a rather ponderous deliberation.

Second, the president was reluctant to make these two decisions because he wanted complete information, and because he wanted to ensure a consensus on the part of his executive team. In both decisions, he held off the clear decisiveness which his management team wanted so badly for him to exhibit.

Third, both the president and the top management team appeared to avoid any bold decision which would result in a radical redirection of the firm. When the president finally made a bold decision, both he and the team seemed either unable or unwilling to execute it.

By contrast, the executives of the successful firms we described earlier were able to resolve a series of paradoxes—rational and quick analysis, powerful CEO and powerful team of VPs, bold yet safe decisions. Unsuccessful firms possessed very few, if any, of these characteristics.

What did we find at Omicron Computers? We chose to describe this firm because it was caught between success and failure, and so fits our description of the "living dead." Omicron exeuctives possessed many characteristics of successful firms. They anticipated impending problems. They conducted a careful analysis of competitive and technology trends, as well as their own distinctive competences. They were a strong team of experienced executives who were markedly united in their core values of how business should be done. Eventually a bold decision was made. But, Omicron decisions were ultimately made too slowly. Their president was both too indecisive and yet too intrusive in functional affairs, and the team did not attend to execution. Very simply, the top management team at Omicron could not resolve the competing tensions required for success.

Omicron need not have succumbed to this eventuality. They began as a winner and dominated their market niche. Several of the executives read the signals for change very early. The other executives were slower to see the competitive changes, but when they did, they were anxious for direction. Although our story takes place during the first real slowdown of the industry, the fact remains that Omicron had competitors that were growing and profitable during the same period. It was possible to do well, and Omicron had been positioned to do so.

What are the implications for managers in fast moving environments? We suggest the following:

• Be alert to weak signals that might suggest a need for strategic or tactical change. The signals could be either internal (e.g., engineering running out of projects) or external (e.g., potential entrants becoming vaguely visible) or both. Often, prior success puts blinders on management.

- Continuously consider alternative options to the present course. These options could respond to the moves of competitors or to changes in technology, demand, or government regulation.
- Capitalize on your managers' instincts to take action. When pressure mounts to address strategic change, do not wait for confirmation from hard data, such as flattening sales figures.
- When both managerial instincts and weak signals indicate a need for strategic change, act boldly. The half-life of your old strategy may be too short to be worth the energy and resources invested in "better execution."
- Above all, act decisively. Busy executives in fast-paced firm environments want a voice, but they also want leadership. Extensive attempts at group consensus may lead to frustration.

Conclusion

There has been increasing interest in the linkage of managing paradox and superior performance by researchers such as Van de Ven[14] and Cameron and Quinn.[15] The story of Omicron Computers helps to illustrate that a careful, analytical decision process, undertaken by a collegial group of executives, is not enough for firms in high-velocity, high-technology environments. Successful firms deal with the competing tensions of analysis and speed, autocratic and collegial power, and innovation and incrementalism. Managing firms in high-speed environments is more like playing a constantly changing video game than it is like playing chess, where the rules are fixed and there is time to contemplate each move. By examining a firm caught in the limbo of the "living dead," we hope to have portrayed some of the problems of managing in such environments.

References

1. This term has been attributed to Franklin ("Pitch") Johnson of Asset Management, a Palo Alto venture capital firm.
2. Alfred D. Chandler, *Strategy and Structure* (Cambridge, MA: M.I.T. Press, 1962); James Brian Quinn, *Strategic Change* (Homewood, IL: Dow Jones-Irwin, 1980); Henry Mintzberg and James A. Waters, "Tracking Strategy in an Entrepreneurial Firm," *Academy of Management Journal*, 25/3 (September 1982):465–499.
3. Jeffrey Pfeffer and Gerald R. Salancik, "Organizational Decision Making as a Political Process: The Case of a University Budget," *Administrative Science Quarterly*, 19/2 (June 1974):135–151; James G. March and Johan P. Olsen, *Ambiguity and Choice in Organizations* (Bergen, Norway: Universitetsforlaget, 1976); Charles E. Lindblom, "The Science of 'Muddling Through,'" *Public Administration Review*, 19 (1959):79–88; Irving L. Janis, *Groupthink* (Boston, MA: Houghton Mifflin, 1982).
4. Victor H. Vroom and Phillip Yetton, *Leadership and Decision Making* (Pittsburgh, PA: University of Pittsburgh Press, 1973); Deborah L. Gladstein and Nora P. Reilly, "Group Decision Making Under Threat: The Tycoon Game," *Academy of Management Journal*, 28/3 (September 1985):613–627.

5. L. J. Bourgeois, III and Kathleen M. Eisenhardt, "Strategic Decision Processes in High Velocity Environments: Four Cases in the Microcomputer Industry," *Management Science* (forthcoming); Kathleen M. Eisenhardt and L. J. Bourgeois, III, "On Designing Top Management Teams," Working Paper, June 1986. The results described in these papers are based on a study of 12 firms in the microcomputer industry undertaken between 1984 and 1986. Our intent was to investigate the process by which top management teams make major decisions in fast-paced high-technology industries. Using a multimethod approach, we obtained extensive qualitative data from over 70 executives, including personality descriptions from their colleagues, the frequency and nature of interactions with each other, as well as descriptions of their decision-making sessions in terms of climate, conflict, cordiality, etc. We also obtained extensive data from questionnaires completed by every executive. We measured firm goals, key decision areas, a variety of interaction patterns, political behavior, and power. We also traced the story of the making of a specific strategic decision in each firm from the perspective of every executive involved. Finally, we gathered secondary source data, including financials and business plans, and we observed the executives in meetings when appropriate.

6. A number of details in the story of Omicron Computer Corporation have been disguised and reflect a collage of the firms in our study whose financial performance places them in the category of the "living dead."

7. John W. Wilson, *The New Venturers* (Reading, MA: Addison-Wesley, 1985), p. 196.

8. This midrange methods approach attempts to triangulate some of the precision of quantitative research with the insights of a qualitative approach.

9. The power maps indicate an individual executive's power relative to major decisions in the key functional areas.

10. Eisenhardt and Bourgeois, op. cit.

11. Lindbloom, op. cit.; Quinn, op. cit.; March and Olsen, op. cit.

12. Vroom and Yetton, op. cit.

13. Janis, op. cit.

14. Andrew H. Van de Ven, "Review of *In Search of Excellence*," *Administrative Science Quarterly,* 28 (1983):621–624.

15. Kim S. Cameron and Robert E. Quinn, "Organizational Paradox and Transformation," in Robert Quinn and Kim Cameron, eds., *Paradox and Transformation: Toward a Theory of Change in Organization and Management* (Cambridge, MA: Ballinger, forthcoming, 1988).

PART III

STRATEGIC ANALYSES OF INDUSTRIES

Chapter 11

New Venture Strategies in the Minicomputer Industry

Elaine Romanelli

ntrepreneurship. Intrapreneurship. Internal Venturing. These are but a few of the buzzwords that signal a growing attention to the processes and pitfalls of new business start-ups in the late 1980s. Reasons behind this emphasis are many. The outset of this decade saw a great concern for the "revitalization" of American industry. Corporations, large and small, looked to the entrepreneurs and the companies they founded for models of how to innovate technologically, how to organize for creativity, how to expand market horizons. New technologies (e.g., robotics, biotechnology) created opportunities for the building of new industries. A general brightening of the economic climate freed resources for entrepreneurial experimentation across diverse strata of domestic and international competition.

Despite all the clamor, critical questions remain unanswered. First, we still know very little about why new ventures succeed or fail. Statistics remain dismal. According to the 1983 *State of Small Business Report to the President*, for every three businesses founded, approximately two fail.[1] A 1980 study of business failures conducted by Dun & Bradstreet showed that 53% of all failures and bankruptcies occur within five years of a firm's establishment; fully 80% of business start-ups fail within ten years from birth.[2] Before we can conclude about the efficacy of the entrepreneurial model, we need to identify the successful model. We need to understand whether and how different models may be appropriate for different kinds of organizational environments.

A second and equally important question pertains to the influence of successful early organization on the subsequent character of the firm and

This research was supported by the Strategy Research Center, Columbia University, and the Business Associates Fund, Fuqua School of Business, Duke University.

165

its opportunities for growth and change. Recently, management scholars have described how large, established organizations experience considerable difficulty in trying to respond quickly or effectively to changes in markets and technologies.[3] Some scholars have argued that in fact a positive performance benefit accrues from "sticking to the knitting" of a dominant competence.[4] Still others have suggested that there exists a middle ground of "corporate entrepreneurship" that can sustain the positive outcomes of existing strategic orientations while extending domains of competence and opportunity.[5] The crucial years of an organization's creation, and the degree and kind of success it achieves early on, establish the basis for understanding a firm's later capacities and opportunities for change.

This chapter examines how the early strategies of 108 firms in the minicomputer industry influenced both early survival and later capacities and directions for change over the period 1957 to 1981. Strategic activity patterns of firms that survived their early years are examined and compared with those of firms that failed. In line with findings presented by Jack Brittain and John Freeman in their study of the semiconductor industry,[6] this investigation shows relationships between kinds of new venture strategies that succeed and characteristics of environment over the industry life cycle. Overall, firms exhibit a strong tendency to persist in early-established strategic activity patterns even as conditions of environment change. Moreover, it appears that more successful or longer-living firms engage in less change than firms which fail. Investigation of strategies that enhance early survival probabilities and examination of the extent to which firms "latch on" to these strategies over time lays a groundwork for understanding the significant role of history in determining organizational options over time.

New Venture Strategies

As discussed by Raymond E. Miles and Charles C. Snow, there is a growing consensus among management scholars about the concept of *fit* among organizational strategy, structure, and internal management processes as the essential criterion for organizational survival.[7] An organization's strategy comprises basic activities—e.g., market segment position and resource-exploiting activities—that describe a firm's alignment with conditions of environment. Structure and processes, as discussed by Alfred D. Chandler in his seminal work on diversification, serve to support the strategic alignment.[8]

A number of recent studies explore strategy-environment alignments that enhance survival probabilities for new organizations. Miles and Snow traced the success of several major corporations (e.g., Carnegie Steel, Sears, Hewlett-Packard) to their *early* discovery and articulation of new organizational forms.[9] Brittain and Freeman, in their study of semiconductor firms, also find that organizations which move quickly to exploit resources as they first become available accrue "first mover advantages" that establish and sustain market position over the long time frame.[10] Being first to market implies a *chance* to gain significant control over available resources in the absence of substantial competition. More generally, however, studies indicate the importance of *rapid and extensive* exploitation of resources when resources are abundant. It refers to the degree of penetration or control over available resources that a firm seeks to achieve.

Somewhat differently, Glenn Carroll, in a study of newspaper publishing, brewing, music recording, and book publishing industries, describes the efficacy of a specialist strategy for young firms when resources become concentrated among a few dominant firms.[11] Specialism/generalism, in contrast to market penetration or depth of resource exploitation, refers to the breadth of market domain that a firm addresses. Specialists identify and concentrate activities on market segments where competitors either cannot or likely will not enter. Generalists, on the other hand, seek position over a broad spectrum of market opportunities.

Figure 1 describes four basic organizational strategies that emerge from association of market-breadth and market-penetration strategic dimensions. As shown, firms may adopt either a broad "generalist" or narrow "specialist" stance with respect to breadth of market served. Independent of market-breadth decisions, firms also may adopt either an "aggressive" penetrating or "conservative" measured approach to exploiting available resources.

Much of the literature on organizational strategies has treated organizations' "positions" on these two dimensions in terms of strategic "types." This implies the existence of some natural association between market-breadth and market-penetration decisions, which is typically predicated on an assumption of "best" relationships. Managers can make separate strategic decisions on these dimensions, however. The question remains open as to whether one or the other of the dimensions is more important to performance and/or whether any relationship between the dimensions enhances an organization's chances for success. By keeping the two dimensions distinct conceptually, we gain the ability to examine their separate and joint influences on organizational performance outcomes.

As indicated in Figure 1, there are several trade-off opportunities that confront managers of an organization as they seek to establish competitive position in the marketplace. Probably first among them is choice on the market-breadth dimension.[12] Depending on the nature of expertise or experience that characterizes the management team, and on the kind and amount of available resources, managers can choose whether to concentrate activities toward exploitation of a narrow or broad band of market opportunities. Contrast, for example, Hewlett-Packard's addressing of the more sophisticated scientific and financial segments of the calculator market with Texas Instruments' positioning in calculators for the general population. Texas Instruments was a generalist; Hewlett-Packard was a specialist. Organizations can then choose whether to exploit resources rapidly in the

Figure 1. Dimensions and Types of Organizational Strategy

Market Breadth

		General	Special
Market Penetration	Aggressive	Firms exploit as many resources as possible as fast as possible over a broad spectrum of market opportunities.	Firms exploit as many resources as possible as fast as possible within a narrow band of market opportunities.
	Conservative	Firms adopt a conservative approach to exploiting resources over a broad spectrum of market opportunities.	Firms adopt conservative approach to exploiting resources within a narrow brand of market opportunities.

given market domain to achieve substantial penetration or share of available resources, or they can adopt a more conservative approach to exploiting available resources. Here contrast Texas Instruments' aggressive advertising campaign and introduction of numerous calculator models (i.e., different prices, memories, and functions) to meet the diverse needs of the general population with Sharp's reliance on a very few, basic models advertised in a limited way to the same very general population. Both companies were generalists. However, where Texas Instruments expended vast R&D and marketing resources to achieve a deep market penetration, Sharp conserved resources, trading off market share for margins.

Fairly obviously, there are numerous cost trade-offs associated with decisions on these two strategic dimensions. Certainly it requires a greater expenditure of resources to exploit resources aggressively over a broad domain of market opportunities than to measure or conserve resources within either a broad or narrow domain. More interesting, however, are the tradeoffs that these decisions imply for future opportunities of the organization. Strategic choices on these dimensions require different investments in personnel, technology, reputation, distribution, and so on that are not easily shed as conditions of environments change. A more conservative approach to resource exploitation, even when resources are abundant, may leave a firm "freer" to change market segments or alter exploitation strategies as new segments emerge and/or as technologies change over time. Resource conservation may be an intelligent choice when uncertainty is high. On the other hand, firms which achieve early and deep position in the marketplace may have substantial ability actually to define the direction of new developments and thus influence the nature of uncertainty in a manner that enhances their survival probabilities. Competences that are required to develop this strong position, however, may constrain them from perceiving new opportunities or being able to implement programs to exploit them.[13]

Organizations exist in a dynamic world. As this brief review of the strategy literature shows, organizations' starting strategic positions may influence the ability of the firm to survive in the near term. Especially for new firms, which possess few slack resources for withstanding effects of major error or too strong competition, kinds and amounts of available resources in the external environment constitute important criteria for selection of an entry strategy. At the same time, however, since the very activities of firms that exploit resources change the nature and availability of resources in environments, managers must also position their firms to respond and be competitive in a future and different environment. Perhaps it is this daunting complexity that accounts for the very high early failure rates of new organizations.

The following section traces the history of events and developments in one industry, the minicomputer industry, from its inception in 1957 through 1981 when demand for minicomputers began to decline. It examines the strategies of three highly successful firms—Digital Equipment Corporation, Data General, and Tandem. These firms were founded, respectively, under emergence (1957–1966), rapid growth (1967–1971), and transition to maturity (1972–1981) conditions.

New Venture Strategies in the Minicomputer Industry

Data for this investigation are drawn from a larger study of organization and environment evolution conducted by Michael L. Tushman and this author.[14] The larger study involved a three-pronged approach to understanding trends and outcomes in the minicomputer industry. First, we compiled a comprehensive review of books and business press articles that charted important events in market, competitive, and technological developments. This effort provided core data for characterizing industry change over time and established a backdrop against which we could examine organizational strategies. Second, we conducted in-depth interviews with founders and other managers of minicomputer firms to gain understanding of their perceptions and responses to industry developments. These interviews provided a solid foundation for devising measures of market breadth and penetration constructs in terms that are specifically relevant to competition in this industry. Finally, in order to bolster these qualitative understandings and more rigorously analyze industry trends and organizational responses, we collected extensive product, market, competitive, and financial data on the total population of minicomputer producers (n = 170). The latter data were collected from 10-Ks, annual reports, and business press articles covering the entire span of the firms' lives through 1981.

Emergence (1957–1966)—The minicomputer industry was unofficially opened in the 1957 when Ken Olsen, a computer scientist at M.I.T., founded Digital Equipment Corporation. Olsen was active as a research scientist in developing computer technology for faster and more efficient data processing. He realized that his research on the large computers of the day would benefit from access to a smaller computer that could be installed on-site. The few small computers that existed in the mid-1950s were "dedicated" to very specialized applications such as machinery process control in industrial settings and data-processing systems for military planes and ships. Olsen needed a "general-purpose" computer that could be re-programmed easily to suit his changing processing requirements. No such computer existed. Olsen envisioned a large market for smaller, general-purpose computers in university, government, and educational laboratories.

The computer world was highly skeptical. At the end of the 1950s, Arthur D. Little's accepted estimate of total demand for computers of any sort was $2.4 billion. Computer producers and industry analysts believed that applications for computer data processing were limited to such very large scale projects as analysis of census and election data. Given the technology of the time, producers thought that these would be handled most efficiently by large, centralized facilities that would be "re-programmed" for each individual job. In actuality, demand for computers between 1955 and 1958 alone increased from $9.3 million to $395 million. The number of shipments soared from 150 in 1955 to 970 in 1959, a 650% increase in just four years. Paradoxically, this burgeoning demand for computers reinforced the belief that ever larger and more sophisticated computers would be needed. Manufacturers did not question their estimates of how many computers would be needed. They revised their assumptions about how large the computers would have to be. Millions of research and development dollars were poured into the building of these "super" computers.

Despite this dubious environment, DEC was founded and quickly pioneered the critical circuit module technology that revolutionized production processes in the computer industry as a whole and paved the way for manufacture of a minicomputer. Circuit modules could be combined to achieve processing capacity for virtually any size or speed.

In 1961, DEC introduced the PDP–1, the first computer ever simply to string circuit modules together and call it a computer. Following Olsen's vision, the PDP–1 was targeted toward scientific and engineering laboratory markets. Because of this market specialization, the PDP–1 was categorized as a "dedicated" computer. Olsen himself believed that uses for the smaller computer were limited to the scientific and technical communities. In fact, the PDP–1 was a general purpose computer that offered both the programming flexibility of a mainframe and the on-site availability of a dedicated computer.

The PDP–1 was immediately successful. Spurred mainly by word-of-mouth advertising, demand for this computer and its immediate successors, the PDPs 4 through 7, increased over 500% annually through 1964. Other companies were founded to exploit this market opportunity, including Systems Engineering Laboratories, Decision Data Corporation, Scientific Data Systems, and Pacific Data Sciences. Computers produced by these companies were also targeted toward the scientific and engineering communities. The sales of these computers were somewhat less spectacular than those of DEC's, but their introduction reinforced a growing recognition that small computers had a place, if a limited place, in the computer industry.

DEC's strategy for exploiting resources in this environment was clearly specialist. Though there was some talk of applications for smaller computers in industrial automation and communications management, DEC concentrated all of its marketing activities toward the scientific and engineering segment of the computer marketplace. This concentration was extremely aggressive, however. Olsen's marketing policy, which still characterizes the company today, emphasized direct and personal attention to the specific computing needs of each and every customer. DEC proliferated a large number of "standard" variations on the basic PDP to facilitate customization. The market-positioning goal of the company was dominance in the scientific and engineering computer marketplace.

In 1966, DEC introduced the PDP–8, the first computer ever to be termed a minicomputer. Though the PDP–8 was also targeted mainly toward scientific and engineering end users, it was the first minicomputer to be recognized as a general purpose computer that could be reprogrammed for all types of applications. The PDP–8 was one of the most successful computers ever introduced. Mainframe manufacturers, including IBM, Burroughs, and Hewlett-Packard, finally took note of the growing demand for minicomputers. They began to introduce their own lines of minicomputers. The concept of the "super" computer was abandoned (at least until the late 1970s); IBM alone had lost $22 million. Minicomputers were at last accepted as a legitimate and highly lucrative segment of the overall computer market.

Rapid Growth (1967–1971)—Demand for minicomputers began to explode. Unit sales increased from an annual average of 566 during the emergent years to 13,000 in 1971. Dollar sales increased to $174 million by 1970. Annual average growth rates in unit and dollar sales over the 1967 to 1971 period were 84% and 45%, respectively. Applications for minicomputers quickly spanned all aspects of business needs including basic computation and analysis, industrial automation, communications management, distributed data processing, and so on.

Two factors drove this tremendous growth. First, the general proliferation of mainframes and minicomputers at customer sites prompted the recipients of data-processing output to increase their usage of the computer and to envision an ever-growing number of applications. Users began to pressure computer manufacturers for products to meet their needs. Second, and perhaps more important, computer engineers began to conceive of new technologies that would permit design of ever faster and more flexible computers for these diverse applications. The success of Digital Equipment Corporation, along with the efforts of other young minicomputer firms, had created a wealth of technical and market expertise that was capable of fueling further growth. These companies served as training grounds for new minicomputer entrepreneurs. Nearly 60 firms were founded during the late 1960s and early 1970s to produce minicomputers. The majority were started by engineers who had worked for DEC or other minicomputer producers. Typically, engineers founded new companies in order to design minicomputers that their former employers would not support.

Most notable among these firms was Data General, founded in 1967 by a team of computer engineers from Digital Equipment Corporation. More than any other minicomputer engineer, Ed de Castro, who headed this team, understood that the minicomputer was a perfectly general form of computer that could be programmed and reprogrammed to handle virtually any requirement business, industry or government. Data General developed the NOVA, a very basic, "stripped down" minicomputer, that was designed explicitly to provide maximum programming and add-on flexibility. The NOVA was targeted initially to Original Equipment Manufacturers (OEMs), which were being founded at an even faster rate than minicomputer producers. OEMs specialized in modifying basic minicomputers for custom or dedicated applications. Typically, they specialized even further according to industry or to particular kinds of applications such as industrial process control or severe environments. Effectively, Data General left the customization work to the OEMs. In targeting the OEM market, Data General efficiently positioned itself as a minicomputer generalist. The company did not ignore the end-user market, however. Data General mounted a massive advertising campaign to attract computer engineers at customer sites to the flexibility of the NOVA. For both markets, Data General, like DEC before them, developed numerous "standard" versions of the NOVA and its immediate successor, the Supernova, in order to have on hand whatever size or configuration of minicomputer that would best meet customer requirements.

Both DEC and Data General adopted very aggressive approaches to exploiting resources in their environments. Each sought dominant position through rapid increases in market share. However, where DEC specialized in one market segment (the scientific and engineering segment), Data General generalized its activities to address the needs of virtually any potential user of a minicomputer.

To some extent it seems obvious that the number of market segments available for exploitation was different for emergence and rapid-growth periods of this industry's development. It is somewhat difficult, however, to separate out the decisions of these firms from the opportunities they encountered. DEC opened the minicomputer industry through its targeting of the scientific and engineering markets. Data General was aided in its targeting of multiple markets by the activities of many firms. Generally speaking, resources were much more abundant during the rapid-growth phase than during the emergence phase. There is evidence, however, to suggest that DEC's choice of the scientific and engineering segment was governed more by the background and experience of Ken Olsen than by conditions of the marketplace. In the early 1960s, Control Data introduced a small, but powerful desktop computer to interface with the Model 164, a mainframe. In a primitive way, given today's standards, the Control Data system approximated distributed data processing, which was to emerge fully more than a decade later. Also during the early 1960s, TRW introduced its Model 300, the first stand-alone, industrial process control computer. To one degree or another, all of the market segments that were opened and flourished during the late 1960s were known much earlier. Olsen's computer scientist background dictated DEC's targeting of the scientific and engineering segment. What distiguished DEC from other competitors of the time was its *aggressive* specialization in its chose segment. Data General, though it faced much clearer opportunities than had DEC for market generalization, was in fact one of only a few during the late 1960s to adopt this approach.

It appears, then, that firms do select their strategic approaches somewhat independent of market conditions. Drawing on the success of these two firms as evidence, we may also say that different strategies have more or less chance of success given different conditions of environment. DEC's specialization strategy, given the highly uncertain viability of the minicomputer during the early 1960s, provided some leeway for the company to understand fully one market segment and, thereby, to establish a foothold in the marketplace. Indeed, DEC established a foothold for the industry as a whole. Once DEC had pioneered this industry and demonstrated the core viability of the minicomputer, Data General was able to exploit abundant other opportunities. A generalist strategy, under these conditions, seems to have facilitated the establishment of strong position in the marketplace.

Transition to Maturity (1972–1981)—Dramatic growth in unit and dollar sales began to slow as the 1970s approached mid-decade. Growth rates averaged at about 20% through 1981, except in 1976 when the distributed data-processing segment was opened. Although growth in demand remained relatively high, particularly given the large unit sales base rate that had developed, other factors signalled an increasingly difficult environment for minicomputer producers, particularly new producers.

Most important were competitive conditions that now characterized the industry. Previously, new firms had opened new markets; new firms had garnered major control of resources in the new markets. During the transition to maturity phase, sales in the new distributed data-processing segment were dominated by existing producers. Though the market was new, the technology for exploiting it represented only a simple extension of earlier technologies. Entry barriers became very high. Unit sales concentration ratios increased rapidly: four-firm ratios topped 65% by 1977; eight-firm ratios neared 85% of unit sales. Tellingly, not one of the firms founded during this third stage of industry development ever made it into the top eight. Bigger and bigger shares of the minicomputer market were held by fewer and fewer, and older and older firms.

While established minicomputer producers consolidated control of available resources within the industry, others began to challenge these competitors for their markets and customers. Mainframe manufacturers began to scale down their computers and to market them as just bigger and better minicomputers. Microchip technology, developed during the early 1970s, established the "desktop" computer market that encroached on the most lucrative of all distributed data-processing segments of the minicomputer industry. Established minicomputer manufacturers began to develop new computers at both ends of the size spectrum. By 1977, industry analysts were predicting a very near obsolescence of the traditional, 16-bit minicomputer. Competitive conditions were "tough" even for established producers.

Despite all of this, nearly 40 firms were founded to produce minicomputers during the mid to late 1970s. Most famous and successful among these was Tandem, founded in 1976 to exploit the severe environments segment of the minicomputer market. The severe environment segment encompasses a broad range of applications including those for which the computer must withstand extreme temperatures such as those experienced in certain automated manufacturing processes, violent movements such as those encountered on military jets and tanks, or where computer breakdown spells catastrophe for company operations as in the insurance, airline reservations, and brokerage industries. As discussed above, this segment was actually opened during the mid-1960s with dedicated computers designed for the military. DEC and Rolm, before Tandem, had sold minicomputers to this market. No company had previously specialized in these computers, however, or expended many resources to exploit or develop opportunities. Tandem developed a unique system of back-up minicomputers which ensured that, whatever breakdowns might occur, a second or third or fourth (through 16) computer would automatically kick in to maintain processing. Tandem, like DEC and Data General, developed a large number of "standard" versions of its system to provide for efficient accommodation of the diverse needs of its special market. Tandem was a specialist. Tandem also adopted an aggressive and rapid approach to exploiting resources in its segment.

In many ways, the response made by Tandem to very different industry conditions appears very similar to that described for Digital Equipment Corporation. Both companies specialized in a single segment of the minicomputer market. Both companies adopted an aggressive posture toward gaining control of resources in the environment. Both were highly successful. The appropriateness of DEC's specialization, however, appears to have been driven by uncertainty. The viability of the minicomputer had to be proved and specialization provided the freedom to gain experience with the needs of one kind of user. Tandem, on the other hand, faced virtually no uncertainty. Hundreds of fortunes had been made on the viability of the minicomputer. Technological innovation of the minicomputer was nearly at a standstill by the time of Tandem's entry. The appropriateness of Tandem's specialization appears to have been driven by competition. Tandem's success hinged on exploiting an opportunity that had been deemed too small to worry about by major producers.

New Venture Strategies and Early Survival

Comparison of the early strategies of the highly-successful Digital Equipment Corporation, Data General, and Tandem, along with the conditions of the environment they faced at birth, provides a basis for some interesting speculation about what kinds of strategies will most likely succeed for new organizations entering at different stages of the industry life cycle. These firms remain to this day as strong competitors in the minicomputer industry.

All three firms adopted a very aggressive, market-penetrating approach to exploiting resources in their domain. With little difficulty, DEC and Data General can be classified as first-movers. Tandem however, entered a market that had been opened long before. Tandem, more than any firm before it, moved aggressively to control resources in the segment. Fast-moverness, not first-moverness, appears to be the common denominator. When resources are abundant, whether in a broad or narrow market domain, aggressive exploitation of resources toward the goal of *controlling* substantial resources establishes for the firm a position in the marketplace that sustains the firm over fairly long time horizons.

The three firms differ, however, with respect to their choices regarding breadth of market to address. Both DEC and Tandem adopted a specialist strategy. Data General was a generalist. When resources are abundant and certain and when competition is relatively weak, a generalist strategy is best for gaining strong position in the marketplace. When resources are either highly uncertain (which characterizes the emergence phase of industry evolution) or when resources are concentrated among a few dominant firms (which characterizes the mature phase of industry evolution), a specialist strategy offers the best chance for establishing a sustainable market position.

Case histories are attractive for trying to understand what makes a firm succeed or fail in that they offer a richness of detail that seems to demonstrate clear conclusions. They are dangerous, however, in that they often focus on atypical firms, usually the biggest successes or the biggest failures. The above case studies are no exception. DEC, Data General, and Tandem are probably the three most famous producers of minicomputers. By anyone's standards, they have been phenomenally successful. They are by no means, however, the only firms to have succeeded, either early in their lives or later. In order to understand why some new firms survive and some fail, we need to compare strategies and survival outcomes over a complete or representative sample of firms that were founded.

Table 1 shows the percentage of firms that survived at least six years of life, broken down by stage of industry life cycle in which they were born and by the kinds of strategies they employed early in their lives. Firms were classified as specialists or generalists based on a median split on the number of market segments in which they offered products by the age of three. Firms were classified as aggressive or conservative in their approach

Table 1. Early Strategies and Early Survival

	Number of Firms Founded	Proportion of Firms Surviving 6 Years of Life
Emergence		
Aggressive-Generalist	2	100%
Aggressive-Specialist	4	100%
Conservative-Generalist	1	0%
Conservative-Specialist	5	60%
	12	
Rapid Growth		
Aggressive-Generalist	6	100%
Aggressive-Specialist	14	71%
Conservative-Generalist	5	20%
Conservative-Specialist	33	76%
	58	
Transition to Maturity*		
Aggressive-Generalist	1	0%
Aggressive-Specialist	13	77%
Conservative-Generalist	4	25%
Conservative-Specialist	20	55%
	38	

* Due to our study ending in 1981, several firms did not have the opportunity to exist for 6 years. We counted these as survivors and the reader should be aware that survival rates for firms in this cohort may be overstated.

to resource exploitation based on the number of product lines they had introduced by the third year of existence.[15] As shown, a somewhat different strategic profile for survival emerges from that identified through case analysis.

First of all, we see that all four strategic types are represented in all three stages of industry development. Managers apparently retain choice regarding strategies for entering an industry, though resource conditions vary considerably over the three stages of industry evolution. We also see, however, that the majority of firms adopted a specialist strategy, even under rapid-growth conditions where Data General's generalist strategy was so very successful. This predominance of a specialist strategy makes sense if we consider that resources are usually scarce for new firms. Concentration on one or a few market segments allows the firm to establish a customer base from which it might branch out later.

Second, with respect to the success of these strategies, we see that firms which adopt a conservative generalist strategy, during *any* stage of industry development, fare much worse than firms adopting any other strategy. This also has some intuitive appeal if we consider that the conservative generalist expends very few resources to try to establish position over a broad domain of market opportunities. In effect, the conservative generalist is a "dabbler." Beyond this finding, however, it appears that firms can survive their early years of life employing a variety of strategic orientations. Overall, specialism seems to provide the greatest chance of survival. Generalists, however, also do well during emergence and rapid-growth phases so long as they simultaneously adopt an aggressive posture toward exploiting available resources.

Note that these conclusions are different from what we would assume if we relied solely on the case histories of the three most famous firms. DEC (an aggressive specialist), Data General (an aggressive generalist), and Tandem (and aggressive specialist) all fall in strategic categories that do well in general. These, however, are by no means the only strategic approaches that can contribute to the early survival of firms. Not only do managers retain choice about the nature of strategy for entering competition, their firms can do well with a variety of strategies.

Strategic Persistence and Survival Over Time

The above results indicate that a variety of new venture strategies can be successful for exploiting diverse conditions of a marketplace. As discussed at the outset of this chapter, we need to inquire still further about the efficacy of these strategies for the long run and about the extent to which they constrain the ability of an organization to adapt to changing environmental conditions. First, we need to consider whether firms persist in the strategies they adopt early in their lives. Second, we need to consider whether firms which accomplish some adaptation fare better or worse than firms which "stick to the knitting."

Our data reveal that the majority of firms which survive their early years of life persist in the strategy adopted during those early years. Of nine firms that survived the emergence period of niche evolution, five exhibited a change of strategy as the industry shifted from either emergence to rapid-growth conditions or from rapid-growth to transition-to-maturity conditions. Of 42 firms that survived establishment during the rapid-growth phase, only 16 changed their strategies as the industry shifted toward maturity.[16] Given the degree of turbulence that characterized these industry shifts, the amount of strategic persistence shown by these firms seems surprising. Apparently, once a strategy has proved successful for exploiting some conditions of environments, organizations tend to concentrate on maintaining that strategy despite changes in environmental conditions.

Two clarifications need to be made regarding the interpretation of these findings. First, strategic persistence on these basic specialist-generalist and aggressive-conservative dimensions does not imply lack of *any* response to environmental changes. The firms in our sample did respond to environmental changes by developing new and more sophisticated computer product lines. A few firms did diversify into superminis or microcomputers. A few firms switched market segments. All of these changes, however, support the basic specialist-generalist or aggressive-conservative strategic stance that had been established earlier. Rarely did a specialist become a generalist, or vice versa. Rarely did an aggressive exploiter of resources become conservative, or vice versa. Firms establish competences on these dimensions and engage in change only to sustain these competences.

Second, where strategic changes *did* occur, there were no discernable patterns in the direction of adaptation. Some aggressive generalists became aggressive specialists; some aggressive generalists became conservative generalists; and so on. In other words, while most firms persist in the strategy that brought them success during their early years, managers again retain choice regarding the nature of strategic change for different environments.

Finally, we examined whether overall persistence or adaptation influenced a firm's chances for survival over the long time frame. Despite the fact that most firms persisted in early-established, strategic activity patterns, it was certainly possible that organizations that accomplished some adaptation earned a better chance for long-term survival. Of four firms founded during the emergence phase that survived to 1981 (the end of our study), three exhibited a strategic change. In all three cases, change occurred on only one of the two strategic dimensions. Of 21 firms founded during the rapid-growth phase that survived to 1981, 11 engaged in a change of basic strategy. Examination of strategies over time for firms that did not survive until 1981 revealed much higher proportions of strategic change. Most firms persisted in an early-established pattern of strategic activity. Apparently, this persistence or concentration on sustaining early activity patterns aids the achievement of long-term survival.

Conclusion

Clearly, the issues that face managers for choosing an early organizational strategy and for assessing the long-term effectiveness of that strategy are complex. New organizations must find a way to survive in the short term. As shown by this study, there are many strategic routes to early survival. Choice of an early strategy, however, portends much for the future of the firm. Once a strategy has been implemented, managers change that basic strategy only at the peril of their firms. These finding support "stick to the knitting" arguments that have been advanced recently. Environments will "tolerate" a number of approaches for exploiting resources. Once a choice has been made regarding a strategy for exploiting resources, firms do best if they concentrate on making those strategies work as opposed to trying to change the strategy itself.

Research on the strategies of new ventures and the implications of those strategies for survival of the firm both early on and later in life is only beginning to be conducted. Numerous questions remain regarding the nature of activities that will support different new venture strategies and the long-term survival of the firm. As this study shows, however, investigation of the creation phase of organizational life shows clear promise for clarifying all manner of questions about organization-environment relationships that have occupied the attention of management scholars for decades.

References

1. *The State of Small Business, Report to the President, Transmitted to the Congress* (Washington, D.C.: U.S. Government Printing Office, 1983).
2. *The Business Failure Record, 1980* (New York, NY: Dun & Bradstreet, Business Economics Division, 1982).
3. Michael T. Hannan & John H. Freeman, "The Population Ecology of Organizations," *American Journal of Sociology*, 82 (1977).
4. Thomas J. Peters & Robert H. Waterman, Jr., *In Search of Excellence: Lessons from America's Best-Run Companies* (New York, NY: Harper & Row, 1982).
5. Robert A. Burgelman, "Designs for Corporate Entrepreneurship in Established Firms," *California Management Review*, 26/3 (Spring 1984):154–166.
6. Jack Brittain & John Freeman, "Organizational Proliferation and Density-Dependent Selection," in John R. Kimberly and Robert H. Miles, eds., *The Organizational Life Cycle* (San Francisco, CA: Jossey-Bass, 1980).
7. Raymond E. Miles & Charles C. Snow, "Fit, Failure, and the Hall of Fame," *California Management Review*, 26/3 (Spring 1984): 10–28.
8. Alfred D. Chandler, *Strategy and Structure: Chapters in the History of the American Industrial Enterprise* (Cambridge, MA: M.I.T. Press, 1962).
9. Ibid.
10. Ibid.
11. Glenn R. Carroll, "The Specialist Strategy," *California Management Review*, 26/3 (Spring 1984):126–137.

12. I use the word "choice" somewhat broadly here. A firm may be constrained by the nature of expertise on its management team or by restrictions imposed by external actors to address either a broad or narrow segment of the marketplace. I assume, however, that managers retain at least some control over the existence or strength of these constraints. Firms, of course, may also "choose" to be "dumb" with respect to their strategic decisions.

13. Barry M. Staw, Lance E. Sandelands, and Jane E. Dutton, "Threat-Rigidity Effects in Organizational Behavior: A Multilevel Analysis," *Administrative Science Quarterly* (December 1981).

14. For more detailed discussion of methods and more rigorous analysis of data, see Elaine Romanelli, "Contexts and Strategies of Organization Creation: Patterns in Performance," Working Paper, Duke University; and Elaine Romanelli, "Organization Persistence and Adaptation: A Comparison of Alternative Theoretical Models," Working Paper, Duke University.

15. Correlations between number of market segments addressed and number of product lines introduced were moderate to low, and largely insignificant.

16. Because our study ended in 1981, we could not examine whether firms born during transition to maturity tended to persist or change their strategic activity patterns.

Chapter 12

Managing Through Networks
In Investment Banking

Robert G. Eccles   **Dwight B. Crane**

Nearly all of the management theory developed in this cen-
tury has been based on research in manufacturing firms.
Despite the general recognition that mature economies
show a pronounced shift to service businesses, such organizations
are vastly underrepresented in the work of business policy and
organizational behavior scholars. Professional service companies, such as
law, consulting, accounting, advertising, and some financial service firms,
have been especially ignored.

The purpose of this chapter is to present results from a study of management
practices used in one particular type of professional service firm—investment
banks. This study included interviews with over 300 investment bankers in
17 U.S. investment banks, plus interviews at selected other firms involved
in the investment banking business in the U.S. and abroad.[1] These firms
play a crucial role in the flow of capital throughout the world's economies.

It is particularly important to understand management practices in U.S.
investment banks now because the management challenges they face have
grown significantly. Over the past decade, many investment banks have
grown from partnerships of a few hundred employees to firms with several
thousand, and they have spread geographically outside the U.S. to London,
Tokyo, and other financial centers. In addition, other companies such as
commercial banks and insurance companies are actively entering the investment banking business either *de novo* or through acquisition.

In spite of this interest, there has been very little research on the management of investment banks. The current high level of controversy surrounding this industry over such issues as insider trading, stock parking, and
investment banking's role in the so-called restructuring of America makes
this an unfortunate oversight. By studying how these firms are managed,
the Invisible Hand can be made visible.

Management Through Networks

The central theoretical point of this chapter is that the underlying concept for managing an investment bank is that of a *dynamic and flexible network*. Most companies are organized as hierarchies in which the organization structure indicates not only the span of responsibility and authority, but also the key linkages that need to be maintained to carry out the business of the firm. Investment banks, on the other hand, maintain a complex set of external ties with customers and competitors. These external ties lead to a corresponding set of internal ties that link the various parts of the firm necessary to execute transactions with customers. This network of ties adapts rapidly to changing market conditions and customer needs, so that a traditional organization chart is relatively meaningless.

Network concepts have been used primarily to study *inter*-organizational phenomena, rather than *intra*-organizational issues, but there are two examples of interest. One is the research of Yoshino and Lifson who argued that the concept of a network is the best way to describe the management of *sogo shosha* (Japanese trading companies).[2] In an earlier work, Blau used networks to describe a children's psychiatric hospital.[3]

Commercial banks have traditionally been managed in a very hierarchical manner. Thus, as they expand their investment baking activities, they will confront the dilemma of how to balance network and hierarchical approaches to management. Investment banks face a similar issue as they expand and spread geographically.

The Investment Banking Function

When economists reverentially speak of the efficiencies of the Capital Markets, they do so in reified terms. However, the efficient allocation of capital they applaud takes place in a socially constructed institutional structure of issuers, investors, and financial intermediaries. Investment banks constitute an important part of this structure in their role as financial intermediary.

The term "issuer" is generally used to describe a corporation or governmental body (e.g., city, state, or federal agency) which needs to obtain funds by issuing or selling a security in the capital markets. The security issued by a corporation can be either a debt instrument (such as a bond) or a share of the company represented by an issue of stock. The issuer's bonds or stock are purchased by "investors," including investment funds, pension funds, insurance companies, commercial banks, thrifts, and individuals. Issuers and investors number in the tens of thousands, ignoring the millions of individual investors who participate directly or through such vehicles as mutual funds.

The purpose of the investment banking function is to manage the flow of capital from those who have it (investors) to those who need it (issuers).

This is done through a three-step process of origination (finding issuers who want to sell part of the company in an equity offering or who want to borrow money through a debt offering), underwriting (buying these securities from the issuer), and distribution (selling these securities to investors, hopefully at a profit). This last step often includes several investment banks in a "syndicate" to achieve broad distribution of the security. All three steps are often referred to as "primary securities underwriting," "securities underwriting," or "financing." Broadly speaking, the investment banking function also includes trading of these securities after they are issued in the "secondary market." In the United States, this function is performed for corporations by investment banks, since the Banking Act of 1933 (the Glass-Steagall Act) precludes commercial banks from engaging in the underwriting of corporate securities.[4]

In addition to facilitating the flow of capital in the form of securities, investment banks also act as intermediaries in mergers, acquisitions, and divestitures. This activity is referred to as "M&A," or, more generally, "advisory work." Often, although certainly not always, when two companies merge or one company acquires all or part of another, both will retain an investment bank to help in the transaction. This assistance comes in the form of identifying companies (or parts of companies) to acquire or to be acquired by, valuing the transaction, and negotiating, consummating, and financing the deal.

For purposes of our discussion, we can extend the issuer and investor terminology to M&A activity since it too involves a flow of capital assets. An issuer is a company considering sale of all or part of itself to another company. The acquirer or buyer is an investor in the issuer's assets.

In working with a security issue or an M&A transaction, the role of investment banks is essentially to facilitate the formation of network ties between issuers and investors. These network ties are based on the flow of capital. In theory, issuers and investors could deal directly with each other, and in fact sometimes do, but there are some obvious efficiencies in creating a specialized industry which consolidates all information on the needs of issuers and investors, arranges for issuer/investor ties, and constitutes these ties by consummating the transaction. Given the large number of issuers, investors, and deals, the resulting network of ties between issuers and investors is incredibly complex. For example, almost 5,000 corporations issued common stock in the U.S. in the 1981-85 period and there are a comparable number of large institutional investors. For an investment bank to be effective in soliciting business and in structuring transactions appropriately, it must constantly obtain information from and supply information to these issuers and investors. Competition with other investment banks for the opportunity to facilitate the formation of these network ties is severe.

Although they compete fiercely, investment banks must also work together in a number of ways. This creates ties between them which adds to the complexity of their relationships with their environment. Very often, a number of investment banks cooperate on a financing in order to ensure a broad and speedy distribution of the securities. They also work together, although on a somewhat competitive basis, in representing companies involved in mergers and acquisitions. Finally, much of the securities trading in the secondary market is between investment banks, where they clearly are competing with each other. The industry is quite distinctive in that the firms both compete for deals and then work together to get them done.

There is some ambiguity to the term "investment banking" as it is used by industry participants. It is often used to refer to the full range of activities in which investment banks are engaged. "Investment banking" is also used in a more narrow sense to refer to the "corporate finance" function, including origination and underwriting for issuers and M&A work for issuers and investors. In this chapter, we will be using investment banking in the narrow sense and focus primarily on the corporate finance function. The other major function, "sales and trading" is responsible for the distribution of underwritten securities in a primary offering and for secondary trading of these securities. Historically these two halves of the investment bank have been composed of very different types of people in terms of social background, education, training, and skills, and they have represented two different and often conflicting cultures.[5]

Task Characteristics of Investment Banking—Five characteristics of the investment banking function—three concerning its task and two concerning its relationship with its environment—create the need for a network approach to management. First, in its role as an intermediary between two sides of a market interface, an investment bank must process prodigious quantities of information in very short periods of time. This information includes needs of issuers and investors across a wide range of products, prices, and other characteristics of recent transactions, as well as knowledge of accounting rules, tax laws, and securities regulations. It is through information that the investment bank gets deals, the execution of which provides further information that can lead to further deals.

The second task characteristic is that the investment banking production function is based on doing unique deals. Each financing or advisory deal can be described in terms of the issuers and investors involved, the individuals in the investment bank who are involved in the deal, the price and structure of the deal, and when it is done. Deals are a particular type of project and therefore present the same kinds of management challenges that projects do in other industries such as construction, oil exploration, publishing, and defense contracting. Every deal, just like every project, is different. Furthermore, these deals are often performed under great time pressure and entail substantial financial stakes for everyone involved. These pressures and financial risks create an air of continual crisis.

Third, the execution of investment banking deals involves substantial interaction with clients, as is the case with some other types of professional services such as medicine, law, and consulting. When the production function takes place at the boundary of the organization, it is impossible to isolate and buffer the firm's central task in order to smooth out environmentally induced fluctuations. This creates the need for great flexibility and adaptability, particularly in a service technology where there are no inventories to provide a buffer. At best there is a backlog, but when all of the deals in the backlog have legitimate claims to priority status, this only reinforces the crisis atmosphere that surrounds getting them done. The first response to dealing with a large backlog is simply to expand capacity by increasing the number of hours worked by the professionals who do these deals, but this too reinforces an operating mode of constant crisis.

Environmental Characteristics—To gather the information required as indicated in the first task characteristic, nearly all of the firm's professionals are directly involved with its environment, including customers, competitors, and experts in accounting, law, and taxes. These professionals dealing with the external environment include both the relationship managers who are responsible for the overall customer relationship and the product specialists who deliver the myriad of financing and advisory services offered to customers. This results in the first environmental characteristic— very porous organizational boundaries between the investment bank and its environment. The need for investment banks to work together also contributes to these porous organizational boundaries.

The second environmental characteristic concerning the investment bank's interaction with its customers is really quite unique compared to other professional service firms. Investment bankers provide to their customers, both at their own initiative and at the customer's request, substantial amounts of information on market prices and trends and advice on potential financing and M&A deals. This information is of value to their clients; however, with a few exceptions, they are only paid when they actually do a deal. Thus, a loose linkage exists between value provided to clients and compensation for this value. This is in contrast to most professional services which are paid for based on time-period (e.g., hourly) fees or lump sum payments for particular tasks in an attempt to ensure a balance between value provided and payment for this value.

Although most customers attempt to treat investment banks fairly over time, the loose linkage between value provided and compensation from a future deal means there is uncertainty about when the compensation will occur and whether the revenue received will exceed or fall short of the cost of the service. This can work both ways. Valuable advice from a time-consuming study might later result in a thin-margin bond underwriting. On the other hand, the customer contact resulting from a stream of thinly

priced bond deals might lead eventually to a very large M&A fee. Because
of loose linkage, it is very difficult to measure customer or even product
profitability except for very large aggregations of customers or deals. Thus,
investment banks focus more on total revenues earned from a customer
across deals over a period of time than on the profits on any given deal.
This focus on revenues is consistent with the industry characteristic that a
large proportion of total costs are variable costs in the form of bonuses to
the professionals who get and do these deals.

A Network Approach to Organizational Design

In order to execute unique deals that involve substantial client interaction
in an environment that is both heterogeneous and dynamic, investment
banks have developed complex and adaptive structures of network ties
based on the exchange of information that cross-cut whatever the formal
hierarchy happens to be. The relative strengths of these internal ties vary in
response to variations in the strengths of the external ties between issuers
and investors and in the characteristics of deals. Because so many people
in an investment bank are directly tied to the environment, changes in the
environment are rapidly translated into changes in organizational structure.
Given uncertainty about the external environment and the need for rapid
changes in external ties, the investment bank must have the capacity to
make or break and strengthen or weaken internal ties as circumstances dictate. For example, when a change in the market place creates an opportunity for a new product, new internal ties are needed to communicate information about the product and to focus marketing emphasis. The development of the new product itself often depends on the creation of new ties.
After the product has matured or the market window has closed, the specially created ties can fade away. Thus, a high degree of organizational
fluidity is needed so that internal ties can adapt to changing external patterns of asset transfers.

These structures have much in common with the organic structures described by Burns and Stalker.[6] What is distinctive about them is how the
large number of ties between members of the organization and its environment, particularly customers, directly shape and reshape these organic
structures. For this reason we describe them as "client-centered" organic
structures in contrast to "task-centered" organic structures as are found in
R&D organizations where there is little direct client contact.

Customer Ties—The foundation of an investment bank's structure is the
ties individuals have with customers. From these, investment banks have
developed an internal network structure that is not at all a well-defined
hierarchy of authority and responsibility. Structural variations from traditional hierarchies are common and include overlapping and shared respon-

sibilities, dual reporting relationships and roles, vague roles and reporting relationships, inverse management hierarchies, and other coordinating mechanisms. These structural characteristics facilitate the creation of network ties to increase the flow of information.

With varying degrees of formality, investment banks assign relationship managers and product specialists to specific corporate customer accounts. These client teams are responsible for soliciting, obtaining, and executing business for their client. This requires the individuals to work together and is an important structural device for specifying network ties. The number of ties is multiplied by introducing heterogeneity in client teams. Product specialists, for example, work on several different teams so that each investment banker gets the opportunity to work with a much larger number of other bankers than would be the case when a fixed team was assigned to a set of clients. Heterogeneity in client teams also contributes to the flow of ideas that worked in one account to other accounts.

Overlapping and Shared Responsibilities—Overlapping responsibility exists when a part of one manager's responsibility is also part of the responsibility of another manager, as illustrated by a new product development group that reports to two different departments. Shared responsibility exists when two managers are both responsible for a unit of the organization. It is common, for example, to have co-heads of a department.

Both overlapping and shared responsibilities increase the number of people to whom information is transmitted. Each manager has his or her own ties (albeit with some overlap) through which to communicate information. The use of co-heads also increases the amount of expertise used in managing a department. This has become especially important due to the increasing complexity of the investment banking business.

Dual Reporting Relationships and Roles—Overlapping or shared responsibilities also lead to dual reporting relationships for employees in the overlapped or shared organizational unit. This increases the amount of information made available to the unit because of the number of network ties that can be maintained by two responsible managers.

In addition to having dual reporting relationships, non-managerial personnel can also have dual roles, as when they are members of more than one department. Dual membership increases the number of ties an individual can form and is another way of disseminating information between these departments.

Other forms of sharing and duality are used by investment banks to increase the flow of information. One is the use of pooled resources, such as a pool of analysts or associates, to work on deals in a variety of departments. Another form of sharing is the use of internal joint ventures between two departments when neither is capable of pursuing an opportunity alone.

Vague Roles and Responsibilities—The mechanisms described above expand a simple hierarchy of responsibilities and relationships by increasing the number of specified ties. The virtue of these mechanisms, such as dual reporting relationships, is that they identify some of the crucial ties or links along which information should flow. To some extent, these ties can be depicted in an organization chart. There is a danger to this identification, however, if individuals interpret unidentified ties as ties that do not need to exist. An overly precise description of points between which communication should take place can preclude communication between other points.

One way of encouraging communication in an organization is to be purposefully vague about roles, responsibilities, and reporting relationships. As Burns and Stalker noted, a precise description of what one is responsible for is also a precise description of what one is not responsible for. When responsibilities are vague, the individual is compelled to take broader responsibility and in doing so increases the number of network ties. Similarly, vagueness in specifying the person or persons to whom an individual is responsible compels him or her to communicate with a broader range of people.

Inverse Management Hierarchies—Vagueness of roles is also reflected in the management of investment banks. A sequence of hierarchical titles exists in these firms, such as analyst, associate, vice president, senior vice president, and managing director. As in other professional service firms, movement up this professional hierarchy does not, however, always imply increased responsibility for internal management of the firm. Management of external relationships to generate deals is so important that much more value is placed on this activity than on internal management. Thus, movement up the hierarchy indicates professional competence and external client responsibility, rather than more authority for internal management. Even the members of an investment bank's management committee, who are responsible for running the firm, spend significant amounts of time meeting with clients and following deals.

In spite of the value placed on external relationships and deals, the fact remains that the organization must be managed in some fashion, particularly as it grows in size and complexity as has been the case in a number of investment banks. One response to this need is to assign management responsibility to "middle levels" of the organization, such as vice presidents and junior managing directors, who oversee the planning and day-to-day management functions. These inverse hierarchical arrangements give more time to the more senior professionals to concentrate on external relationships.

Structural Dynamics—While techniques such as overlapping, shared, and vague roles and responsibilities are useful in the development of networks, a dynamic organizational structure is also important. When departmental lines are rigidly maintained in a static organization, for example, there is a natural tendency for a departmental boundary to become a barrier to ties that might be formed across it. Thus, it is not surprising that all of the investment banks in this study were in continuous flux to varying degrees. Because of the frequency of change, structural snapshots of investment banks are less informative than the general characteristics described above and the reasons for frequent restructurings.

Structural change, rotational training programs, and cross-departmental career paths all contribute to the formation of network ties. Training programs, such as two-year rotations for new associates, have as an avowed purpose the development of the skills needed to be an effective investment banker. But, they are also a way of introducing new associates to a number of more senior people in the firm, thus helping new people learn whom to approach for help and information in the future.

Cross-departmental career paths play a similar role in building network ties across departments. When people move from one department to another they establish new ties and become a conduit of information between their new department and their old one. The cumulative effect of rotational training programs, the placement of cohort members in different departments, and diagonal career paths across departments leads to a rich set of interdepartmental ties.

Moving from one position to another is simply one form of changing one's responsibilities. Even within a position, the activities and the people with whom one interacts change as responsibilities are added and deleted. The vagueness of roles, discussed above, is due in part to constant role redefinitions that expand the number and alter the strength of ties one has in the organization.

Reorganizations of individual jobs are often accompanied by major reorganizations within the firm in response to changes in the flow of capital between issuers and investors. Periodic reorganizations also strengthen internal ties that have weakened and prevent clique formation and structural ossification. Preventing clique formation is important to keep a group from building a power base and a claim on resources that may not be justified under changed business conditions. Preventing ossification is important since it results in a network of internal ties that can respond adequately to changes in the external environment.

The picture of an investment bank's organizational structure that emerges is one with dispersed authority that is ambiguous, flexible, loose, and constantly changing. Network, not hierarchy, is the best name for such a structure because the network image emphasizes the importance of horizontal ties. In a traditional hierarchy, vertical ties are more important.

Each individual has a large number of ties with others in the organization. In many cases the ties are stronger across groups than they are within groups. These ties are based on current and past deals that were worked on together, as well as expectations about future opportunities. Giving and receiving information and rendering task assistance lead to a high degree of interdependence within these networks.

These interdependencies result in substantial potential for conflict because they often involve trade-offs among the goals of the individuals involved. Fortunately, working together also leads to an implicit record of debits and credits between individuals that can contribute to the resolution of conflicts. The multiple points of interaction between individuals make it possible to balance these debits and credits across the various issues of interest, providing a number of opportunities for resolving this conflict.

Evidence of the importance of these debits and credits is the emphasis individual bankers place on "personality" over "structure" in both understanding how the organization works and how to work effectively within it. In other words, few general guidelines exist on how interdependencies between individuals should be managed. The complex and changing environment makes it impossible to specify what the network of ties should be. Instead, individuals establish a set of working arrangements with each other that are adapted to personal strengths, weaknesses, and preferences, and which balance out the debits and credits over time.

Externally Oriented Systems

In contrast to their ill-defined organizational structures, investment banks, especially the larger ones, have well-defined management control systems that are client oriented. These systems focus both on effort and resources expended and on the outcomes achieved. They function as an exoskeleton that anchors the bank on ends to be obtained in its particular environment. This provides definition for the flexible endoskeleton of organizational structure that provides the means. When well-defined systems are combined with ill-defined structures, individuals focus on ends and are able to adopt means that are most appropriate for accomplishing them.

Many of the systems' reports provide data on a client or client category to direct bankers' attention to the external customer environment. There are, however, limitations on what these systems can measure, given the loose linkage between value provided and payment received. In particular, it is very difficult to generate measures of client and product profitability.

Investment Banking Marketing Efforts—Beyond direct observation of an investment banker's activities, a primary source of information regarding effort expended is provided by the call reports used by a number of investment banks. Details of call report systems vary, with the large firms using more formal systems than the small investment banks. Objectives for calling effort are often set according to customer priority categories. A company would be placed in the high-priority group, for example, if it generated a large number of investment banking transactions and if the bank had either a substantial relationship with that company or hopes of establishing such a relationship. Relationship managers and others who deal directly with clients fill out these call reports which summarize briefly the purpose of the call, the topics discussed, and the potential for future business. The reports are aggregated into calling activity reports that measure the amount of client contact, both by individual company and by client segments such as industries or priority groups. These reports provide management with some indication of the intensity of the firm's marketing efforts.

Call reports serve other purposes as well. They are another way of communicating information to management and to colleagues and are therefore distributed to a number of people. Ideas mentioned in a call report by a banker may be useful to other bankers with their clients. Filing call reports also indicates to bankers that their activity is being monitored and creates an incentive for them to continue this activity. A number of managers pointed out the utility of call reports, despite the lucrative financial rewards bankers can earn. They felt that these rewards were not a satisfactory motivation in light of the long lead times between the calling effort and getting a deal. Since investment bankers do not receive the kind of short-term feedback available to sales and trading personnel, some managers believed call reports help to provide the motivation needed.

Investment Banking Outcomes—The outcomes of these marketing efforts are measured primarily in terms of deals won and deals lost to competitors. (Some even attempt to assess the potential for deals that could have been done but no bank did.) In contrast with other industries, the emphasis placed on "deals done away" is quite significant. Given the loose linkage between value provided and revenue earned, lost deals represent foregone opportunities to reduce this gap. Those responsible for a client are often asked to explain why the firm did not get a particular piece of business. The most acceptable reason is that another firm submitted a "suicidal" bid (although it is unlikely the other firm perceived its bid as such). The least acceptable reason is that those responsible did not know the deal was coming up and found out about it only after another firm had already won it. The emphasis on deals done away is a strong incentive for those with client contact to have as complete information as possible about what is going on at a client company. It is a signal that information not obtained is as important as information obtained, since lost deals represent lost opportunities for getting information that can lead to future deals.

Another reason for the emphasis on deals done away is that it measures the bank's "market share" of a client's business relative to other banks. Now that companies typically have more than one investment bank, it is important for a bank to know its relative position with each of its clients. Competing banks that have done little or no business with a customer attempt to wedge themselves in by getting a piece of business in one product area and then expanding into other product areas. Thus, keeping track of deals done away is a way of identifying the product fronts on which battle is being waged by competitors.

A record is also kept of the revenues or fees earned on deals won. Since many deals involve more than one department of the bank, the revenue is either split among the relevant departments or each department receives full credit in a double-counting, or multiple-counting, system when more than two departments are involved. Fee splits, a variation on the always vexing transfer pricing problem, are a common source of dispute. Investment bankers have recognized the futility of finding a technical solution to this problem that will be acceptable to everybody. Instead, they use very simple fee-splitting rules; the most typical is dividing the revenues evenly among the departments involved.

An increasingly common practice is giving each department full credit for the deal. This multiple counting eliminates much of the potential conflict over whether or not a department has been fairly credited for its contribution to a deal. It is also a system useful in reinforcing the interdependence of units within the investment bank. Since each banker gets full credit for each deal to which he or she makes a significant contribution, there is substantial incentive to look for ways to assist other departments.

There are some obvious advantages to simple rules for fee splitting or for multiple counting. By their obvious imprecision and inaccuracy, they signal that criteria other than fees earned are considered in evaluating and rewarding performance. When a great deal of effort is expended in developing and implementing sophisticated fee-splitting or transfer-pricing techniques, the managers affected regard these measures as crucial. They then have an incentive to invest time and energy gaming these internal measures, even at the expense of pursuing external opportunities.

Limitations on Measuring Outcomes—Although revenues are measured, little effort is made to deduct marketing and other expenses from them in order to arrive at profitability figures, whether on a customer or a product basis, except at fairly aggregate levels. There are four principal reasons for this, all based on the loose linkage between value received by the customer and payment made to the investment bank:

- the potentially large size of fees earned,
- the difficulty of assessing the relationship between effort expended and deals won,
- an emphasis on doing one deal as a way of getting other deals, and
- the use of one business to enhance the bank's performance in other businesses.

Investment banking, particularly when serving large and sophisticated clients that do a variety of deals, is often described as a fee or revenue-driven business. The primary expense category is personnel costs, and relatively modest base salaries limit the fixed-cost portion of this category. Far greater are the variable cost bonuses, but these are tied to revenues earned. Furthermore, capacity can be expanded by increasing the number of hours worked by bankers, which helps limit excess capacity costs. Moreover, the size of fees earned in some businesses, such as large M&A deals, simply overwhelms concern about costs. Rather than worrying about expenses, bankers focus on getting deals and on putting resources in place to pursue and process them.

It is difficult to match precisely effort expended with deals won. The selection of an investment bank for a particular deal may be based on marketing efforts made in the past, on well-regarded presentations for deals that were not awarded, on advice from professionals in other departments of the investment bank, as well as the current marketing efforts by the department that won the actual deal. Although the customer obviously has some perspective on the reasons why the bank was awarded the deal, the reasons are not always precise or clearly communicated to the investment bank.

Sometimes, perhaps often, certain types of deals are undertaken in the hope of receiving more lucrative ones in the future. A bank may compete for a low-margin debt offering as a way of establishing contact and building credibility which it hopes to translate into M&A or other fees later on. Whether or not a bank is willing to actually lose money for the sake of preserving or improving its position with a certain customer is hard to determine. That banks often accuse others of doing so, however, reveals a common tendency to look more at total fees earned for a particular customer than on the fees earned on a deal-by-deal basis.

Engaging in less profitable businesses as a way of enhancing one's competitive position in more profitable businesses is a common strategy. Investment banks, for example, actively compete for commercial paper business even though it has very low margins. As a customer's commercial paper agent, the bank has daily contact that can be used to generate information that might lead to other deals. Another example is underwriting large volumes of investment grade debt in order to obtain the advantages of a high market share, including improved access to information—being in the "deal stream"—and the secondary trading profits. Such inter-product relationships make an emphasis on product-by-product revenues or profits an artificial exercise.

The Bonus Determination Process

The third element of organizational design, which integrates the network structure and externally oriented systems, is the bonus determination process. Given the large size of these bonuses, which can be multiples of five or even ten times a base salary, and the variances in them, they are a very powerful integrating mechanism. One of the most notable differences between investment banks and any other organization is the size and variance in bonuses, and the extent to which these bonuses are decoupled from seniority or formal hierarchical position. This makes their role as an integrating mechanism much greater than is the case in any other kind of organization.

The bonus determination process, like the structures and systems described above, emphasizes the importance of being responsive to customers, reinforces the formation of internal network ties, and focuses on maximizing interdependent outcomes. For example, bonus calculations are based upon aggregate levels of performance. Individuals are rewarded on the basis of revenues earned, their standing vis-à-vis competitors, their professional competence, their marketing efforts and client relationship management, and their contributions to the development of the organization (recruiting, training, and teamwork). Data from a variety of sources are used to make these assessments: reports generated from the management control systems discussed above, self-evaluation memoranda, cross-evaluation surveys, third-party surveys (by Greenwich Associates and McLagan Partners), and the subjective judgement of relevant managers.

The dominant practice is to calculate bonuses based on aggregate levels of performance as determined by revenues or profits. Investment banks that used to calculate separate bonus pools on a departmental basis have recently shifted to a more aggregate approach. All of the firm's relationship managers and product specialists are considered members of one large bonus pool. The obvious problem with separate bonus pools is that they encourage local optimization at the expense of global performance. In today's environment of complex deals and strategic relationships among businesses, such suboptimization can seriously interfere with a bank's competitive effectiveness.

A valuable source of data for measuring and evaluating individuals' performance is input from their colleagues. In some of the larger banks this is done quite formally, through cross-evaluation surveys of people who have worked together on one or more deals. Relationship managers and product specialists evaluate each other on various technical and interpersonal criteria in order to provide data on their professional competence and their ability to work with others. Each is also asked about how others' technical and interpersonal skills contribute to marketing and servicing clients. In some cases, individuals are asked how well they know the person being evaluated in order to place a proper weight on the responses. The number of individuals a banker is asked to evaluate (and who therefore evaluate him or her) can be quite large. One senior banker said he was part of an 80-person cross-evaluation survey.

These cross-evaluation surveys fulfill a number of functions in addition to providing input into the performance evaluation and bonus determination process. Since senior managers receive surveys on all personnel, they find out who has worked with whom and, perhaps, how intensively. This gives top managers some information on the working organization which is so imperfectly and incompletely described in the organization chart. These cross evaluations also enable them to identify potential problems, either by person (when there is general agreement that a person is weak or difficult to work for) or between persons (when two people rate each other much lower on all criteria than the average rating either receives from all raters combined). Finally, these cross evaluations are helpful in comparing and even rank-ordering bankers, although the later must obviously be done with some care and an awareness that the measures are imperfect.

Third-party surveys are also used in evaluating performance. Greenwich Associates conducts an annual survey on investment banking in which customers are asked to evaluate investment banks along a number of dimensions, including quality of calling effort. These data are provided for specific product categories and so can be used to assess a firm's product specialists. Since these data are also presented according to industry categories, some rough assessment of relationship managers can be made by matching the categories with the bankers responsible for covering each industry. Banks can also order so-called "special action reports" for a specified set of clients. A bank can, for example, order special action reports on each of its relationship managers and product specialists.

These third-party surveys and evaluations also serve the purpose of emphasizing to investment banking professionals the importance of the client, i.e., the external network ties. Like the call reports, they too emphasize that the primary purpose of one's efforts is to satisfy client needs.

The size of bonuses in investment banking and the amount of data that must be interpreted in arriving at them make bonus determination a complex and time-consuming process. It typically begins with a self-evaluation memorandum, or "puff sheet" as it is called in one bank, in which the banker details his or her contributions over the past year. It includes deals worked on (where it is common to take full credit for all revenues), marketing efforts for which the banker hopes to receive future business, and time spent on recruiting and training.

The senior managers who are responsible for determining bonuses review these self-evaluations, management information systems reports, cross-evaluation surveys, and third-party surveys and evaluations. They add their own knowledge of the individual based on direct experience or conversations with others. They must also assess the value of marketing efforts which have not resulted in deals, compared to deals actually completed. All the quantitative and qualitative evidence is weighed to come up with an overall evaluation of the individual's contribution to the bank over the past year.

An individual's bonus depends upon this evaluation, his rank in the organization, bonuses expected to be awarded to counterparts in other banks, and bonuses paid within the organization. The size of a bonus depends, to some extent, on the individual's rank in the firm's hierarchy. But while the average associate or vice president receives a smaller bonus than the average managing director, an exceptional individual may receive a higher bonus than average or poor performers at a higher level. Senior management also attempts to match the bonuses it expects other banks to pay in order not to lose employees. Market data on salaries are obtained informally and through compensation surveys conducted by McLagan Partners. Finally, attention is paid to the relative sizes of bonuses since they can be as important as the absolute amount. Bonuses are not only consumption dollars, but also represent the organization's evaluation of the individual's professional competence and thus they confer status and honor. This is especially important since promotion up the management hierarchy is not a primary objective of many or even most investment bankers.

Evaluating an individual's contribution and determining a reward for it in an organization which emphasizes interdependence as much as an investment bank does, and where the financial returns are potentially so great, are a source of major dissension. The need to exercise a substantial amount of subjective judgment in weighing all of the relevant data creates the possibility that individuals will perceive bonuses as unfair. This can be extremely detrimental in the investment banking business where individuals can so easily change firms or reduce the quality and quantity of their effort. One way management copes with the problem is to spend significant amounts of time at year-end on bonus determination, and to make the organization aware that it is doing so. This increases both the reality and the perception that bonuses are being properly determined.

Management Challenges

The fluid and dynamic network approach to management described above works best when the organization is relatively small, when everybody is in one location, and when the firm has developed it over time. Currently the largest investment banks, particularly those which have expanded rapidly in London and Tokyo, and the commercial banks which have been most aggressive about entering the investment banking business, are feeling strains in implementing this management approach. These organizations are confronting the dilemma of how to balance network and hierarchical approaches to management. Those which are most successful in doing so will be the likely winners in the expected consolidation over the next decade.

Increased Size—During the past few years, the major investment banks have grown tremendously. In the four-year period from 1982 to 1986, the employment at four leading firms doubled, increasing from an average of 2,462 employees per firm to 5,059.[7] Thus, these and other firms have faced problems of both rapid growth—a topic about which management theory has disappointing little to say—and increased size. Since the number of potential ties grows geometrically as the number of people grows arithmetically, this increase in size has greatly complicated the task of coordinating the efforts of individuals in the investment banking firm. Other problems of size have emerged—including recruiting, training, establishing career paths, and maintaining the perception of fairness in compensation.

When a firm is small it is easy for all of these activities to be performed by professional investment bankers who remain heavily involved in managing clients and doing deals. The increase in size over the past five years has been primarily at more junior levels; while the number of managing director or senior positions have increased, they have not done so at nearly the same rate. This creates pressures on senior bankers to spend a larger proportion of their time on internal management issues, versus managing clients and doing deals. This can detract from their effectiveness as bankers.

A potential solution to this is to assign formal management responsibility to individuals who concentrate on managing the firm and who spend little or no time managing clients and doing deals. The dilemma here is whether to assign these management responsibilities to senior bankers or to bring in professional managers from outside the firm. The problem with the first solution is that in a business of deal doers, few of whom entered the investment banking business with an interest in becoming managers, there may not be enough people with the interest or talent in giving up deal responsibility for management responsibility—the classical problem of promoting a terrific individual contributor to a management position and having him or her fail.

This suggests that perhaps it will prove more effective to recruit people from outside the industry who have proven management skills. Of course, the problem here is that these managers will not know the business and will have a very difficult time earning the respect of professional investment bankers. For these reasons, managers hired from outside will have a difficult time establishing credibility and gaining control of the organization.

Whether individuals assigned management responsibility are from within the firm, or at least the industry, or are from other industries, they face the obvious temptation of implementing traditional hierarchical management methods. This temptation is especially great since without client management responsibility or involvement in deals, these managers both lack a base of expert authority and need something to do. If they perceive the solution to both of these problems to be the creation of hierarchical control mechanisms, to some extent the effectiveness of the firm will suffer. Thus, their challenge is to find ways of executing their management responsibilities without interfering with the adaptive and dynamic network structures that are the essence of a successful investment bank.

Geographical Dispersion—The growth in size of the major investment banks has been accompanied by a shift in the proportion of personnel located away from the headquarters office in New York City. This includes both so-called regional offices in major U.S. cities (e.g., Chicago, Dallas,

Los Angeles, and San Francisco) and foreign locations, particularly London and Tokyo. Geographical dispersion makes it difficult to implement a network approach to management since it depends so much on high levels of communication. While much of this can be done over the telephone, face-to-face communication is more effective.

The problem of geographical dispersion is most severe in the London and Tokyo offices. Growth in these locations has been greatest, exceeding the rapid growth of these firms as a whole. For example, Morgan Stanley's London office grew from less than 50 employees in 1976 to nearly 800 in 1987. Similarly, its Tokyo office employed fewer than 30 in 1984, but three years later had close to 400. Differences in time zones make conversations difficult, and for the first time these firms are faced with the myriad complex problems involved in managing foreign locations. The need for coordination across locations is as great as the need for coordination within a location, since these firms are attempting to implement global strategies in response to the global nature of the world's capital markets.

It is difficult to maintain the cultural homogeneity which so facilitates a network approach when the firm begins hiring large numbers of people from different countries. Tensions concerning disproportionate representations of U.S. citizens in the management of foreign locations, compensation under different country wage patterns and tax codes, and career paths of foreign nationals are inevitable. Although such tensions are never completely eliminated, they need to be managed in such a way that reinforces the advantages of the network approach.

From Commercial Banking to Investment Banking—To varying degrees, most of the major U.S. commercial banks have made a commitment to build their capabilities in the investment banking business. While they have been able to engage in this business overseas to the extent foreign regulations permit, they have been prevented from most forms of securities underwriting in the United States since 1933. However, they have always been permitted to engage in advisory business and there is a general expectation that Glass-Steagall will be ultimately, or at least effectively, repealed.

The large money center commercial banks have an advantage over the large investment banks in that they are used to managing organizations of large size that are geographically dispersed. However, they have used very traditional hierarchical methods in doing so. In fact, commercial banks are almost a stereotype of the hierarchical or mechanistic organization. Obviously, if they are to be successful, they will have to make some fundamental changes in how they are managed. This is not to ignore the even more basic problem of upgrading the financial skills of their personnel—either through training or outside recruiting—in order to have even a chance of becoming important competitors in the underwriting and related aspects of this industry.

Commercial banks must make changes in structure, systems, and bonus determination to successfully shift from the annuities of commercial lending to the deals of investment banking. Traditional hierarchical structures of simple and clearly defined reporting lines and position-based authority must be replaced with complex vague network structures of diffuse authority. Systems which emphasize profit margins must be replaced with systems which emphasize revenues and market share. Bonuses of small size and low variance based largely on hierarchical position must be replaced by potentially much larger bonuses of greater variance based on careful assessments of actual performance. A near total transformation in management method is necessary. Those commercial banks which have been most successful in making inroads into the investment banking business have indeed moved toward the network management approach used by investment banks.

A Concluding Note on Competition—The largest investment banks are now roughly the same size as the parts of the major commercial banks devoted to investment banking. An interesting competitive battle has been shaping up for some time between these two types of firms. How well each type will do, and particular firms within each type, depends upon its relative success in capitalizing on its strengths while overcoming its weaknesses. Investment banks have experience in network management and it is second nature to individuals in them. But they are only recently confronting problems of large size and geographical dispersion, particularly in foreign locations. Commercial banks, in contrast, have experience managing large organizations located in a number of countries, but have little or no experience in network management. The efforts of practitioners to combine these management experiences provide an excellent opportunity to advance management theory.

References

1. In addition to the U.S. investment banks, we also conducted 34 interviews in two U.S. commercial banks which have been particularly successful in the investment banking business and 31 interviews in 10 merchant or universal banks in the United Kingdom, Germany, and Switzerland. All of these firms were strikingly similar in their management practices compared to U.S. investment banks, despite obvious opportunities for differences based on differences in national culture and the fact that seven of these twelve firms conducted their investment banking business in the context of a commercial bank. Finally, in collaboration with Dr. Wayne E. Baker, we conducted interviews with general and financial managers in 21 issuing customer organizations. This enabled us to obtain both the customer and the investment banker perspective on the delivery of investment banking services.
2. M.Y. Yoshino and Thomas B. Lifson, *The Invisible Link* (Cambridge, MA: The M.I.T. Press, 1986).
3. Judith Blau, "Paradoxical Consequences of Excess in Structural Complexity: A Study of a State Children's Psychiatric Hospital," *Sociology of Health and Illness*, 2/3 (1980):277–292.

4. Commercial banks are allowed to underwrite these securities abroad and to underwrite some governmental securities in the U.S., including Federal securities and instruments backed by the "full faith and credit" of state and local governments.

5. For a case study of the tensions between the corporate finance and sales and trading functions at Lehman Brothers prior to its acquisition (not only do investment banks advise companies which are being acquired, but they can be acquired themselves) by Shearson/American Express, see Ken Auletta, *Greed and Glory on Wall Street* (New York, NY: Random House, 1986).

6. Tom Burns and G.M. Stalker, *The Management of Innovation* (London: Tavistock Publications, 1961).

7. These employment figures were obtained from the April 1983-1987 issues of *Institutional Investor* for Salomon Brothers, Morgan Stanley, First Boston Corporation, and Goldman, Sachs.

Editors and Contributors

Editors and Contributors

Glenn R. Carroll is an Associate Professor at the School of Business Administration at the University of California, Berkeley. He is also an affiliated faculty member in the University's Department of Sociology and a research associate at the University's Institute of Industrial Relations. He is an editorial board member of *Administrative Science Quarterly* and *Industrial Relations*. He is the author of *Publish and Perish: The Organizational Ecology of Newspaper Industries* (JAI Press, 1987), co-editor of *Strategy and Organization: A West Coast Perspective* (Pitman, 1984), and editor of *Ecological Models of Organizations* (forthcoming in 1988 from Ballinger).

David Vogel is a Professor at the School of Business Administration at the University of California, Berkeley, and has served as the editor of the *California Management Review* since 1982. His books include *Ethics and Profits* (with Leonard Silk), *Ethics in the Education of Business Managers* (with Charles Powers), *Lobbying the Corporation*, and *National Styles of Regulation: Environmental Policy in Great Britain and the United States* (Cornell University Press, 1986).

Contributors

Homa Bahrami is a Lecturer in Organizational Behavior at the School of Business, University of California, Berkeley, and a Research Associate in the Graduate School of Business, Stanford. She holds a Ph.D. in Organizational Behavior and Strategy from Aston University, U.K. Her primary research interests include organizational design and strategy making in high-technology firms. She is the co-author (with Harold J. Leavitt) of the fifth edition of *Managerial Psychology: Managing Behavior in Organizations* (University of Chicago Press, January 1988).

L.J. Bourgeois, III is an Associate Professor at the Colgate Darden Graduate School of Business, University of Virginia. His research concerns strategic management in volatile environments, top management group processes, and strategy implementation. He has published in *Strategic Management Journal, Academy of Management Journal, Academy Management Review, California Management Review,* and *Management Science*. He is a frequent speaker on corporate culture and managing in high-technology environments, and he consults for a variety of international firms.

201

John Child is the Dean of the Management Centre at Aston University, Birmingham, England, where he was previously Director of the Work Organization Research Centre. His recent research has focussed on organizational changes associated with information technology and on the international dimension of management, including management development in socialist countries.

Dwight B. Crane is a Professor at the Harvard Business School. For the past three years, he has been conducting research with Robert G. Eccles on management in the investment banking industry, and they are currently writing a book tentatively titled *Doing Deals: Management in the Investment Banking Industry* (forthcoming in 1988 from the Harvard Business School Press).

Robert G. Eccles is an Associate Professor at the Harvard Business School. For the past three years, he has been conducting research with Dwight B. Crane on management in the investment banking industry, and they are currently writing a book tentatively titled *Doing Deals: Management in the Investment Banking Industry* (forthcoming in 1988 from the Harvard Business School Press).

Kathleen M. Eisenhardt is an Assistant Professor in the Industrial Engineering and Engineering Management Department at Stanford University. Her research interests focus on management in high-speed, high-technology environments. She has published in *Management Science, Organizational Dynamics*, and *Columbia Journal of World Business*.

Stuart Evans is a Visiting Scholar at the Graduate School of Business, Stanford University. He is currently on sabbatical leave from a small venture capital firm, which specializes in early-stage high-technology ventures. Previously, he was with SRI International and Bain and Company, both in Menlo Park, California. He completed his Ph.D. at Aston University, U.K. His research interests focus on strategic management of high-technology firms.

Michael Gerlach is an Assistant Professor of Business and Public Policy at the Graduate School of Business Administration, University of California, Berkeley. He is co-author (with David DeVries, Ann Morrison, and Sandy Shullman) of *Performance Appraisal on the Line* (John Wiley, 1981). His current interests, which are based on several years of research in Tokyo, focus on Japanese industrial organization and corporate strategy.

Donald C. Hambrick is the Samuel Bronfman Professor of Democratic Business Enterprise at Columbia University's Graduate School of Business. He is also Director of the Strategy Research Center at the School. His research interests are in the areas of executive leadership, top management teams, and business strategy.

J. Richard Harrison is an Assistant Professor in the School of Management at the University of Texas at Dallas and an affiliated faculty member in the University's School of Social Sciences. His current research focuses on corporate governance, the use of committees in organizations, and organizational decision making.

Henry Mintzberg is the Bronfman Professor of Management at McGill University. He is the author of *The Nature of Managerial Work, The Structuring of Organizations,* and *Power in and around Organizations* (all published by Prentice-Hall). He is currently preparing a two-volume book on *Strategy Formation*.

Walter W. Powell is currently a fellow at the Center for Advanced Study in the Behavioral Sciences. In January of 1988, he will join the Business and Sociology faculties at the University of Arizona. He has previously taught at the management schools at M.I.T. and Yale. His research has focused on organizational processes in culture-producing industries (book publishing, television) and on the diffusion of organizational forms and practices.

Elaine Romanelli is an Assistant Professor of Business at the Fuqua School of Business, Duke University. Her research interests focus on new venture strategies and organizational evolution.